Praise for *The New Slavemasters*

"Bishop George McKinney has once again hit the mark! This masterful and inspired work should be read by every parent, teacher, and all others who seek divine insights into the New Slavemasters that stalk all of us today—especially our children. Thank you, Bishop McKinney, for this strategy for victory!

Bishop Gilbert E. Patterson
Presiding Bishop, COGIC Inc.

"Bishop George McKinney is one of the wisest men in the world, and we need his wisdom today more than ever. In *The New Slavemasters*, he shows you how to help kids get free and live free of the evils that so easily ensnare them. If you're a parent, teacher, pastor, or anyone who works with young people, you need this book."

Harald Bredesen
Author, Need a Miracle? *and* Yes, Lord

"Drugs, gangs, teen pregnancy, pornography—they wrap scaly tentacles around our families, our churches, our friends, and drag them into dark places. Bishop McKinney's book will help you bring light to those places and help God bring glorious freedom. You owe it to everyone you influence to read *The New Slavemasters*."

Dr. Charles McKinney
Director of Educational Services and Assistant to the President,
Florida Gulf Coast University

"Through the metaphor of slavery, Dr. George McKinney boldly yet sensitively identifies and addresses a painful and pertinent issue facing the African American community—which is self-imposed slavery! He speaks the truth in love. With compassion but without compromise, he forces the reader to examine realities of present-day enslavement of those who fought and even died for freedom only to exercise that freedom to choose slavery once again in a different form. Although his immediate audience is his own African American community, the principles and standards he raises are relevant and applicable to the broader culture that wrestles and struggles to survive under the same imprisonments. He speaks to the cravings of a generation submitting themselves again to the bondage of contemporary destructive slave-masters."

Bishop Kenneth Ulmer
Senior Pastor, Faithful Central Missionary Baptist Church
Instructor, Grace Theological Seminary, Fuller Theological Seminary,
Pepperdine University, United Theological Seminary,
and The Kings College and Seminary

"This powerful book reports the sad news that many are in slavery today. However, it also communicates the good news that Jesus Christ is available to set people free from slavery of every kind. Bishop McKinney has been a model of this kind of vital ministry over the years. This book is a great gift to the Church and to all of us who will read this urgent message and then reach out to those in slavery with the love of Jesus Christ!"

Dr. Paul A. Cedar
Chairman, Mission America Coalition

"In his book *The New Slavemasters,* Bishop George D. McKinney correctly and persuasively points to the elements that now threaten to enslave the black community and much of our society—drugs, materialism, instant gratification, rage, and gangs. But far from merely decrying these satanic forces, Bishop McKinney provides a thoughtful process for addressing and overcoming them. His discussion and prescription for the family, for couples, for single parents, and for the unmarried offers a blueprint for restoration to health for a society that I believe to be in moral and spiritual freefall. This is a worthwhile publication."

Robert L. Woodson, Sr.
President, National Center for Neighborhood Enterprise

THE NEW
SLAVE
MASTERS

BISHOP GEORGE D.
MCKINNEY

LIFE JOURNEY®

Bringing Home the Message for Life

COOK COMMUNICATIONS MINISTRIES
Colorado Springs, Colorado • Paris, Ontario
KINGSWAY COMMUNICATIONS LTD
Eastbourne, England

Life Journey® is an imprint of
Cook Communications Ministries, Colorado Springs, CO 80918
Cook Communications, Paris, Ontario
Kingsway Communications, Eastbourne, England

THE NEW SLAVEMASTERS
© 2005 by Bishop George D. McKinney and Bill Kritlow

First printing, 2005
Printed in Canada
Printing/Year
10 9 8 7 6 5 4 3 2 / 05 06 07 08 09

The author uses examples from real life in this book; however, the people's names have been changed to protect their privacy.

Cover Design by: Happy Day Design/Ray Moore

Unless otherwise noted, Scripture quotations are taken from the HOLY BIBLE, NEW INTERNATIONAL VERSION®. Copyright © 1973, 1978, 1984 International Bible Society. Used by permission of Zondervan. All rights reserved. Excerpted from *Compton's Interactive Bible NIV.* Copyright © 1994, 1995, 1996 SoftKey Multimedia Inc. All rights reserved. Scripture quotations marked KJV are taken from the King James Version of the Bible. Italics in Scripture quotations are added by the author for emphasis.

The Web site addresses recommended throughout this book are offered as a resource to you. These Web sites are not intended in any way to be or imply an endorsement on the part of Cook Communications Ministries, nor do we vouch for their content.

Library of Congress Cataloging-in-Publication Data

McKinney, George D., 1932-
   The new slavemasters / By George D. McKinney.
      p. cm.
   Includes bibliographical references.
   ISBN 0-7814-4060-2 (hardcover)
   1. African Americans--Religion. 2. African Americans--Social conditions. I. Title.
BR563.N4M3515 2005
277.3'083'08996073--dc22
                                        2004026637

This book is respectfully dedicated to

Sister Jean Carleen Brown McKinney,

my beloved wife of 47 years who
"graduated to Glory" on June 2, 2004.

Sister Jean was my soul mate, my life partner, and my best friend. Together, we reared five sons who love God. Our sons and their wives are bringing up their children in the fear and nurture of God also. From the day our lives were joined together in marriage to her date of graduation, Sister Jean was intimately involved with me in urban ministry. Trained as an educator and counselor, she used her skills, talents, and abilities to enrich the lives of children and families. Her constant endeavor was to "know Christ and make Him known to others." She demonstrated excellence as she served Christ as nursery school director, school principal (K–12), women's ministry director, and copastor of St. Stephen's Church.

Sister Jean was a precious gift from God to me, our family, and the church. We honor her life and ministry with this dedication.

CONTENTS

INTRODUCTION

Nearly two centuries ago, Satan used mankind's deeply rooted sin and resulting inhumanity to enslave a race of God's creation—*African Americans*. Through those dark centuries of numbered tags and iron shackles, Satan worked to keep African Americans in cruel bondage. Babies were torn from their mothers' arms; husbands from the strong, supportive embrace of their wives; brothers and sisters from their siblings' trust. It was an enslavement that shattered all hopes and dreams and destroyed a normally staunch and resilient spirit, while it shattered God's natural defense to slavery's horrific effects—*the family*.

But in spite of the terror that stalked those dark days, God was faithful to sustain African Americans by ministering to their deep, painful hurts. Then His mercy was further revealed when, largely through the protestations of scripturally inspired abolitionists and a devastating civil war, the slave masters ceased their dreadful profession and institutional black slavery ended. And with its demise a great land became a better, more righteous nation.

So what has happened to the African American family since those days? Prejudice produced deep and scarring injustices—oppression, lynchings, and segregation—that prevailed for a century beyond slavery's "end." Then social awareness spawned the Civil Rights Movement, and justice for African Americans took great leaps forward. But have we arrived?

In this new day, when African Americans unquestionably enjoy complete freedom, there are new, insidious Slavemasters at work in society. These New Slavemasters work outside civilized law and labor to ensnare black families—and, for that matter, families of all races. The

New Slavemasters, however, are even more threatening than were their whip-wielding predecessors. While the latter were content to enslave the physical being, these New Slavemasters are satisfied only with the imprisonment of mind and spirit as well.

As you turn these pages, I challenge you to look deeply into the works of these New Slavemasters and, in so doing, to inoculate yourself and those you love against their bitter influences. If those near you are already ensnared, this book will help you to understand the world in which they find themselves and to assist them physically, emotionally, and spiritually to break their bonds, so that all of us may proclaim and rejoice that we are truly "free at last"!

CHAPTER ONE

CRACK!

*For our struggle is not against flesh and blood, but against the rulers,
against the authorities, against the powers of this dark world and against
the spiritual forces of evil in the heavenly realms.*

—Ephesians 6:12

*Mr. Gore then, without consultation or deliberation with
any one, not even giving Demby an additional call, raised his musket to his face,
taking deadly aim at his standing victim, and
in an instant poor Demby was no more.*

—Autobiography of Frederick Douglass, an escaped slave

As Frederick Douglass wrote in his autobiography more than a century and a half ago, Mr. Gore, a slave overseer, decided that the slave Demby needed discipline—needed the whip. A cruel weapon, the whip had a handle about three feet long—the butt end of which was weighted with lead—and cowhide lashes six or seven feet long. It took little effort for the practitioner to tear the flesh and leave deep, gruesome scars—stripes. It was with such a whip that Mr. Gore disciplined Demby. But after receiving only a few stripes, Demby plunged into a shoulder-deep creek and refused to come out. Mr. Gore grabbed a musket and told Demby that if he didn't come out after the third call, he

11

would be shot. As the excerpt above testifies, Demby remained in the water, and Mr. Gore made good his threat.[1]

Now, these many years later, that same cold, sudden, merciless death still stalks us. And just as the cruel Mr. Gore cloaked it in the guise of "essential discipline," it now shadows our neighborhoods masked as gang shootings, domestic violence, and child abuse. Of course, my predominantly African American neighborhood in south San Diego is not immune, and when this menace assaults us—no matter what the heartrending circumstances—I always hope the victim's funeral will initiate a season of much-needed emotional and spiritual healing.

It was not to be so this time. Not at the funeral that followed the terrible drama I am about to describe. Instead of hearing the solemn prayers and grief-cleansed memories whispered over the coffin that day, I heard a sound I have heard far too often—the distinct glacial crack of that same flesh-gnawing whip—this time wielded by the *New* Slavemasters.

THE NEW SLAVEMASTERS

This tragedy erupted from the clash of four family members. First was Edward. At age thirty, he was deeply troubled, his life twisted and wounded by his own irresponsibility and drug use. Edward lived with his mother, Rachel—a small Christian woman who wanted nothing more than to see her younger son drug free, productive, and safe in the arms of Jesus. But so far her frequent prayers seemingly had gone unanswered.

Next was Edward's father, Robert. Many years earlier he had left his wife and two sons and moved to South Carolina. Rachel repeatedly asked him to take Edward to live with him, but Robert always refused.

The fourth was Edward's older brother, Jacob. Jacob was a respected deacon in our church, St. Stephen's of the Church of God in Christ, in the San Diego, California, Jurisdiction. Like his mother, Jacob loved his brother and prayed for him often. He and Edward had been close as children, which made the vigil over Edward's self-destruction that much more painful.

Edward somehow had got hold of nearly $2,500 in cash. He decided to transform the money, a "nickel bag" at a time, into crack cocaine and ride its smoke all the way to death's door. Hiding the money in his room, he began to work his plan. It didn't take his mother long to notice Edward's decline, and a quick search uncovered the money. When Edward came home, she put herself between her son and the cash.

Edward became unhinged. When his frantic shouts and threats failed to dislodge her, he attacked his mother. My wife, Jean, and I have five sons, and I have no idea what it would be like if one of them attacked either of us. But Rachel knows, for she experienced it as Edward grabbed her by the shoulders and tried to push her out of the way.

But this diminutive woman would not be easily pushed. She was literally fighting for her son's life. She knew if he got into that bedroom he would hide the money somewhere else and use it to kill himself even faster. Frantic to prevent that tragedy, she struggled with the very soul of desperation to keep herself between her son and his money. But no matter how hard she fought, she was no match for the much larger man, and she knew that any second she would be thrown out of the way like a rag doll.

Just then, Jacob stepped through the front door. He could never be sure what he would find when he visited his mother's house, but he never expected to discover an all-out war. Crossing the room in a few quick strides, he positioned himself behind his brother and wrapped firm, restraining arms around him. But Edward would not be restrained. Maybe the drugs "kicked in," or maybe a reservoir of bottled-up rage broke loose, but whatever the reason, Edward released his mother and spun ferociously in Jacob's arms. Now facing him, without a heartbeat's hesitation, he plunged his thumbs into Jacob's eye sockets.

Having charged into a firestorm, Jacob was instantly over-whelmed—emotionally and physically. This was his brother, the kid he had grown up with, helped, taken the blame for, shot hoops with, and loved—and now such savagery—all focused on one aim, to destroy him.

And the pain. Searing. Like none he had ever experienced. Survival instincts blistered and erupted. Reacting blindly, Jacob brought up flailing arms to beat at his brother's arms and wrists. His counterattack must have worked; Jacob abruptly found himself behind Edward, his arm beneath Edward's chin pressed against his neck. "Stop!" Jacob cried. "You have to stop!"

But Edward wouldn't stop. Jacob, determined to remain behind his brother, held Edward even tighter, then tighter still. When Edward finally did settle down, Jacob released him, and Edward dropped to the floor breathing heavily. After lying there a moment, he began to vomit. Jacob, his eyes still on fire, figured the worst was over and started looking after his mother. Neither realized, until it was too late, that Edward had stopped breathing. The struggle had overtaken his drug-depressed system; he had choked to death on his own vomit.

The police said later that Jacob had acted in self-defense. Even his mother, distraught at one son's death but now focused on the other's emotional recovery, said that Jacob had reacted the only way he could. But Jacob would not be consoled.

"Because I've killed my brother," Jacob told anyone who attempted to console him, "I cannot forgive myself." He was determined to sweep all comfort and encouragement aside so that he could bear every ounce of deep withering guilt and spiritual confusion. And through it all, he just couldn't stop asking God: "Why? How could I have done this? How could You have let me do this, Lord?"

Edward's funeral was held a few days later, and by that time Jacob and I had spent several difficult hours working to shore him up spiritually and emotionally. Although I saw nothing in the tragedy for which Jacob could be blamed, it took a lot of counseling to bring him anywhere near a place of comfort and acceptance. As the day of the funeral dawned, Jacob had nearly forgiven himself and had decided, as a way of saying good-bye and expressing what tenderness he could to his brother, to be one of Edward's pallbearers.

But that was not to be.

His father, Robert, flew in for the funeral, and the moment Jacob moved to touch Edward's casket, Robert sprang angrily from his seat. Pointing a finger at Jacob, he cried out bitterly: "Murderer! Get away from my son. How dare you touch that casket? You murdered him. You murdered my son."

Jacob, shocked by the sudden assault, battered again by the intense guilt, pulled his hand back as if from a hot stove. Finally, buried beneath waves of remorse and despair, Jacob shrank away and joined me at the edge of the gathering; his hope to somehow reach out and touch his brother once more swept away.

THE CRACK OF THE WHIP

Does this look anything like your family? I sincerely hope not. Of course, your family dynamic may be even more difficult. But whether you have just recognized the seeds of destruction being sown or whether the New Slavemasters have invaded your life as completely as they invaded the lives of these four people, this book has been written for you.

In the following pages, we will discover exactly who these Slavemasters are; but first let's take a look at why they have slithered back into our neighborhoods.

In Ephesians 6:12, Paul writes that we are engaged in a mammoth spiritual struggle, one that pits us "against the rulers, against the authorities, against the powers of this dark world and against the spiritual forces of evil in the heavenly realms." You have just read about a battle in that war, and if you didn't think so before, I hope you realize it now—this war is serious. Our enemy plays for keeps. Lives, both physical and

His strategy was simple—keep us weak, alone, and in pain, so we would lack the focus and energy to search for God.

spiritual, teeter in the balance, and Satan, the opposing general, is anxious to shove us over the edge into oblivion.

One potent way he has managed to exert his hellish influence over the African American community was to cruelly enslave us. For centuries he tore us away from our native lands and held us in the most vicious circumstances. At the beginning of this chapter I gave you just a glimpse of its horror. His strategy was simple—keep us weak, alone, and in pain, so we would lack the focus and energy to search for God. And if we found Him, we would be so sick with rage and loathing we would reject His influence over us—no matter how tender and benevolent it might be.

For Satan, the stakes couldn't be higher. When he loses this war, he and his followers will be tossed into an eternity of complete darkness where not a single ray of God's loving radiance will ever find them again. Therefore, for him, this is total war.

Keep that fact in mind. The moment you begin to think that Satan is merely playing a game with us, that his goal is just to *disrupt* our lives, you will be reminded that our enemy wants to destroy us (John 10:10). Satan's goal is not just to disrupt the communications between you and your spouse; he aims to destroy it. And those discussions you now have with your children? Satan would like to see those tender moments of training and instruction change into angry, violent, polarizing confrontations (Ephesians 6:4). In fact, he won't be satisfied until you have given up on God and His divine plan for your family.

Satan does not want us to rely on God—or on Jesus, our only pathway to Him.

Just as centuries ago his strategy was to have slaves suffer the flesh-gnawing, spirit-breaking whips of slavery, today his strategy is the same. He wants to enslave us. Like Mr. Gore and his kind, our New Slavemasters work cruelly and tirelessly to keep us alone, weak, and in pain. Whenever possible, they whisper in our ears that it's all God's fault. Edward, Rachel, Jacob, and Robert were all victims of these vicious New Slavemasters.

Let's meet them now individually.

WHO ARE THE NEW SLAVEMASTERS?

They are the plagues of our inner cities, the plagues of our suburbs, the plagues of our youth and wage earners and even our well-to-do—all those who are physically and spiritually broken and emotionally bruised and depressed. We have met one of the New Slavemasters already—drugs. And there are others, among them materialism, the mindless pursuit of pleasure, the drive for instant gratification, and racism. All of them sow the seeds that lead to perhaps even more destructive New Slavemasters: teen pregnancy; domestic violence; adult and child pornography; gangs; and overpowering, step-directing rage.

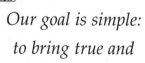

Our goal is simple: to bring true and absolute freedom.

Within these pages, we will examine each of these forces, how each enslaves, and how we can keep from becoming ensnared by them—or, if we have already been enslaved by them, how we can break free. This book is about our journey through a treacherous landscape, one that seeks to isolate and weaken us as it did Edward and, I believe, his father, Robert. Ultimately, our story will be about Jesus, the One who accompanies His people along the way. He was there for Rachel and Jacob. And because He was with them, both are now on their way to emotional and spiritual healing.

Our goal is simple: to bring true and absolute freedom. And our journey to that goal begins on the next page.

CHAPTER TWO

A PROUD, DYNAMIC, SENSITIVE— DANGEROUS PEOPLE

For we are God's workmanship, created in Christ Jesus to do good works,
which God prepared in advance for us to do.
—Ephesians 2:10

Olduvai Gorge: a series of startling discoveries in this area suggest that the most
important and fascinating developments in human history took place in the Dark
Continent. Discoveries by Dr. L. S. B. Leakey and other scholars indicate that
man was born in Africa, that he began to use tools there and that this
seminal invention spread to Europe and Asia.
—Lerone Bennett Jr.
Before the Mayflower: A History of the Negro in America—1619–1966

As the quote above from Lerone Bennett's fine book suggests, anthropologists are finally catching up to what we Christians have known all along: This area of the world is the cradle of civilization *and* its womb.[1] The first words in Genesis, penned thousands of years ago, confirm this truth. I begin here to bring credibility to what now follows. And what follows, I believe, tells us why we were so dangerous to Satan and why God has been so faithful to us through our trials.

Bennett goes on to write that in the Nile Valley, in Sudan, archaeological finds prove "that people of a Negro type were influential contributors to that cradle of civilization—Egypt."[2] Bennett also states that the civilization of our ancestors "manufactured pottery before pottery was made in the world's earliest known city."[3]

And there's more:

The Sahara: Henri Lhote, French explorer, discovers rock paintings which suggest to author Basil Davidson that "peoples of a Negro type were painting men and women with a beautiful and sensitive realism before 3,000 B.C. and were, perhaps, the originators of naturalistic human portraiture."[4]

> *We were exactly the kind of people God could use. Those same attributes made us exceedingly dangerous to God's enemies.*

What do these discoveries tell us? It says we as a people were inventive, creative, and imaginative, *and* that we were practical, sensitive, and expressive. To paint naturalistically and sensitively on cave walls, we were tenacious. We were exactly the kind of people God could use—and obviously did use early on—to enhance and further civilization within His earthly kingdom.

Those same attributes made us exceedingly dangerous to God's enemies, particularly Satan. He knew that in our hands the Gospel would be a powerful weapon against him, so he seized upon an opportunity to make us too weak, too isolated, to be the danger to him that we could have been.

Two facts must be remembered here: Man had fallen in the Garden of Eden (Genesis 3:1–24), and man was accustomed to using beasts of burden. Economies flourished because men used donkeys and horses to carry what they could not. In the early 1500s, when it was learned that the native populations in the newly discovered West Indies could not do the work the Spanish wanted done, they looked around for the beasts of burden who would be able to do that backbreaking labor. Satan planted within the hearts of white Europeans the notion that black Africans were the beasts of burden for which they were searching. In 1555, Captain John Lok wrote about our ancestors, describing them as "a people of beastly living, without a God, lawe [sic], religion, or common wealth, and so scortched [sic] by the heat of the sunne [sic], that in many places they curse it when it riseth."[5]

Europe had its new beasts of burden. And although much of Europe participated in the slave trade, "the English, according to some authorities, during the two and a half centuries they were engaged in that traffic, took more than double the number of Negroes from the coast of Africa than all other nations combined."[6]

To be fair, Africa was also ruled by nature's law, "eat or be eaten,"[7] which made it easy for Satan to plant within the minds of our own people the idea that to sell their captives and other undesirables into slavery was perfectly moral and legal.

The stage was set, therefore, to inaugurate slavery in America. In 1619, Dutch traders sold twenty of our beloved into the English settlement of Jamestown, Virginia, to begin this heinous activity with the British colonies.

I could go on and expand on that history begun that terrible day so many years ago. Instead, I would like to expand upon the more personal history of our ancestors written on their backs by the whips of the slavers and now on the backs of their descendants by the New Slavemasters. For it is by throwing off those shackles that true freedom comes.

ALONE AND WEAK

For I am convinced that neither death nor life, neither angels nor demons,
neither the present nor the future, nor any powers, neither height nor depth,
nor anything else in all creation, will be able to separate us from
the love of God that is in Christ Jesus our Lord.

—Romans 8:38–39

Though the field was some distance from the house, I could hear every
crack of the whip, and every groan and cry of my poor mother.

—Autobiography of William Wells Brown, an escaped slave

William Wells Brown, born a slave in Kentucky in the early 1800s, was whisked off with his mother, Elizabeth, to Missouri when still an infant. As the years passed, William worked as a house slave while his mother toiled in the fields. One dark morning, he awoke to the sound of his mother's voice. But not her soft, love-filled whispers, the supportive, encouraging sound that so often embraced his heart. No, these were distant, anguished cries. A few minutes late to the fields, she was receiving ten lashes from the overseer. His mother was the one person William loved, the one person who loved him, the only member of his family he knew, the only person he trusted. And now he sat in the bitter darkness balanced on the edge of his wood-framed bed as leather thongs ripped his mother's flesh. And there was nothing he could do about it but weep.[1]

He felt absolutely *alone.* There was no one to help, no one to complain to, no one to take his part even if he did complain, no one to comfort him or salve his mother's wounds.

No one to care.

At that moment, and for many moments to come in William Brown's life, Satan seemed to be winning. As I mentioned at the end of chapter 1, I firmly believe the reason our precious African American families were enslaved centuries ago, and the reason they experience enslavement today, is that Satan wants to see us alone and weak.

Let's understand why *alone* first.

> *Satan only has to keep us from seeing our need for a savior and who that Savior is.*

WHY ALONE?

Satan doesn't need us to embrace him. He claims victory if he merely drives a wedge—a permanent separation—between God and us. Satan only has to keep us from seeing our need for a savior and who that Savior is. By doing so, he keeps us from crying out to Jesus for salvation. It is this cry that snatches us from Satan's cruel bondage and translates us into God's protective, loving arms. This wedge separating us from God is pounded into our hearts by a very big hammer fashioned of lies.

By my count, there are four corrosive, debilitating lies the Devil uses to keep us feeling alone. And each time he whispers one of them in our ear, the hammer slams down. But for that wedge to pierce the heart and take hold, those lies must be believed—and lived. I am convinced we are most vulnerable to those lies when we are alone.

SOMETIMES WE ALL FEEL ALONE

At times we all feel alone. This is particularly true when we are children, when it is so easy to feel forsaken by our parents and friends. But usually Mom wraps consoling arms around us, or Dad pats us on the back, and suddenly our sense of abandonment dissolves. But many children grow into adulthood believing no one cares. They feel as if they are on their own physically; emotionally; and, especially, spiritually. For them, Satan's four big lies appear true.

As they did to Farrah.

Farrah's grandmother, Selma, went to our church. Farrah never knew her dad, although she knew the father of her little sister, Carol. Carol's father lived with them until Farrah was ten. That's when he and her mother robbed a convenience store. When their father and mother ended up in prison, Farrah and Carol became their grandmother's responsibility. Selma took her new responsibilities seriously, making sure, among other things, that Farrah and Carol went to church.

Carol loved church. Even from the nursery, she seemed to belong. When she was eight, she went to summer camp and was saved. She met her husband-to-be at one of our youth group meetings. And through all of it, she remained faithful to Jesus and His Church. When her son, Henry, was born, she made sure he attended church, and when he was old enough, she made sure he was enrolled in our elementary school. Although life has been difficult since her husband left her, Carol and her Lord walk it together.

That's not true for Farrah. She was thirteen when their mother died in prison—a drug overdose that some called suicide. And from the moment she and Carol learned of it, Farrah no longer seemed to care that her grandmother and sister loved her. Farrah's eyes turned cold and bitter, and she began to behave as if she were alone on the planet. She came to church occasionally, and there was a period of time when she and I spoke. As we did, I began to understand the lies Satan was telling Farrah—lies that she believed.

Lie #1: All people are out for themselves.

To Farrah, not only did the world not care if she lived, died, or merely existed, it was worse—the world was *hostile*. It had taken her mother and the only father she had ever known. "Even Grandma only cares about

> *To Farrah, not only did the world not care if she lived, died, or merely existed, it was worse—the world was* hostile.

us because her precious church friends might talk if she didn't," she said. When Farrah believed the lie, she began to see people as fundamentally selfish. And why shouldn't they be? They had their own lives and didn't want anyone like her in the way. Farrah became isolated emotionally.

Lie #2: Since no one cares about you, you needn't care about anyone.

Farrah wasn't about to care about or help anyone else; she was too busy taking care of herself. And if they did need help, they could get it where she did, from within. That's what Farrah thought when Carol asked her to pick up her son, Henry, from school.

Carol's husband abandoned her when Henry was six. One night her Honda Civic died when she was late to pick up Henry at school; we were due to close any minute. Selma wasn't home, so she called Farrah, reluctantly. Farrah never had been much help to her, but maybe this time would be different. But without apology, Farrah refused. She was fighting with her boyfriend and didn't want to miss his phone call. Carol was very close to writing her sister off after that episode.

She *did* write her off after this next one.

Lie #3: To get what you need, you must take it.

The first two lies taint others' motives. It makes them look callous and self-centered, living at our expense. As a result, we become their victims, and victims are owed. And what we are owed, we have a right to.

This lie allows us to be active in our selfishness; we take what we need from others to satisfy those needs and to get a little revenge at the same time. It is an irresistible combination. But, when we put feet to this lie, we inevitably hurt those closest to us the way Farrah hurt Carol.

About a year after Farrah refused to pick up Henry, Carol discovered what Farrah had done.

"You had an affair with Conner?" Carol gasped. "My husband? And you say it like that?"

"Like what?"

They were alone in Carol's kitchen. Carol had invited Farrah to dinner in an attempt to patch things up. "Like you're ordering a Big Mac or something. You had an affair with my husband?"

"I don't like Big Macs. Anyway, he's been gone three years. What do you care? He wasn't all that happy. He would have left anyway."

"He was my husband, Farrah. My husband!"

"It wasn't my fault. I'd just dumped that guy who used to hit me. I needed somebody. You wouldn't have wanted me to go back to being hit, would you?"

That night Carol severed her relationship with Farrah. No one could blame her, of course. Maybe someday she will be able to forgive Farrah and love her again as the Savior commands. But until then, her Gospel witness to Farrah has ended, which means that Farrah, like most who live this lie, burned at least one of the bridges that may have carried her to Jesus.

Satan crafted these first three lies to sever our earthly relationships, which is easy to do when we believe ourselves to be alone anyway. He has crafted the next one to sever our relationship with our Creator—and Farrah, as have so many others I have counseled over the years, believed it wholeheartedly.

Lie #4: No one could love you; there's something about you that is just unlovable.

We see others married or in serious relationships. They seem to be happy and a part of each other's lives. Farrah saw it in the relationships Carol, Selma, and Henry had with one another. No matter what happened, they were there for each other. Yet she was alone. Her relationships always ended. People like her mom and her dad always left, but those who stayed ended up violent, or hating her, or just making her life miserable.

"You know," I said when we happened to see each other at a wedding, "it could be you make your relationships go bad. You can't expect an affair with your sister's husband to end well."

She shook her head. "It's not that," she said. "There's something wrong with me. Something people just don't like. Maybe something evil. And that's why people end up leaving me. Who wants to be around that?"

And then she took this lie to a more destructive depth. "I don't think even God could love me. It's true, you know. God couldn't love me."

Of course I protested, but she wasn't listening. The lie had closed her spiritual ears.

Farrah was just where Satan wanted her: alone and cut off from those who might present the Truth to her.

But for Satan, alone isn't enough. People alone still have the power to make a difference. After all, *The Terminator* worked alone. And while they stumble around, they might just stumble over to God.

WHY DOES HE WANT US WEAK?

Satan also wants us *weak*.

William Wells Brown, that terrible morning when he heard his mother's back being slashed by the Negro whip, certainly saw himself as *weak*, totally impotent not just in that horrific moment, but in life itself. You can almost hear him groan: "What good am I? I can't even help my mother when she needs me."

Those thoughts and ones like them make us susceptible to more of Satan's lies:

Lie #5: You are powerless.

William Brown felt powerless to help his mother, and later he wrote that he felt powerless to become free. For a time this lie lived within him, just as it lived within Farrah. It didn't matter

> *Satan wants us to close our eyes, plant our feet firmly beneath us, and stay put.*

what she did, whom she befriended, what hoops she jumped through; she was powerless to achieve what she always had been denied—to be loved. And when we are powerless, we don't even try. That's where Satan wants us. He wants us to feel so powerless that we stop trying. Satan wants us to close our eyes, plant our feet firmly beneath us, and stay put.

But the lie eats even deeper. When William Brown was stripped of his power to help his mother, he was stripped of his power to be a man with dignity who strives after the good. I believe Farrah came to a similar place. She became powerless to be a woman. Proverbs 31:10–31, particularly verses 25 and 26, describes the woman Farrah believes she will never be:

> She is clothed with strength and dignity; she can laugh at the days to come. She speaks with wisdom, and faithful instruction is on her tongue.

Even as contemporary and streetwise as she seemed to be, I believe Farrah would claim this definition for herself if she thought she could. But I think she has fallen prey to the lie and has given up.

Lie #6: You are at the mercy of evil.

Edward, Jacob's brother, had to believe this lie. Consumed by an overpowering hunger for what those drugs brought, he drifted along at their mercy until finally they showed him no mercy at all. William Brown's mother believed this lie. When she went out to that field ten minutes late, she knew what awaited her, yet she went anyway—because she was at the mercy of the overseer. Earlier, when she went to the white man's bed where William was conceived, she didn't resist. There was no belief that she could. And when we don't resist, evil has its way with us, which makes us even less of what we could be—what God would have us be—and we sink even more deeply into the quicksand of spiritual defeat.

Lie #7: You are worthless.

What a terrible lie to believe. Yet I am convinced that millions do just that. It is a harsh lie, and weakness helps us accept it. Can't you just hear the ruler of this world taunting William Brown? "If you can't help your mother at a time like this, you're no better than a dog." In his memoir he describes the murder of a male slave. The man was running from unjust punishment and dove into a river near a riverboat to escape. He ended up drowning, and when his pursuers got him back on the docks, they just left him there. His body was later picked up with the trash and just carted off like worthless refuse,[2] as worthless as William undoubtedly felt as he listened to his mother's cries for help and mercy.

Have you ever heard this lie whispered in your ear? I suppose we all have at least once in our lives. But did you believe it, make it part of your life, and begin to live as if it were true? I think Farrah did. Later, Farrah's grandmother asked me to pray for her eldest granddaughter. Farrah had entered into another violent relationship, this time ending up in the emergency room—and she was talking about going back with the guy. "I just can't help myself" was what she had told her grandmother. If she had thought herself worth anything, she could have.

A DESTRUCTIVE RESULT

Isolation and weakness have another debilitating effect—fear and pain. There is nothing more fearsome in a hostile world than to face it alone. And the fact that we are alone, that we have no involved family; friends; or loving, supportive husbands or wives, brings pain—worse than pain, real, honest-to-goodness agony; the hurt of abandonment and betrayal, of inadequacy, of unworthiness.

And when we are afraid and in pain, when we are hanging by our fingernails, we instinctively grab for lifelines. We reach out for anything that will bring safety and peace, even for a little while. We tell ourselves that we will deal with the collateral damage later. Satan loves this kind of desperate situation. Who among us has time for good judgment and long-term spiritual planning when our fingernails are about to break and the alligators are nipping at our toes? And which lifeline does the Devil throw us? One of the New Slavemasters.

In the next few chapters, we will take a look at these New Slavemasters and see how, if obeyed, they firmly anchor that wedge in our heart and keep us from the love of Christ and the wondrous world God has created for us.

CHAPTER FOUR

NEW SLAVEMASTER:
DRUGS

*"He who overcomes will, like them, be dressed in white. I will
never blot out his name from the book of life, but will acknowledge his
name before my Father and his angels."*
—Revelation 3:5

*This, at the time, I thought to be one of the
most cruel acts that could be committed upon my rights;
and I received several very severe whippings for telling people that
my name was William, after orders were given to change it.*
—Autobiography of William Wells Brown, an escaped slave

We met Edward in chapter 1 and saw his dreadful end plus his
brother's and mother's anguish, before and after his death. Did
Edward make wise choices in those last years of his life? How about his
decision to buy crack with the $2,500? Or each time he lit the crack pipe
and drew the smoke into his lungs—into his soul—was that a good
choice?

Hardly. Stepping in front of a speeding bus would have been a better choice. He would have gone more quickly and experienced *and
inflicted* far less pain. All of us know that a hundred miles from illegal
drugs is too close. If they ensnare us, they tie us in knots and drag us

away with them. They harm us physically; sometimes they kill us, as with Edward, and if we survive them, they devastate us emotionally. But the physical and emotional toll on the user is only a small measure of the damage they do. Just ask the wife of an alcoholic.

WHEN THE HEAD FALLS

Stan was in his mid-thirties; married to Glenda; and had two girls, Tierra and Cassandra. Besides being a family man, Stan was a cabinetmaker. He loved to work with wood, to shape patterns and apply delicate stains to bring out the wood's natural grain and luster. His kitchens had won design awards and been featured in *Architectural Digest* magazine. He was at the top of his game—until his right hand was crushed.

The kitchen wall was too rotten, and the cabinet fell on his hand, breaking every bone. After the surgery, he never regained complete feeling or full use of it.

Stan went to church every Sunday, read his Bible faithfully, tried to raise Christian kids, and adored Glenda. By any measure, life had been sweet. But after the accident, when he first tried to fashion a particularly delicate edge to a cabinet door, he knew life had soured. Stan prided himself on his intricate edges, yet now he couldn't even feel the router, let alone hold it firmly enough to work the edge he wanted. That night he stopped at the bar he passed every night on the way home and got drunk.

He was deeply embarrassed when he finally faced Glenda, but she understood. She had mourned losses before. She understood the next night, too. The third night, however, she got concerned. And the fourth night, she confronted him. He blew up. He told her to mind her own business. He said she didn't understand and he needed time to adjust, to figure out what it all meant, what he was going to do with the rest of his life. The alcohol slurred his words, but the meaning came out clearly. He wanted to be left alone.

Over the next year, he got his wish. First to lose heart was Tierra.

Birthdays were always a very special time for the kids, and this year Tierra's should have been extra special: she was turning thirteen. But her daddy came home that night absolutely wasted. Worse still, for the first time they couldn't afford a special birthday. Her mother let it slip they were almost broke. Mom took her out to a little restaurant, but it wasn't quite as satisfying as she had hoped.

Next, Stan lost Cassandra and Glenda on the same night. From the moment her father began to drink, Cassandra began to work to please her parents. She just couldn't do enough for them. She made them breakfast, fed the dog, made sure her room sparkled and her homework was done before dinner. She worked like a demon to be their little angel. But there was one element of her life that she kept to herself—gymnastics.

Every Saturday morning, Cassandra headed for the Girl's Club. For the next two hours, she practiced. If asked what she liked about gymnastics, she would say tumbling, or the parallel bars, but I suspect she really liked being on her own and working so hard there was no time to think about what was happening to her family. One day, though, all that intruded. Suddenly, in the middle of her workout, she heard loud voices. Her father stood in the half-open doorway yelling raw obscenities at her mother, who tried to stop him from entering. The fight ended abruptly when he struck her mother, who went sprawling. Her father then stumbled backward and hit the hardwood floor with a thick crack. After her mother ushered Cassandra home, her father moved out.

This isn't an unusual story when alcohol or drugs are involved. The cost to everyone is astronomical. Marriages are destroyed, relationships between parents and children shattered. Careers evaporate. Hopes for the future wither on the vine as love gives up the ghost, and horizons grow dark and stormy.

But more is destroyed than the relationships themselves. The good these relationships have been created to do is destroyed as well. Later

Satan's victory is huge when he launches an entire family down that destructive path usually walked by individuals.

we will talk about the various roles members of families are called to play, but when those roles go unfulfilled, lessons go untaught, guidance goes ungiven, examples never occur, and God's hope for the family goes unrealized. Family members, especially children, quickly become estranged from one another. The family grows weak and ineffective. Satan's victory is huge when he launches an entire family down that destructive path usually walked by individuals.

THE FAMILY AS A CASUALTY

Although we think in terms of Satan corrupting individuals, his sights are always on the family as a whole. He loves to shatter the whole into a number of isolated, warring parts, as he did through the old slave masters. Frederick Douglass, an escaped slave, was born in Maryland sometime around 1818, a date Frederick never knew. "By far the larger part of the slaves know as little of their ages as horses know of theirs," he wrote, adding that slave masters saw their slaves' interest in their ages as "impertinent, and evidence of a restless spirit."[1] They were right about Frederick. His spirit was indeed restless.

In 1838, after an arduous, sometimes violent life, he threw off his chains and escaped to New York. While there, and later in Boston, he became one of the most articulate and influential African Americans in the fight against slavery. He writes of his mother, Harriet Bailey, and his father, whom he suspected as being the white man who owned him. Before he was a year old, his mother was taken from him, "before I even knew her as my mother,"[2] and forced to work on a farm some twelve miles away. It was a common custom, used to break the bond between mother and child, so when either was mistreated, neither would give assistance. In all his young life he saw her only four or five times, "and each of these times was at night and was very short in duration"[3]—when her fieldwork was through and she could manage the twelve-mile walk to her son's side.

Slavery, by its very nature, was horrifically cruel, but breaking up families—husbands from wives, mothers from children, brothers and sisters from their siblings—was devastatingly so. It tore what was left of their slave hearts right out of them.

It would be wonderful to say families are safe from that kind of abuse today. But they are not. Today, as you read these words, the New Slavemasters still rip families apart, still grind hearts and futures beneath cold, thick souls.

That was certainly true of Stan's family. Tierra, a teenager with a battleground for a home, is now hanging out with gang types. Cassandra, unable to assure her future by being perfect, seems to have just crawled inside herself. I haven't seen her smile in a very long time. Glenda, too, has built an emotional fortress around herself. It is more ironclad than Cassandra's, more impenetrable, and except for the occasional Sunday service, Glenda has become pretty much a stranger here.

Stan traded everything he professed to hold dear for booze.

Why? To anesthetize the pain. His sense of who he was and who he wanted to become were tied to what his hands could do. But now his hands could no longer work. The emotional pain was severe—and it grew as his income diminished. And who could help? No one. Sure, there were people to talk to, but none could make his hand work again,

Satan wants you to become someone those closest to you no longer know—and no longer want to be around.

and that was the only help he wanted. He couldn't even go to God—after all, God could have kept his hand from being hurt in the first place, and once hurt, He could have healed it. If He could raise His Son back to life, He could certainly heal a hand. With his manhood setting like a blood-red sun, he became terrified. And just as booze covered over the pain, it dampened his fear. It became what kept him going—while it kept him dying.

WHEN A CHILD FALLS

Stan was the head of his family, so it is understandable that the family would be thrown into turmoil by his allegiance to the bottle. When a child develops a substance-abuse problem, the effects can be just as disastrous. Parents can drive themselves to distraction and the poorhouse trying to turn a child around. And they should; they might be successful. Yet the resources they expend—their time, energy, and money—are resources the rest of the family needs. Unless resources are spent

Just as the old slave masters demanded absolute obedience, so the New Slavemasters claim absolute sovereignty.

wisely and balanced against what the other family members need, scars develop. One member of our flock got a call to go bail his wayward son out of jail just before he was supposed to step into his daughter's piano recital. It took a number of years for his daughter to recover from seeing her father choose her brother's needs over hers—yet again. If that choice is made often enough, "good" children begin to wonder what being good gets them.

That's the goal of the New Slavemasters.

Just as the old slave masters demanded absolute obedience, so the New Slavemasters claim absolute sovereignty. Your life is their life. They want to "jerk you around" and take you away anytime they want.

In fact, their claim on you goes even deeper.

THEY TAKE AWAY WHO YOU WERE

William Brown was named William at birth, but when he became Dr. Young's slave, all that changed. Although childless, Dr. Young had a nephew who came to stay with him. That boy's name was also William. William Brown's mother was ordered to change her son's name to Sandford. "This, at the time, I thought to be one of the most cruel acts that could be committed upon my rights; and I received several very severe whippings for telling people that my name was William, after orders were given to change it. Though young, I was old enough to place a high appreciation upon my name."[4] Later, when he escaped, although now known as Sandford, he changed his name back to William.

The slave masters—old and new—want all of us, everything that makes us who we are. Then they want to bend us to their will. That was certainly true for Stan and Edward and for all those locked in the dungeon of substance abuse. They lost "who they were" and became *whom their slave masters wanted them to be*. That is what Satan wants for you. He wants you to become someone those closest to you no longer know—and no longer want to be around.

But just as William Brown escaped and reclaimed his name, so also can those who are locked behind addiction's thick walls escape and reclaim the life they once had. Instead of grabbing the death-line that leads to dependence, grab the lifeline that leads to freedom—grab hold of Jesus.

But substance abuse isn't the only New Slavemaster ravaging our homes, communities, and churches. We will meet another in the next chapter.

CHAPTER FIVE

NEW SLAVEMASTER:
MATERIALISM

"And why do you worry about clothes? See how the lilies of the field grow. They do not labor or spin. Yet I tell you that not even Solomon in all his splendor was dressed like one of these."
—Matthew 6:28–29

[T]*he child again commenced crying. Walker stepped up to her* [the child's mother], *and told her to give the child to him. The mother tremblingly obeyed. He took the child by one arm, as you would a cat by the leg, walked into the house, and said to the lady, "Madam, I will make you a present of this little n——r; it keeps such a noise that I can't bear it."*

"Thank you, sir," said the lady.

—Autobiography of William Wells Brown, an escaped slave

At the tender age of twelve, Barbara decided she would marry a doctor. For the next ten years, the only question that remained was which one. By the time I met her, she was engaged to a pediatrician.

"Money can't buy happiness," she would say, "but it can buy what makes you happy. And doctors have money." In a way she is right. We all do need *things*: food to eat, a bed to sleep in, clothes to wear. Sometimes we need *nice* things—an anniversary dinner, a sparkling wedding ring, a new fishing pole—just to show we are alive. Things *are* important. Without certain things, life is a monumental struggle. And maybe today we need things even more than we did in the past. What used to be luxuries have become almost necessities. Who can survive without television, in fact, without cable? All teens need cell phones. And all offices need fax machines, FedEx accounts, and computers. The Internet, hardly used ten years ago, is now indispensable. Without it, some people couldn't find a date or talk to their families. And let's not forget, the world itself is a *thing*, and none of us could exist without *it*.

So to minimize our need for things would be silly.

But to make them too important is equally silly.

That is what Barbara did. But we could hardly blame her. When Barbara was still a toddler, her mother ran off to New York with a local disk jockey, deserting Barbara and her three older brothers. Her father worked in a garage, and her mother thought he should have done better.

Barbara explained: "He didn't have the drive to do anything but change other people's oil. Mom just wanted a few of the nicer things. I can't blame her. Disk jockeys make more than oil changers. And doctors make more than both of 'em."

Barbara and her brothers never went hungry, but they never had luxuries either. Of course, all four of them complained, but her father didn't care. To change would mean that he would have to work harder and that his wife was right, and he wouldn't allow either of those things. To be fair, though, not having things was only an irritant until Barbara was seven and her fifteen-year-old brother, Clarence, got his sixteen-year-old neighbor pregnant.

"He was actually excited," Barbara said incredulously, "like he was finally a man, or like it took some maturity or skill. Men can be such idiots. The excitement lasted only a few months though. The girl started telling people it was some other guy's kid." The "other guy" was an older boy who could afford more things because he had graduated and was already working. "When Clarence confronted her, she said: 'Who's to say it's not his? He seems to like the idea. And he has money, and me and my baby need support.'

After all, a new house wouldn't betray her, a mink stole wouldn't hurt her, and a Hawaiian cruise definitely wouldn't desert her.

"See," Barbara went on, "money matters. It cost Clarence his kid. And it cost me my mom."

For Barbara and many like her, life is about things and the appearance things gives them. To Barbara, relationships are not between her and others, but between her and what others can provide her. And they last as long as they provide what she wants. Interestingly, all other relationships are seen in the same light. Her brother lost his child because he had no money. Losing the child had nothing to do with a moral choice he had made. It was all about things and the appearance that he could afford them.

Barbara became a slave to materialism because things seemed safe. After all, a new house wouldn't betray her, a mink stole wouldn't hurt her, and a Hawaiian cruise definitely wouldn't desert her. And because things are safe, she allowed herself to be enslaved in order to fill the empty places in her life with those very safe things. Things brought her *a strong sense of fulfillment.*

FULFILLMENT

One way God pokes and prods us through life is by planting within our hearts goals for which we strive, a place we want to go, something we want to do. And when we get to it, we feel *fulfillment*. We experience a rightness about having arrived. We have climbed the mountain, crossed the finish line, reached the goal. As Christians we feel God's blessing; we have done what He wants us to. Then, after a few days of feeling at loose ends, another goal bubbles up before us. Maybe we want to graduate from high school. Then we do. What now? Then the desire to go to college ignites, and we have another objective to reach. Life becomes a series of moving from one God-given goal to the next, one sense of fulfillment to the next.

Of course, we would like our goals to have a *nobility* to them, because reaching them makes us better; it means that we have proved ourselves worthy in some way by achieving them. Life becomes up the "up" staircase. If we are living the Christian life, those steps should move us ever closer to God and to the likeness of His Son (Romans 8:29)—which is our ultimate goal and fulfillment.

For the slave to materialism, like Barbara, fulfillment is different.

For instance, instead of feeling fulfilled when her family feels comfortable, warm, and safe in her home, the slave to materialism smiles contentedly when her house is envied, which to her shows power and a sense of style.

Why? Because the lord of this world is whispering in her ear a few more of his lies: "You've been hurt so badly, you deserve everything you can get. People only want what you have, so it's okay to take what you can. What matters is what you can get in this life; don't worry about who you are."

And just as things fulfill her, the people in her life are things as well.

PEOPLE BECOME THINGS

When William Brown was a young man of marrying age, he became Mrs. Price's servant. Mrs. Price was "proud" of her servants and kept the few she had well dressed, so they all turned out in grand style. Maria, a young woman, was also her slave. Mrs. Price soon decided that William and Maria should marry. She impressed upon William continually the importance of marriage and the necessity of having a wife. William, however, had no intention of marrying. He wanted to escape, and a wife would slow him down, make escape more difficult. When Mrs. Price finally realized that William wasn't going to marry Maria, she decided the reason was that William wanted to marry Eliza, who was owned by another. But before purchasing Eliza, she sat William down and asked his plans for courtship and marriage.[1]

In that delicate situation, William had to walk a tightrope. Afraid to set off alarm bells, he tried to remain positive but not too positive. He told her he really did want a wife, but not right at that moment. "But how do you feel about Eliza?" she asked. William expressed mild interest, and the next thing he knew Mrs. Price had bought Eliza, and she had become part of the family.

Since William wanted freedom so badly, his tightrope walking became a high-wire act. To remain on good terms with Mrs. Price, he promised to marry Eliza, but just not immediately. And since he wanted Mrs. Price to believe he had feelings for Eliza, he had to remain on good terms with her, too, even though his sense of honor kept him from leading her on.

For the old slave masters, even an institution as sacred and intimate as marriage was merely an arrangement among property. Slaves were merely things. They urged these *things* to marry, but only in order to produce more *things*, and then to shackle them and make it more difficult for them to escape. If a slave was sold, the spouse (without benefit of divorce) was urged to marry again. *Things* can't be bigamists.

To the materialistic Slavemaster, people are merely things—things acquired, things cherished, and things sought. Let's look at Barbara again. The pediatrician will be Barbara's second marriage. Her first, a biology major in college, was a pre-med student for a time. He gave up the idea of becoming a doctor after deciding his heart was in teaching for the Lord. He came to work for us, instructing one of our lower grades. He was quite happy, until Barbara decided that their apartment was too small. Of course, he didn't make enough to afford a larger one.

He went to teach in public school. But alas, he didn't make enough there either. When they failed to earn enough money to buy a home, Barbara found reasons to end the marriage.

I haven't met the man to whom she is now engaged. I am sure he is a fine fellow. But what is he to Barbara? She tells everyone she loves him, but he might find the heat turned up at home if he ever decides to become a missionary or even a teacher.

To the materialistic person, marriage is merely an entry point, a gateway to all the things that lay behind it: the big house, the luxury car, the expensive jewelry—all that stuff by which materialists measure their worth. The more stuff they have, the more important they are. And spending money gives them a sense of power, especially if they can exert influence over someone by spending it.

The point is that we who are slaves to materialism simply believe ourselves to be better than those who have less than we do. If I drive a Lexus and you drive a Ford Taurus, I am better than you are. If I wear Armani suits, and yours come from Sears, I am better than you are. We all play *The Price Is Right,* and the higher the price, the "righter" whatever it is. Little value is placed on the issues of the heart.

AND WHEN WE DON'T GET WHAT WE WANT?

William Brown's master, Mr. Walker, bought a farm, then took William on a trip to buy slaves to work it. After buying twenty-three men and women, Walker bought another woman who had a six-week-old baby in her arms. Finding no boats available to take them down the Missouri River, they started out by land: Walker and William Brown on horseback, the slaves chained together on foot. Only the woman with the child was left unchained; it was thought unlikely that she would try to run away with a baby.

The road was deeply rutted, and the baby, frequently jarred by

Mom's missteps, became uncomfortable and started crying, which it kept up most of the day. Walker often told the woman to keep the child quiet, but she couldn't. Finally, they arrived at the home of a friend of Mr. Walker, where they stayed the night.

The next morning, soon after the slaves were assembled, the baby began to cry again. As the quotation at the beginning to the chapter tells us, Walker coldly took the baby from its mother and handed it as a gift to his friend as if giving away a mongrel pup. In spite of the mother's frantic pleas, Walker was stead-fast in his cruelty. This was no human baby he was giving away; it was merely property. For the remainder of the walk to the farm, the now-childless woman was chained up with the rest of Walker's property.[2]

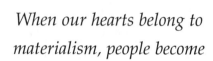

When our hearts belong to materialism, people become expendable.

Just as the evil Mr. Walker gave away that woman's precious baby, we materialists, as Barbara did, discard those who fail to give us what we want. A heartless thing to say? Perhaps. Doubly heartless when compared to what Walker did nearly two centuries ago, but truth is truth. When our hearts belong to materialism, people become expendable, no matter how close or important they once may have been to us. If a husband fails to provide the level of support a materialistic wife requires, he is history. If a wife fails to be the servant a materialistic husband requires, he will help her pack. If parents fail to keep materialistic children satisfied, even after those children reach adulthood, they will call home only when their bank account runs dry. Of course, there are always excuses for breaking off such relationships.

"You don't love me anymore."

"I didn't have time to call."

"The dog ate your phone number."

"I need to go out and find myself."

Slaves to materialism may have all the marbles, but they inevitably play alone.

But the real reason is far simpler. Slaves to materialism don't establish the intimate connections that keep people in their lives—those connections that feed relationships and keep them strong and vital. In the end, slaves to materialism may have all the marbles, but they inevitably play alone.

A DOUBLE-EDGED SWORD

As you can imagine, this sword of materialism has two very sharp edges. Just as we feel superior to those who have less than we do, we also feel inferior to those who have more: "You have more than I have, so I am less than you are."

This opposite edge cuts very deeply. It may cause us to reach beyond our means in an attempt to catch up. Or it may cause us to climb inside ourselves and give up on life's natural competitiveness. "There's no way I can compete. It's just too hard to even try."

And, worst of all, it can tell us that God isn't blessing us anymore. He has rejected us because there is something wrong with us, and our lack of things proves it. What's more, there is no reason even to try to better ourselves. God won't let it happen anyway. Life becomes the ultimate defeat.

WHY ARE WE SLAVES TO MATERIALISM?

This New Slavemaster is no different from the others. His first goal is to keep us alone. And he does a masterful job. By keeping our focus on things, he keeps us from connecting on an intimate level to those close to us. We never see them for the wondrous creations they are. But more than souring our relationships with others, this New Slavemaster's goal is to sour our relationship with God. Materialists focus on the temporal—things seen and held, bought and sold. And because our eyes are fixed there ...

◆ It keeps us from relating to a spiritual God.

◆ It keeps us from thinking about our sin.

◆ It keeps us from seeing the goodness of God apart from what He gives us.

◆ It causes us to focus on acquiring *things* and achieving *our* goals instead of seeking God and His will for us.

◆ It keeps us from seeing our need for a spiritual Savior.

Materialism keeps us from seeing God, which is our New Slavemaster's ultimate goal. Does this sound at all like you? There is a little of the materialist in all of us, so I am sure some of it does. But are you a slave to materialism? Do you choose things over relationships? Is God just asking you to give up too much? If so, then keep reading; there may be other Slavemasters' whips cracking across your shoulders.

If materialism isn't an issue with you, keep reading anyway. Maybe on the next page we will reveal the whip that is tearing at your back.

CHAPTER SIX

NEW SLAVEMASTER:
RACISM

So God created man in his own image, in the image of God
he created him; male and female he created them.
—Genesis 1:27

Randall said that the task was too great or he should have done it. Cook said it
made no difference — he should whip him. Randall stood silent for a moment, and
then said, "Mr. Cook, I have always tried to please you since you have been on the
plantation, and I find you are determined not to be satisfied with my work,
let me do as well as I may. No man has laid hands on me, to whip me, for the last
ten years, and I have long since come to the conclusion not to be whipped by any
man living." Cook, finding by Randall's determined look and gestures,
that he would resist, called three of the hands from their work,
and commanded them to seize Randall, and tie him.

—Autobiography of William Wells Brown, an escaped slave

We have all hit our thumb with a hammer, and if we haven't, we
know someone who has. The first time we do it, it hurts; the next
time the pain is sharper; and the next, excruciating. It is like that with
racism. The first time a tender bruise on the heart forms, and each time we
suffer it again, the hurt builds and builds. It was like that with Marcus.

The first time this New Slavemaster's whip cracked across his back
was in elementary school. Marcus played the trumpet in the orchestra, and

for an eleven-year-old, he played it pretty well. His parents couldn't afford his own instrument, so he rented one from the school. About halfway through the year, his teacher asked him to switch to the trombone. Eager to learn something new, Marcus jumped at the chance. He turned in his trumpet and grabbed the much more imposing slide trombone.

I define racism as the institutionalized expression of a controlling group's prejudices.

A white student was waiting to get the trumpet, and as Marcus walked away with the new instrument, he heard the kid balk, "You don't think my lips are going to be where that black kid's lips were?"

But what made the moment even worse, instead of reprimanding the child, the teacher merely said: "That's okay. I've got a new mouthpiece in the back."

Marcus was devastated. He had thought the teacher liked him. Over the next few weeks his interest in music waned.

Dr. Billy Graham put it this way:

Racism in the world and in the church is one of the greatest barriers to world evangelism. Racial and ethnic hostility is the foremost social problem facing our world today. From the systematic horror of "ethnic cleansing" in Bosnia to the random violence ravaging our inner cities, our world seems caught up in a tidal wave of racial and ethnic tension. This hostility threatens the very foundation of modern society.

We must not underestimate the devastating effects of racism on our world. Daily headlines chronicle its grim toll: divided nations and families, devastating wars and human suffering on an unimaginable scale, a constant downward spiral of poverty and hopelessness, children cruelly broken in body and warped in heart and mind. The list is long, but for the sensitive Christian, it is even longer: whole peoples poisoned by violence and racial hatred and closed to the gospel as a result; indifference and resistance by Christians who are intolerant toward those of other backgrounds, ignoring their spiritual and physical needs.[1]

But what is racism? I define racism as the institutionalized expression of a controlling group's prejudices. Racism is *prejudice* plus *power*. The Jewish scholar Abraham J. Heschel declared that racism is worse than idolatry. It is Satanism, an unmitigated evil, a treacherous denial of the existence of God. It is blasphemy.[2]

Man's fallen state is raucously proclaimed by his universal tendency to gather into groups, then declare his particular group superior—more intelligent, more righteous, more highly favored by his god(s)—than all others. Having common ethnicity, skin color, religion, social class, economic status, social or political philosophy, when their group gains political, social, or economic power, they attempt to impose their beliefs and practices on the powerless. When they do so, they practice racism.

Racism in America is systemic. No institution is free from its influence. No family, no community, no social group has escaped the diabolical poison of its hatred, indifference, and violence. Nowhere is its influence so vividly demonstrated than in today's Church. Whether liberal or conservative, this telltale reality remains the same: Sunday morning is the most segregated time in America. During this hour of worship, believers should affirm God's lordship and presence among them to a watching world. They should proclaim that God is One, that Christ is Redeemer and Savior, and that the Holy Spirit is present in the hearts of *all* His people—and all His people make up one, and only one, spiritual family regardless of external differences. The Church's failure to overcome this racism in worship is reflected in its failure to demonstrate love and unity in its kingdom works.

Sunday morning is the most segregated time in America.

The practice of apartheid in the American Christian church is part of a schizophrenic pattern; there is great concern for doctrinal purity, theological orthodoxy, and liturgical correctness with no corresponding concern for biblical righteousness or social, environmental, and economic justice and human rights here and around the world. The New Slavemaster is alive and thriving.

While there have always been isolated Christian groups that have openly renounced racism as sin, it has only been recently that major Christian bodies have adopted resolutions declaring such a position. Until now, too many churches have batted the problem away, assuming their own righteousness by declaring racism to be society's problem, to be addressed by social, economic, and political solutions.

The United States has clearly demonstrated that social, economic, and political solutions are not effective in solving what is essentially a spiritual problem.

But after 400 years, the United States has clearly demonstrated that social, economic, and political solutions are not effective in solving what is essentially a spiritual problem. Yet many Christians still adopt an attitude of indifference to racial problems. Sociologists J. M. Winger and G. E. Simpson have astutely observed that, although the Protestant churches stress the dignity and worth of the individual and espouse the brotherhood of man, negative racial behavior patterns persist.[3]

Interestingly, a convincing argument can be made that racism is a secular religion that competes on the world stage with other religions. Samuel Koranteng-Pipim states:

As a religion, racism shares all the essential characteristics of every other religion, secular or supernatural. Racism has its own:

1. Sacred artifacts—tangible object, such as a Confederate or Nazi flag, or even a person, Adolf Hitler or Elijah Muhammad

2. Sets of beliefs—creeds and myths that attempt to explain the origin and nature of reality

3. Practices—active observable aides of religion and may include acts of discrimination, violence, segregation, rituals and ceremonies, such as wearing a special kind of clothing or hairstyles

4. Community of worshipers—the social group that shares the beliefs and practice the racist religion; the racist community may be a church, a tribe, a gang, whether respectable, like the apartheid government of South Africa, or ignoble, like Skinheads or the Ku Klux Klan, or a nation where the civil religion becomes known as fascism

5. Moral values—the racist community's sense of right and wrong, which it seeks to preserve and transmit to future generations for the group's survival. For instance, the view that it is wrong to integrate churches and schools, or marry people of other races, or employ qualified workers of the other races.

Racism justifies the discrimination, exploitation, and dehumanization of one group by another; one group believes the other is less valuable, less than human, are their intellectual and moral inferiors. Historically, those inferior groups have been Blacks, Jews, Native Americans, Gypsies, and women—although other groups have also felt the sting of prejudice, have been despised and treated as subhuman: criminals, the chronically ill, the obese, the physically handicapped, the mentally retarded, and unwanted babies.[4]

MARCUS

By the time Marcus graduated from high school, life had changed a lot for him. His mother had left the family to live in Saint Louis with some guy she had met on the Internet. Marcus now lived with his father and older brother. His father seemed angry all the time, and his brother worked at various jobs but mostly hung out with his buddies at a few of the local bars. Marcus came to church now and again—said he liked the way it made him feel—but he had never truly committed himself to Jesus. He felt his future lay in getting a job and making money and working his way up to making even more money. He liked being independent from the vagaries of parents. The instant he received his diploma, he got a job at a warehouse and committed himself to one day running the place.

Working hard, it didn't take long before he got his first raise, and after six months he had worked his way up to being a fully qualified forklift operator. Next stop supervisor. As you can imagine, when one works around merchandise with tons of mechanized steel, one tries not to break things. Black marks appear on employee records when employees break things. Marcus never did. But others did—others who were white. And they were the ones who got promoted to supervisor. Over Marcus, and over and over again. Demoralized, after two years he finally quit.

RACISM IS SIN

Racism proclaims that God's favor and access to Him is based on *race*. The Bible says it is based on *grace*: "For the grace of God that brings salvation has appeared to all men" (Titus 2:11). "All men" means black men, white men, up folks and down folks—all folks.

Which simply means: *racism is sin*—for several reasons. Chief among them is that it is a clear violation of God's command that we should love one another (John 15:12). We don't love when we enslave, impoverish, and oppress people. We love when we uplift and minister to people, which is the very opposite of racism. Racism is rebellion against God for our own purposes—ego, greed, a lust for power—and it denies that we are all created in God's image and that God's image is fully expressed in a wealth of diversity.

So God created man in his own image, in the image of God he created him; male and female he created them.   —Genesis 1:27

God created man. He didn't create a superior man and an inferior man. To imply that He did is to accuse God of making a shoddy product. Obviously some people are smarter than others, but God didn't pass out intelligence, or any other attribute, based on race. If we "buy into" that lie, we say that God created inferiors—some to be "hewers of wood and drawers of water" (Joshua 9:21 KJV).

When I was a young man in segregated Arkansas, the state legislature would pass smaller appropriations for black schools than for white schools. Its reasoning: "When you educate a black man, you ruin a good cotton picker." Such an attitude tells a terrible lie about God—that He was prejudicial in His act of creation. Nothing could be further from the truth.

Racism is sin because it teaches that man's dignity and worth are determined by his skin color and not by his relationship to God. God's Word declares that man's worth and dignity are derived from his being a child of God by creation:

... because those who are led by the Spirit of God are sons of God. For you did not receive a spirit that makes you a slave again to fear, but you received the Spirit of sonship. And by him we cry, "*Abba*, Father." The Spirit himself testifies with our spirit that we are God's children. Now if we are children, then we are heirs—heirs of God and co-heirs with Christ, if indeed we share in his sufferings in order that we may also share in his glory.
                                                        —Romans 8:14–17

We are one family: black, white, yellow, red—the blood of our Savior runs through all our veins.

Racism is sin because it teaches the lie that grace is racially motivated—that instead of looking at the heart, God looks at color—that it's not our sin, but our skin. Such belief places culture and custom above God's inspired Word.

Racism is sin because it says that we can be excluded from God's abundant blessings based solely on culture. God's ownership of and sovereignty over all things is denied. It is culture that metes out justice, not God. My friend John Perkins puts it this way: "Justice is the question of who owns what." The wealth of this world and the privileges it conveys do not really belong to those who have it. It is not the property of the needy or the greedy, but "the earth is the LORD's, and the fullness thereof; the world, and they that dwell therein" (Psalm 24:1 KJV). Since God owns everything, it is presumptuous for one group to deny prejudiciously, covetously, and selfishly to another group access to that which belongs to God and which He provides for all His people. As it is stated in Ecclesiastes 5:9, "Moreover the profit of the earth is for all" (KJV).

THE CHURCH HAS FAILED

Often the Church is charged with the stewardship of what God provides His people. And for far too long the Church, the very one charged with protecting and proclaiming God's Word, has failed to use that Word to deal with racism.

We need to use it now.

God's Word is a powerful tool (Hebrews 4:12), a firm rock upon which we can build mighty structures of love, tolerance, and inclusion. The racists, however, stand on the quicksand of vacillating customs, ever-changing laws, and fickle societal norms. But when we stand on Scripture, we are firmly anchored to the truth (John 17:17). And that truth proclaims that it is not God's will that any should perish, but that everyone should come to repentance (2 Peter 3:9). All have equal access to God by grace through faith in His Son Jesus Christ (Ephesians 2:8; Hebrews 4:14–16).

How strange it is that the Church allowed itself to drift away from such a fundamental truth and tie itself to the buoy of prevailing cultural whims. It is time to throw off that line and return to God's anchorage—to Scripture that declares His love for all peoples. That is as true today as it was when Jesus told the story of the Good Samaritan—a man culturally hated by Jesus' audience, yet declared by Jesus to be their neighbor and, as they were, one of God's children (Luke 10:25–37).

When we realize that racism is sin, we expose one of Satan's great lies. Over the centuries he has convinced Christians that racism is merely a social problem, like poverty or ignorance. And since there is no biblical prohibition against them, there must be none against racism. But by acknowledging racism as sin, we place it under the spotlight of God's Word. It becomes what it is, like murder, adultery, stealing, coveting. It becomes unprotected behavior, behavior that soils our hearts and demands repentance.

But What about the Victims of Racism?

But what about the victims of racism—the slaves to this terrible Slavemaster?

They are much like Randall, a large, muscular slave who worked on a plantation with William Wells Brown. Even though the master told Cook, the overseer, not to whip Randall, Cook soon became determined to do so. As racists do, Cook had to prove his superiority. Trumping up an excuse, he confronted Randall, who, as the quotation at the top of this chapter tells us, refused to be whipped.[5] And when Cook called out three workers to help him subdue Randall, the slave told them: "Boys, you all know me; you know that I can handle any three of you, and the man that lays hands on me shall die. This white man can't whip me himself, and therefore he has called you to help him."[6]

Randall prevailed. The three men refused to lay a hand on Randall to help Cook. But that wasn't the end of it. The racist can't stand to be thwarted by the object of his prejudice. About a week later, aided by three friends, Cook confronted Randall again. When Randall refused to allow himself to be cornered, three of them attacked him, while the fourth drew a pistol and fired. The wound brought Randall to the ground. Now weakened, Randall received a beating on his head and face with clubs and was then tied up to a beam and given a hundred lashes with the cowhide whip. After his wounds were cleaned with saltwater and he was left hanging there overnight, he was then taken to a blacksmith's shop and fitted with an iron ball and chain. For the rest of his days he was forced to work in the fields dragging the heavy iron— the amount of work required of him was same as the others who labored *without* ball and chain.[7]

Cook's racism could not allow this black man to live any other way but with profound pain and humiliation.

The New Slavemaster—racism—leaves its victims in this same condition—beaten and brutalized, the rest of their lives handicapped by the weight racism demands its victims carry wherever they go.

Marcus carried that weight. After he had quit his job at the warehouse, a bitter anger flamed deep inside him. Stoked by his father's directionless rage and his brother's indifference, Marcus's bitterness caused him to lose one job after another. Soon his anger at everyone and everything rivaled his father's. And it was a painful rage, one embedded in a sense of great loss. He knew he had real talent, real skill, real worth, yet none of his ability mattered. He could have been anything and everything he ever wanted to be, if it were not that all the doors before him seem locked and all their keys given to others—white others. He began to drink. It took about four beers to dull the pain. And after six, the bottle pressed to his lips didn't feel like the mouthpiece of that trumpet anymore at all.

Marcus hasn't yet broken free of this terrible Slavemaster. But if you are a slave to racism, you can. To cut the chain and kick the iron ball away requires a renewal of your strength and confidence and the realization that you are not alone. As you turn these pages, you will learn what fuels that renewal and what brings about that realization.

TWO NEW SLAVEMASTERS:
INSTANT GRATIFICATION
AND THE MINDLESS
PURSUIT OF PLEASURE

*"The rain came down, the streams rose, and the winds
blew and beat against that house; yet it did not fall,
because it had its foundation on the rock."*
—Matthew 7:25

*But, alas! This kind heart had but a short time to remain such.
The fatal poison of irresponsible power was already in her hands,
and soon commenced its infernal work. That cheerful eye, under
the influence of slavery, soon became red with rage.*
—Autobiography of Frederick Douglass, an escaped slave

INSTANT GRATIFICATION

Even though we will start with this New Slavemaster, the issue we are about to examine might actually have us feeling the sting of both whips.

Sarah was married nearly fourteen years, and she and Gerald had three children, eleven-year-old twin boys and a girl a year younger. If she had been asked if her marriage was good before she got that call from Mailboxes, Etc., Sarah would have cried out, "Yes!" She and Gerald seldom argued, and he was home most nights, except when he was at the men's group meetings or at work. A staunch Christian, he loved the kids and worked hard, but only from eight to five. It was a real shock, then, when the clerk who called asked if they wanted to keep their postal box. "The payment's a week behind," he told Sarah. "You need to pay, or we'll send the mail back. Not that I wouldn't want to send that stuff back anyway."

Sarah was confused. She knew of no postal box.

Curious and more than a bit troubled, Sarah went to see what all this was about. After one quick glance at what was in the box, she wanted to send the stuff back too: folded up in there were a half-dozen pornographic magazines. "My son was addicted to that stuff for a while," the clerk, a woman about ten years older than Sarah, said sympathetically. "I'd burn it if I was free to do so."

Sarah stared at her with a long, pained expression.

Sarah said nothing to Gerald until after the children were asleep. Then, as he sat in his recliner doing the morning paper's crossword puzzle, she pulled the magazines from beneath her quilting basket, where she had stashed them, walked purposely over to him, and when his questioning eyes finally looked up, she dropped the magazines like an anvil into his lap. "I think these are yours," she said, her eyes burning with betrayal.

Instant gratification at first seems ... well ... gratifying.

Gerald looked up, an epicenter of shock radiating from his core. For a fleeting instant he wondered how he got himself into all this mess. When he first began to dabble in pornography, he actually didn't know what all the fuss was about. Even though he knew everyone from his mother to his wife had come out against it, it just didn't seem wrong to him. What harm could there be in it? In fact, there were benefits. His needs were easily satisfied, and he didn't have to bother anyone else to satisfy them. The pictures were readily available, and, frankly, they were stimulating. Yet now the woman he loved was in emotional agony, and the guilt he felt probably would be the same he would have felt if he had committed murder.

Slavemasters can be that way. They can start out feeling like friends, boon companions, then suddenly turn on you.

Slavemasters can start out feeling like friends, boon companions, then suddenly turn on you.

Nearly two centuries ago Frederick Douglass found that to be true. There was a time in his slave life when he served "a woman of kindest heart and finest feelings." Mrs. Auld had never owned a slave before Frederick came into her possession. Having been independent before her marriage, she was a woman of industry and self-reliance who seemed to genuinely disapprove of slaves behaving around her with "crouching servility." She wanted slaves to look her in her face as if they had human dignity and strength of spirit most whites saw as threatening. As such, most slaves felt fully at ease with her, and none left without feeling better for having seen her. She even went so far as to begin teaching her slaves to read.

But after a strong word of caution from Mr. Auld, she stopped teaching and soon stopped behaving humanely to her slaves at all. As Frederick Douglass relates:

> But, alas! This kind heart had but a short time to remain such. The fatal poison of irresponsible power was already in her hands, and soon commenced its infernal work. That cheerful eye, under the influence of slavery, soon became red with rage; that voice, made all of sweet accord, changed to one of harsh and horrid discord; and that angelic face gave place to that of a demon.[1]

The same was true for Gerald. As he peered down at the several magazines that lay as an emotional and spiritual weight in his lap, he knew everything about them was changing. The fun was gone; the sense of fulfillment those terrible images brought was evaporating; his insides, that part of him that usually leaped with a sort of forbidden delight at the very thought of them, lay heavy and sour. The same demon that had infected Mrs. Auld so long ago was beginning to rise up dark and destructive from between those foul pages.

It was as if he could actually see it. And his eyes remain fixed there—on the magazines and at the evil that lived there—as he spoke. "I'm sorry," he said. But it wasn't the tone of someone repentant, someone beseeching another to help him change into someone better. It was a gloomy, resolute sound that told Sarah he was filled with regret, but was powerless to change; he was defeated.

Unfortunately, Gerald is far from alone. Porn attacks all ages and both sexes, the rich and the poor, college grads and high school dropouts, mechanics and secretaries, sophisticates and commoners. I once counseled a woman with a university education, the wife of a doctor, a person who attended gala fundraisers for underprivileged children and fashionable diseases. She suddenly found herself addicted to Internet pornography. The last time I spoke with her, her marriage was crumbling.

This scene occurs far too frequently these days in homes throughout our country. And, tragically, Christian homes are not immune. They are ripped apart as often as homes that reject Jesus and fly the banner of the world's philosophies. And because Gerald had allowed those worldly influences to build a home in his heart, his eyes, and his hands, he had quite effectively shot the love Sarah had for him right through the heart!

Gerald's gun, of course, had been pornography; for others it may be the lure of easy credit or gambling or shoplifting or just unbridled spending. In all these cases, people spend their resources to get what they want, denying those nearest them what they need.

In Sarah's case, the instant she saw those filthy pictures she felt the bullet of betrayal tear into her. Sarah had become a victim of pornography, and we will see a little later how she and Gerald ended up. Pornography has its psychological roots in a number of different areas—

Members of this cult of instant gratification often find themselves in a desperate effort to keep their emotional house from toppling off its foundation.

power and control, inability to be intimate, among others—but we want to examine it here because, above all, this Slavemaster belongs to the cruel cult of instant gratification.

The cult of instant gratification

This cult has a chaotic membership. We have already seen one sect; another that seems to be growing uncontrollably is the Slavemaster that enslaves many to credit cards. One friend suddenly found himself $43,000 in credit card debt with nothing tangible to show for it. Just to make minimum payments he needed to set aside, above food, rent, clothing, and utilities, nearly $1,200 a month. He found himself working two jobs—jobs that took him away from his wife and children, wore him out physically, and severely limited his availability for ministry. The crack of this Slavemaster's whip was very painful, and the weight he shouldered out in the fields was immense.

But there is another way this Slavemaster works us. Members of this cult of instant gratification, like my debt-ridden friend, often find themselves in a desperate effort to keep their emotional house from toppling off its foundation. If they are sad, they run somewhere to get happy; if they need money, they borrow it; if they want companionship, they find someone with whom to spend time. Every plan is short term, every solution short lived. And those dragged along with them, like Sarah, find their own needs unmet, even ignored. Loved ones can take this kind of abuse for only so long before they simply leave. The ones enslaved soon find that their selfishness has rendered them alone.

THE MINDLESS PURSUIT OF PLEASURE

Like instant gratification, the mindless pursuit of pleasure is an emotional drug. Those enslaved by it crave the excitement; the chaos; the sense of belonging; and, simultaneously, the sense of detachment these pleasures bring. As with instant gratification, there is some justification for this pursuit, in moderation. We all need some fun now and then to recharge our batteries, refresh us, and make life's difficulties easier to bear. But there is something drastically wrong when that is all we want.

Are you a slave to instant gratification or the mindless pursuit of pleasure? Do you find yourself in the chaos of pornography, rising debt, gambling, or any number of other pursuits that can seem to regenerate you? Do you have someone like Sarah in your life, someone who loves you but who is being driven away by your insensitive, destructive, all too selfish behavior? If so, the Slavemaster's whip is clawing its bloody stripes across your exposed back.

Stop the chaos.

Do what these Slavemasters reject. They want you too distracted to reach out for something better, too tired to seek redemption, too intent on your own temporal requirements to be aware of your greatest needs of all—your spiritual needs, your eternal place in this universe.

Unlike the slaves of old, you have control of that whip and can stop the beating anytime you want. And when you do, you will find that you have *gratified* yourself *instantly*—your fleeting *pleasures* have turned to purest *joy*. By turning to Jesus, and through Him to the Father, you will be seeking what truly satisfies and sets you free.

Now let's take a look at another couple of Slavemasters we need to watch out for.

CHAPTER EIGHT

NEW SLAVEMASTER:
RAGE

Get rid of all bitterness, rage and anger, brawling and slander, along with every
form of malice.
—Ephesians 4:31

If any one thing in my experience, more than another, served to deepen my convic-
tion of the infernal character of slavery, and to fill me with unutterable loathing
for slaveholders, it was their base ingratitude to my poor old grandmother.
—Autobiography of Frederick Douglass, an escaped slave

ENRAGED

At times as we read Frederick Douglass' autobiography, we can feel the anger boiling around his words. One of those times is when he writes about the murder of slaves. He tells the dreadful story of how a Mr. Thomas Lanman of Talbot County, Maryland, killed two slaves, one of whom he attacked with a hatchet. "He used to boast of the commission of the awful and bloody deed. I have heard him do so laughing." He tells of another murder—of his wife's cousin. She was a girl of fifteen or sixteen, and she had been ordered to mind Mrs. Hicks' baby during the night. Since she had been up with the child the past few nights, she was tired and fell asleep. The baby awoke and started crying, but the girl slept through the noise. Mrs. Hicks didn't. The woman grabbed an oak stick and beat the poor girl, breaking her nose and breastbone. She died a few hours later and was quickly buried. Neither Mr. Lanman nor Mrs. Hicks was ever charged with a crime, a fact that angered Frederick Douglass.[1]

But his rage at those incidents pales when he writes about this next one. If you haven't already done so, read the Frederick Douglass quotation above.[2] Feel the rage in his words. It is like the words bubble up from a seething volcano—hot, boiling like lava. His grandmother had served her master faithfully "from youth to old age." Her work had brought her master wealth; her children and their children and their children's children had worked his plantation. When he died, she was left a slave to watch her children, grandchildren, and great-grandchildren divided up like "so many sheep," without being allowed a word to shape their own destinies. Then, to put the final punctuation on the long death sentence of her life, when she grew unable to perform the duties required of her, they took her to the forest, built her a drafty little shack, and then made her live there and support herself with her own twisted, arthritic hands.

Does reading that story make you angry? It makes me angry. Although it pains me to admit it, I am not a youngster anymore, and just the thought of being turned out to a very cruel and unforgiving pasture, as that poor lady was, makes me boil inside. And since I boil just reading it, Frederick Douglass must have become volcanic living it—actually watching his sainted grandmother treated so barbarously.

Has something ever turned your fleshy heart to stone, your insides to molten lava, and your every sinew to steel, making you want to reach out and strike someone?

Has anything like that ever happened to you? Has something ever turned your fleshy heart to stone, your insides to molten lava, and your every sinew to steel, making you want to reach out and strike someone? If you have never experienced such almost uncontrollable rage, perhaps you are not human. I am sure all of us have been that enraged at least once in our life.

For me, anger is born from injustice. It flares when I am treated as less than I believe myself to be. That was probably true of Frederick Douglass as well. He rightly believed himself human, to have the heart, soul, and just claim to freedom of any other man. But then he and his grandmother were treated with the cruelty one might reserve for beasts, for insects. Rage flared within him. And since he wrote these words long after his grandmother's death, he obviously carried his rage for many years.

That is the kind of rage I am focusing on here, not the momentary bursts of anger we all experience and quickly deal with. I am referring to the kind of rage that begins as early as infancy and is borne from injustices and violations that we continue to experience long after the events that caused it are forgotten—or if not forgotten, enshrined in dark, seething memory. This kind of anger is nourished by smaller, even insignificant, injustices and violations, and in the end, it robs us of so many wonderful experiences and joys.

As it did with James.

JAMES

James seemed angry all the time. Little things set him off: slow service in a restaurant, even the slightest disrespect from his boss. When he went shopping with his girlfriend, Jenna, and she diverted her attention from what they specifically were looking for, he started to grumble: "You said all you wanted to do was return that blouse. You did that. Why are we looking for shoes now?" If James' sparks of rage flashed too quickly and too often, the fires would light and flame, and he could hardly keep from strangling somebody. "I told you this would happen," he would flare. "Two pairs of shoes. And different colors! Now you're gonna want pants and after that a new jacket, maybe two. I don't want to shop. I don't like to shop. I'm outta here."

And as he stomped away, Jenna would feel that she had been strangled.

But Jenna saw some good in James. He worked hard, went to church, only drank the occasional beer, seemed faithful, and liked kids. But his constant anger took its toll on her. "You know," she would say to him, "one day you're going to push me just once too often, and I'm the one who'll be out of here."

Then James would apologize, with a halfhearted attempt at sincerity, and add, "But I hate to shop, you know that."

"Well, I like to shop. I'm telling you, I don't have to take this."

James's "buried" anger was about to cost him someone very precious, and it probably wasn't the first time.

ANGER

Remember Edward in chapter 1? There were a number of ways he could have reacted to his mother's planting herself between him and his crack money. He could have run away and avoided the situation. He could have realized that his mother was just trying to save him from himself and sought help for his addiction. He could have just tried to get Mom and his brother Jacob out of the way. Instead, with his emotional restraints weakened by the drugs, he unleashed his buried rage. Why he was so angry is anyone's guess, but he let the anger-animal out of its cage, and he, and it, tried to gouge out Jacob's eyes. It was definitely an attempt to permanently and horribly injure his brother.

Buried rage is powerful. And when that vicious animal is loosed, it doesn't care a whit about consequences, only about retribution.

Buried rage is

powerful. And when that vicious animal is loosed, it doesn't care a whit about consequences, only about retribution. The money was the furthest thing from Edward's mind as he plunged his thumbs into Jacob's eyes. I believe at that instant Jacob stood for every injustice Edward had every experienced: every violation, every slight, every time he had been treated with less-than-complete respect and as a valued human being.

> *And while anger crouches in the depths of our souls, we are slaves to it.*

James doesn't remember why he's angry. I asked him about it once, and he looked at me like I had camels squeezing out of my ears. "Angry? I'm not angry. It's a beautiful day. What have I got to be angry about? You're crazy if you think I'm angry. You want to see angry? Just say that I'm angry again, and I'll show you angry." Not only did he not have any idea why that caged animal was prowling around inside him, but he also denied that the animal even existed.

When I get angry, justified or not, I know exactly who and what "got my goat."

James doesn't.

Edward didn't.

Edward's anger appears to have snuffed out his future. James's seems to stand between him and his future.

Where did it come from, though? Counselors suggest a couple of possibilities. It may have resulted from a single, psyche-rattling past injustice, perhaps a horrific act of abuse. Or it may have originated from a series of less dramatic injustices that over the years piled up like highly flammable cordwood. It still remains caged beneath the surface, white hot and waiting for its chance to proclaim itself and seek revenge.

While anger crouches in the depths of our souls, we are slaves to it. By its mere presence, it colors and dampens so many important elements of our lives—our joy, our sense of well-being, our ability to sympathize and empathize. Physically, it wears us out. It takes so much energy to keep that animal caged and under control that life becomes drudgery. And when this New Slavemaster decides to break loose, the whip it carries cuts deep. See how deeply it cut into Edward's back? How deeply it may cut into James's back?

Is this New Slavemaster cracking its whip across *your* back? Here are some ways to tell.

WHAT ANGER'S CRACK FEELS LIKE

Although buried deep, there are surface indicators that anger is buried down there. In addition to the fact that little annoyances become major disruptions, and legitimate anger becomes inappropriately explosive, there are others.

We often feel sorry for ourselves.

The issues that caused our buried anger often make us feel put upon. If we were abused as children, for instance, and others we know weren't, we may believe their lives are far better than ours. And maybe we are right. Those things that have made us angry may be real. But feeling sorry for ourselves, although understandable, doesn't solve our problems; it merely keeps us mired in them much longer.

Our other emotions seem bottled up within us.

This New Slavemaster of buried rage acts like a cork in a bottle filled with wonderful, life-affirming emotions and keeps them from being felt and appreciated. We begin to believe nothing good ever happens to us. And in a way, we are right. Good does happen, but we never experience the accompanying rush of good feelings that should accompany it. To put it another way, our life's garden blooms with joy and sadness. But unless we feel the full, glorious impact of life's joy, those moments of devastating sadness will never be offset. Sadness will eventually overwhelm us.

We do not feel too warmly toward others.

Anger, even buried anger, has a target—the person responsible. Who among us can feel warm and welcoming toward the object of our anger? In spite of the fifth commandment to honor our father and mother, if we are filled with buried anger, we are often cool, even hostile, toward our parents. Even if they weren't directly responsible for our anger, often we believe they should have protected us.

We see God as a stern Father.

If we see our parents as all rules and no relationship, we will probably see God the same way. That attitude doesn't make us bad Christians, but it does cause us to miss out on so many blessings. We see God as One who wields the rod, even the sword, and exercises swift retribution for any infraction. No wonder we fear Him far more than love Him. Of course, God is loving and forgiving. I can't count the times He has held me in the warmth of His arms when I have deserved His rebuke. No one is more understanding, more generous and gracious with us. He, of course, wants our obedience, but no one knows better than He does the struggle we go through to give it. He works with us firmly, but also gently, filling us with every good thing as we move ever close to Him and to the likeness of His Son (Proverbs 3:27; Romans 8:29).

Do you see anger as one of your Slavemasters? If so, all that rage caged deep inside you makes you vulnerable to three more of Satan's lies.

Lie #1: You—and only you—can right the injustices that have oppressed you. Revenge. "Let's turn those tables. We have been cheated, victimized. And because no one cares about our suffering, only we can make things right." That is not to say that there aren't positives that can result. In William Wells Brown's case, only his rage at the injustice of slavery drove him to face the dangers of escape, and only his drive to right the wrongs he had suffered caused him to carry the truth about slavery to sympathetic ears in the North.

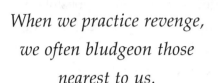

When we practice revenge, we often bludgeon those nearest to us.

But there is another side to this coin, and it often comes up. Edward's rage drove his thumbs into Jacob's eye sockets, and I believe Farrah's rage caused her to tell Carol about the affair with her husband. When we practice revenge, we often bludgeon those nearest to us, not necessarily those most responsible for our pain and anger.

Lie #2: Rage gives you power. We will talk about forgiveness later, but for now, this lie is crusted in truth. Rage does give us power. It keeps adrenaline pumping; it keeps us focused. Edward's rage exploded all over the place. When the thumbs in the eyes didn't work, he continued to struggle. When one escape attempt failed for William Wells Brown, he devised another.

Rage keeps *purpose* beating in our breast. And where weakness proclaims worthlessness, purpose gives us back our sense of worth, which, on the surface, sounds pretty good.

But this sense of power is destructive. It keeps us mired in our anger and in the reason for it. When we should leave our rage behind and use our energy to forge a new life-affirming foundation, we scheme and plot and scheme some more and in the end are no closer to a better life than when we started. The firmer foundation for the better life never gets built.

Finally, there is this lie. Every time I read it, I can hear the hiss of words in my ear, a sound tightly laced with seduction and contempt.

Lie #3: God betrayed you. Rage looks for a scapegoat.

"Someone did this to me. Oh, sure, I may have contributed to the problem, but if it wasn't for that other person, I would have been fine."

And who better to blame than God? No matter what has happened to us, He is powerful enough to have kept us safe. It is God's fault no matter who actually hurt us. It is God's fault that Dad left or that Mom killed herself. It is God's fault that we lost our job, that the house burned down, that we went broke, that we had a terrible thirst for alcohol or appetite for drugs.

It is all God's fault. He betrayed us.

We want the fear to end and the misery to stop. And until it does so, we have every right to be angry. In our wrath, I believe Satan achieves what may be his final goal: the wedge between our Creator and us is firmly set in place. It is highly unlikely we will call on Jesus humbly and fervently when we are consumed with self-affirming rage.

The crack of this Slavemaster's whip is powerful, the stripe it lays is long and deep, and all too often we submit to it willingly.

CHAPTER NINE

NEW SLAVEMASTER:
GANGS

"A voice is heard in Ramah,
mourning and great weeping,
Rachel weeping for her children
and refusing to be comforted,
because her children are no more."
—Jeremiah 31:15

The secret of master's cruelty toward "Henny" is found in
the fact of her being almost helpless.
—Autobiography of Frederick Douglass, an escaped slave

Melanie awoke from an anxious sleep a little after midnight. Outside it was dark, her city locked down; the streets lay in a kind of electric calm. At first she wasn't sure why she had awakened, but then as the fog of sleep cleared she remembered the rattle of the front door closing. Taylor, her sixteen-year-old son, the only other person in the house, must have left. Of course, he was supposed to be sleeping. Where was he going? Then a deep, defeated sigh—she knew.

The gang.

Her heart heaved, then constricted to a tight, wet knot.

What did they call themselves? The Imperial something; it didn't matter. Nothing mattered but her son, and right now her son was walking into a snare, one from which he might never free himself. The wet knot soured, then rose to stick in her throat.

Over the past month she had repeatedly warned Taylor about them. "They're a gang, and gangs are bad. Do you hear me? Gangs are bad." But he listened less and less. That friend of his—Brick or Rock, something hard and stupid, Blockhead probably—kept dragging him in. Blockhead called her precious son *Cutter.* She shuttered as to why. She and Taylor had battled this afternoon. He wanted freedom. "I'm no kid, Mom. I can make my own decisions. I'll do what I want to do." He was nearly six feet tall with shoulders like a football player's. He towered over her five-four frame, and his arrogance reminded her of his father.

In Los Angeles alone there are more than 1,100 gangs and 100,000 gang members.

There was no telling what trouble was searching for him; some of it reached out far beyond the point of no return. Which gave her no choice. She threw on some clothes and pushed out into the night.

GANGS

I have met hundreds of mothers like Melanie. Gangs are everywhere. They have been active in every state in the union since the mid-1980s. In Los Angeles alone there are more than 1,100 gangs and 100,000 gang members. One, the 18th Street Gang, has more than 10,000 members. They are in several states besides California and have spread south through Mexico down as far as El Salvador.[1]

When gangs invade a community, they suck the lifeblood right out of it. First, they take our boys *and* girls and turn them into drug traffickers, extortionists, even murderers. Law-enforcement officials estimate that half of gang members engage in at least one of these activities. Then they turn our neighborhoods into jungles of fear and violence: gang fights, drive-by shootings, innocents caught in the crossfire. And when community residents rise up to testify against them, they are threatened, intimidated, even killed.

With the brittle nature of their moral fiber, why wouldn't gangs react with violence? The stakes are high on the streets. The prosecution of a single element of the 18th Street Gang resulted in twenty-four federal convictions and $2 million in drugs confiscated, as well as the confiscation of several luxury cars, homes, and jewelry.[2] With all that money and expensive "stuff" involved, you would think the average gang member joins to escape poverty. But no. Gangs aren't isolated to poorer neighborhoods. The 311 Boyz come from an affluent section of Las Vegas. Brandishing the iron cross of Nazi Germany, they have been credited with at least nine violent acts, including one beating that ended with its victim requiring a titanium plate in his head.[3]

And gang activities seem to be on the rise. To pinpoint Los Angeles again, in the mid-1960s there were fewer than 200 people slain by gang members; in 1995 there were 807. And when you realize that only one individual dies for each ten to fifteen people wounded, the numbers of violent crimes becomes staggering.[4]

CUTTER

Melanie, on the other hand, had only one violent crime to think about that night, the one she hoped she would be in time to prevent. Before she left the house, her prayers overflowed with pleading.

When she reached the sidewalk, Taylor was nowhere in sight. There was nothing either way but older two-story homes, small yards, some ragged and unkempt, all sharply drawn in black shadows and sterile light from the three working streetlights. She took fewer than five more steps when she heard gunshots. She spun around. Two more shots came from the same direction. "Taylor?" she heard her tight, quivering lips whisper as she darted in frantic steps toward the gunfire. After a half-block she heard a sharp wail of sirens, then saw two bodies in a crumpled heap. She joined the growing knot of bystanders and heard a spatter of gravelly whispers.

"Who did it?"

"You know a *Cutter*? He did one of 'em, I hear." Her heart tightened; her knees went to rubber. Taylor did this? Her baby?

She watched the police secure the scene as more officers arrived with the coroner's van. Had she heard anyone else named as the shooter she would have let them know it somehow. But she couldn't "finger" her own son. She wouldn't even know how to say the words.

This was her worst nightmare—certainly no answered prayer.

THE BIG LIE

Why do kids join gangs? You would think that groveling at the feet of this New Slavemaster would be the last place they would want to be. The rules are strict, the initiation painful and demeaning. No "go to your room" for an errant gang member. Instead, it's "go to your grave." Yet join they do. And since drug use and violence take them places from which they will never return unscathed or unscarred, the instant they cross that terrible threshold, their lives grow dark.

And that's why I hate this New Slavemaster most of all.

It preys on our weakest and at the time when they are their most desperate for love, care, and acceptance. There is so much cruelty in the gang's lies—cruelty found in Captain Thomas Auld, one of Frederick Douglass' slave masters. He is described this way: "The leading trait in his character was meanness; and if there were any other element in his nature, it was made subject to this."[5] Henny was a young slave woman who worked with Frederick in Auld's kitchen. This brutal man would tie up poor Henny and whip her unmercifully. Sometimes he would tie her up before breakfast, whip her, then have breakfast and go to the store. Upon his return, he would whip her again, reopening the raw wounds that had begun healing. Frederick believed his master's cruelty to Henny lay in the fact that she was nearly helpless.[6] As a child, she had fallen into a fire and been terribly burned. The flames had consumed her hands so completely that she lost use of them, which made her an economic burden to Auld.

Young gang recruits aren't such a burden, and it is also hard to think of gang members as helpless. Many I have seen are lean and muscular, with determined, hate-hardened eyes. For them, the gang is largely a business. But perhaps at one time even they were like Taylor—or like Henny—emotionally weak and vulnerable, someone who needed love and acceptance. Of course, that's what we all need. And this New Slavemaster, like the old one, preys on these needs with an eye toward dragging our young people into a world of hate, isolation, and ultimately death.

If that is their future, why are 100,000 Los Angeles kids and young adults eager to join such gangs? I asked Taylor this question one afternoon a few weeks later. He confirmed what I already knew: "The gangs say they're family. And they act like family. Have fun and stuff." It was easy to see that being part of a family meant a great deal to him. "My mom tries. But we're on our own, and I work and she works, because my dad don't. So there's no time, for, like, family stuff."

"The gang is your family."

It is an intoxicating lie when young people, like Taylor, see their *real* families in shambles, when fathers have deserted them, and mothers work all hours to make those elusive ends meet. Or, unlike Taylor, they have never known their fathers, and their mothers are mothers in name only. Young people, from toddlers to teens, want to belong to well-structured, loving, disciplined families. We are created that way. And when our families aren't that way, we seek one that is. Gangs fill the bill—or at least they say they do.

And they say it four ways.

81

FOUR LIES OF THE GANGS

Gang Lie #1: "We accept you."

"You know what's neat about the Imperial Street Gang?" Taylor told me the first lie. *"They accept me.* I can be whatever I want, and they'll accept me. That's just plain cool."

It is cool, and it's a powerful message many children ache to hear. It says: "Whatever you want, whatever you aspire to, no matter how anti-social, even criminal, it's okay, go for it."

"I loved it when they talked to me like that," Taylor said. "And if I got into trouble, they said they'd be right there for me. My dad said that to me once. Just before he piled into his car and left for good. My 'homies' wouldn't leave me like that."

Gang Lie #2: "We support you."

That's the second "family" lie: *"Your gang family will be right there if you ever get in trouble.* Whatever you get into, we're here to support you. And not just with encouragement or prayers. We'll lie, cheat, steal, even kill to get you free."

Strong talk. And they generally back it up. Their record of intimidation and witness tampering proves that fact. If this "family" lie is believed, young people like Taylor are convinced they will never stand alone, even in their darkest hour. Of course, only God can make a promise like that stick. But to young people who have seen their real families crumble before their eyes, this lie is profoundly inviting.

Gang Lie #3: "We are loyal to you."

"Sure they wanted me to be loyal," Taylor responded to my question. "If I'm in, I'm in. But this is a good kind of loyalty. They said they'd be loyal to me. And I believe 'em." This third "family" lie says: *"We demand a good kind of loyalty; we're loyal to those who are loyal to us."*

Don't we all want to be loyal to those who will do anything for us when we need them? Of course we do. But there is a price to be paid for such "loyalty." A guy named Richard paid it. Called Little Richie by his "homeboys," he was only sixteen and a little on the short side. Although from San Diego, his body was found in Miami, Florida, with two bullets in the head. Word had it that he had been sent there to murder a guy who owed money to his gang. He had failed.

Gang Lie #4: "We love you."

But there is another price—maybe even stiffer—a complete and unquestioning loyalty to evil. And if a gang member should decide the price is too high and wants to quit the gang, what then? He comes to realize that this next, and last, "family" lie is a total fraud.

"The guy we called Stone Killer looked me right in the eyes and said, *'The Imperials love you, Cutter. That's what all this means—we love you.'*" Taylor, like millions of other kids, sees his family in turmoil and comes to the only conclusion he can: Love in his family may have been there once, but it's gone now. "Dad doesn't love Mom anymore, Mom doesn't love Dad anymore, and neither loves me—and maybe they never did."

Even Christian families with two Christians at the helm, Christians who have told their children repeatedly—before and after breaking up—that God loves them no matter what, only show their children that love leaves. Longing to feel accepted and connected, children drift to where they believe they are accepted and connected, then mistake those feelings of acceptance and connection for love. We, of course, know that whatever the gangs provide, it is something very different from love. We know this because ...

Love is patient, love is kind. It does not envy, it does not boast, it is not proud. It is not rude, it is not self-seeking, it is not easily angered, it keeps no record of wrongs. Love does not delight in evil but rejoices with the truth. It always protects, always trusts, always hopes, always perseveres.

Love never fails. —1 Corinthians 13:4–8

These kids want to be supported, protected, and nurtured.

Love is the New Slavemaster's cruelest lie of all. These kids, even the most hardened among them, want to be loved; they want to be supported, protected, and nurtured. They want someone to work hard for them, to sacrifice for them, and to give them only what's best. And they want it even when the best, the discipline, may hurt and require change. Deep down inside, they know this truth. What the gang offers is neither. The "love" that sent Little Richie 3,000 miles away to murder another did not "delight in … truth," nor did it "always protect."

MELANIE'S CHOICE

Melanie's love, on the other hand, did both. And more. As she made her way back to her home, she struggled with the thought that *love is kind*. Kindness includes wanting the best for the people you love. And she desperately wanted the best for Taylor. God tells us through Paul to "pray without ceasing" (1 Thessalonians 5:17 KJV), and that's exactly what Melanie did. At times talking audibly, she asked God over and over again what to do. Should she tell the police what she had overheard? Or should she try to convince Taylor to turn himself in? Or should she just pretend she had heard nothing? What was best for Taylor? What if he had killed that man?

"Oh, Lord, why have You done this to Taylor?" she asked. "Why did You even give me a son if You were going to allow this to happen?"

Somewhere on her walk back, her answer came. Reaching her home, she was just about to step through the front door and dial 911, when a squad car pulled up out front. Two officers slid from the front seats, and Taylor unfolded from the back. The officers said they would be back in the morning for his statement and drove off.

Without waiting for the rear lights to fade, a much-relieved Melanie wrapped her arms around Taylor, and after a long, precious moment, asked him what happened.

I am convinced that one reason God instituted prayer is that He wants to reveal Himself to us, to show us by His actions that He loves us and is there with us whatever our situation or circumstances. He revealed Himself to Melanie early that morning. Her faith was rewarded by a personal glimpse of the Lord's mercy to an anxious mother.

What had happened when Taylor left the house? He had seen Blockhead a block away in a group of five or six boys. As Taylor approached, a group of guys he hadn't seen gunned down two of the boys who stood with Blockhead. Heartsick and terrified, Taylor ran away and flagged down a police car. The bystanders who whispered his name must have seen him running.

In the spiritual war for our youth, gangs are Satan's nuclear bomb.

When he got home, he asked Melanie to pray with him. About a week later, Taylor recommitted himself to Christ.

For Taylor, the sharp crack of the New Slavemaster's whip—the horrific sound of those gunshots—was a wakeup call. For too many others, it's a death knell. In the spiritual war for our youth, gangs are Satan's nuclear bomb, one of his ultimate weapons against the most vulnerable among us, our confused and searching teens. Through lies, coercion, intimidation, and brutality, by appealing to pride and a hunger for power and purpose, this New Slavemaster draws these poor souls in and binds them there.

Fortunately God can break those bonds. And before this book ends, you will know how.

OUR PEOPLE, OUR FAMILIES, OUR COMMUNITIES IN CRISIS

Thus far in this book, we have been introduced to at least some of the

New Slavemasters and have seen how they work. Now it is time to see how terribly effective they have been. Over the next few chapters we are going to take a look at the crisis they have brought to our families and communities.

CHAPTER TEN

THE NEW SLAVEMASTER'S WAR AGAINST THE CHILDREN

Sons are a heritage from the LORD,
children a reward from him.
—Psalm 127:3

He peopled my young mind with unclean images, such as only a vile monster could
think of. I turned from him with disgust and hatred. But he was my master. I was
compelled to live under the same roof with him — where I saw a man forty years my
senior daily violating the most sacred commandments of nature.
—Autobiography of Linda Brent, a former slave

Linda Brent was six before she knew she was a slave. Her father was
a fine carpenter whose skill was needed in the Old South. He was
allowed to work unhindered and support himself. Linda lived with her
parents in a nice home, never dreaming that she could be snatched from
them at any time. Her father's goal was always to buy his children's
freedom, but he could never manage it.

Then Linda turned twelve. Her mother had died a few years earlier,
and her kindly mistress raised her afterward. But then she died, too, and
left Linda to her five-year-old niece. She and her young mistress played

happily together as friends. Her future seemed reasonably bright and secure for a slave, a fact that seemed affirmed when the five-year-old's father, Dr. Flint, was asked if Linda was for sale. He had replied that Linda was his daughter's property and was not his to sell.

But Linda's horizons darkened when she reached her fifteenth birthday and began to appear sexually desirable. That's when Dr. Flint began his base pursuits.[1] In her memoir, Linda says:

> But where could I turn for protection? No matter whether the slave girl be as black as ebony or as fair as her mistress. In either case, there is no shadow of law to protect her from insult, from violence, or even from death; all these are inflicted by fiends who bear the shape of men. The mistress, who ought to protect the helpless victim, has no other feelings toward her but those of jealousy and rage.[2]

Satan is no fool. He knows the easiest way to keep a people enslaved, isolated, and weak is to defeat their children. If he can shatter their hopes, keep their not-so-distant horizons filled with ravaging storms, then he believes they are his forever. And so Linda Brent was emotionally and spiritually shredded as a child. That destructive war against our children is still being waged—by the New Slavemasters this time. The evidence of this war is unmistakable, and, as then, we adults bring the greatest havoc.

First, some tragic statistics: Every year more than 1.5 million children fall prey to abortion—war casualties that have yet to leave the womb; seven of ten African American babies are born outside an intact family.[3] Pornography and child prostitution combine to be a $10 billion-a-year business—to create even more severely wounded children. And domestic violence accounts for thousands of children murdered every year by their parents.

Reread those statistics.

Now focus on the pain, the sense of alienation and weakness that each incident inflicts upon those whom it touches. And how much more severe the pain when we, as a community, absorb that collective blow. We will examine why the pain is inflicted later, but now let's take a closer look at these statistics.

REJECTED GIFTS

One million, five hundred thousand abortions a year—1.5 million silent cries. Although a dreadful number, it is not that surprising when we realize that nearly 70 percent of all young people are sexually active by their mid-teens. Tragically, this rate of sexual activity is just as high among our church kids.

Ripped unceremoniously from the womb, these are human beings, little you and little I. When one of our own suffers, don't we all suffer? But we also suffer the loss of all that those lives would have achieved. The contribution my children and grandchildren make to my life is huge and to be without a single one of them would be an unfathomable loss. Oh, how casually some among us discard God's divinely wonderful gifts!

The aborted children's mothers navigate some painful seas as well. Although the media and the proabortion lobby would like those moms to believe their pain is limited to the operation's minor discomfort, there may be considerable lingering emotional trauma that resurrects even years later.

A young couple came to me for premarital counseling. It was the first marriage for both. The woman privately disclosed that since the age of fourteen she had had six abortions and no spiritual or psychological counseling. Physically, she had received a clean bill of health, but emotionally and spiritually she was in severe distress. Her sense of self-worth was teetering on the edge of bankruptcy. She believed herself unworthy of a good man's love or even of God's love. Although in our counseling times together she tried to find a stronger spiritual direction, the damage was too great. It sabotaged any hope she had for a faithful, giving husband and children of her own. The marriage ended after just a few months.

Abortion brings pain to the fathers of the aborted children, too, as it does to the parents of the mothers and fathers. But for now, let's examine the damage inflicted by the next statistic: *seven of ten African American babies are born outside the marriage bond.*

SEVEN OF TEN

Although the parents of these babies have signed up for decades of difficulties, the real victims are the children. How painful is it for children to know their fathers don't love them enough to build a warm, supportive home for them? We will take a closer look at these "men" later, but for now let's just simply say that in each of these families, the father is gone. And because he is, what pain will the mother inflict upon their children merely because she is overwhelmed, pushed over the edge by having to be both mother and father? Will punishments be more severe, or will the kids be the targets of unreasonable anger and frustration? Will they be less likely to receive little gifts and big hugs? Just feel the pain in the words "Where's Daddy?" The pain builds.

> *How painful is it for children to know their fathers don't love them enough to build a warm, supportive home for them?*

CHILD PROSTITUTION—AND MORE

Young girls and boys, still young enough to look for Barbie and G.I. Joe under the Christmas tree, are dragged from bed to bed, used and abused worse than animals—over and over again. Those who should be their protectors—adults—treat them that way.

A few paragraphs ago we met a woman who had had six abortions and whose self-image was so cor- roded that she was unable to live a normal life as a married woman and mother. How much greater and more emotionally raw are the wounds inflicted on mere children plundered by prostitution's heartless indifference?

Kids hardly able to deal with their legitimate emotions are now on fire with emotions ignited by drugs.

And there's more. Drugs have reached deep into our elementary schools. Kids hardly able to deal with their legitimate emotions are now on fire with emotions ignited by drugs. Like most addictions, drugs drag these young users from all the critical supportive people and "things" in their lives: parents, friends, pastors, teachers. Prisoners of their own secret worlds, the young addicts face a deep erosion of life's quality and the death of their dreams and the sense of connection that helps those dreams flourish.

And all that disconnection—the promiscuity; the drugs; the sense of alienation and weakness; and, finally, the salving of all the resulting pain with drugs and alcohol—seems to gravitate to the catchall cure: gangs. It is within gangs that the great lie is told: *"We are family."*

We have already discussed gangs, but when considering the war against children, gangs hold a special place in Satan's arsenal. When a child crosses that threshold and becomes one of them, the damage is immediate. That is not to say that God doesn't work within the hearts of gang members. I have seen some remarkable cases of rebirth and redemption within gangs. But these are glorious exceptions. Gangs and their overwhelmingly thorough influence on children generally turn these young, vulnerable hearts stone cold. And no wonder—at very tender ages these children begin to deal in the businesses of death.

But that's only half the human toll. The families of these child drug users and gang members reside at the epicenter of this bone-rattling quake. Sometimes they shatter. Society also pays a huge price for the crime gangs and drug users perpetrate; the cost of theft and violence; the medical and therapy bills drug users generate; and, for many, the huge economic and personal cost of incarceration when gangs and drug involvement land them behind bars.

It is during this very incarceration that our youngest become even harder, even more prone to reject what family and society have to offer. There is the greatest cost of all—the productive lives that are lost to the family, the community, and the nation, which results in more agony and alienation that weaken us all.

But Why Does Satan War Against the Children?

As already suggested, pain, and the sense of being alone and weak, ranks high in Satan's spiritual warfare strategy. And his war on the children is vital within that strategy. Notice what the Old Testament prophet said of God when he was faced with all the dilemmas of his age:

> Yet, O LORD, you are our Father. We are the clay, you are the potter; we are all the work of your hand.   —Isaiah 64:8

If Satan can get to the children and build within them a hard, frightened core, then the work that God, our spiritual potter, must do to save His people will be that much more difficult. For instance, if children do not trust authority, isn't it more difficult for a teacher or pastor to share the Gospel with them? If children fear those closest to them, won't it be harder for a saved aunt, uncle, or sibling to win them to Christ? The scars borne by children can be very deep, their wounds truly difficult to uncover and heal.

The war against our children also perpetuates the activity and influence of the New Slavemasters. It drives our children to drugs; to instant gratification; to the mindless pursuit of pleasure; to gangs, prostitution, and pornography; thus making them willing subjects for the slaver's whip.

And as those leather thongs claw their exposed backs, especially when they are our children, we question God's existence and certainly God's love for us and them: *How could He love us yet allow us and our children to go through such agony? And if He is all-powerful, why doesn't He protect His children and ours from this pain?* We see God as unconcerned about our kids, which forces us to turn to other places for relief. The Psychic Network certainly seems to offer immediate, caring help. Like the warmth of the sun as a storm blows in, God becomes less and less a part of our lives.

But, again, Satan also wants to destroy the Christian influence within our communities. And when he goes after our children, he can succeed several ways. Well-behaved children are strong witnesses for Christ. People naturally want to know why such children are so good, so their goodness reflects well on them and on their parents as well. Poorly behaved children have the same effect on others; their behavior serves as a witness that the Christian God is weak, unable to keep His wayward children on the right path. Well-behaved children give their parents more time to spend being light and salt to their community (Matthew 5:13–15). Rebellious children, and especially lawbreakers, tie a family in knots and sap the family's witnessing energy and time.

Finally, the world can hardly wait to label Christians as hypocrites, as people who don't "walk their talk." What greater way for the world to use the rebellion of our children against us? The greater the rebellion, the greater the attack can be. It gives others one more reason not to listen to us. It makes our salt tasteless and our light dim.

And when our light goes out, the Enemy wins.

BUT HE DOESN'T WIN

Scripture is clear. Satan was vanquished at the cross and will be thrown into the lake of fire, into hell, on the Last Day (Colossians 2:15; Revelation 20:10). Our clear victory should give us even greater confidence as we face our spiritual enemy. We *will* win. Of course, not every step we take will seem like a victory. At this writing, three Christian missionaries have just been gunned down overseas. I wish this were an unusual tragedy. But it is not. Christians are always being tortured and murdered somewhere. Which means that our personal victory may not be here on earth, but it will be somewhere. One day all God's people, and may we all be among them, will hear His precious voice as He reaches down a supportive, welcoming hand and says to each of us, "Well done, good and faithful servant" (Matthew 25:23). Oh, how I long to hear those wondrous words!

Our clear victory should give us even greater confidence as we face our spiritual enemy.

PAIN, ALIENATION, AND WEAKNESS DISSOLVE IN LOVE

But until then, there is work to be done.

In Romans 12:1 the apostle Paul describes it as presenting our lives as living sacrifices to God. Then, in Hebrews 12:1, we are told to throw off the sin that hinders us and run the race God has marked out for us. What marks the route? Good works, works that bring praise and glory to God, works that God has prepared in advance for us to do (Ephesians 2:10).

Those good works are all built on a firm foundation of *love*. Just as sugar dissolves in water, so pain, alienation, and weakness dissolve in love—in all its simplicity, in all its profound depth. Which follows from this simple fact: God *is* love, and our good works express it. Our grandest work, of course, is to point to Jesus those whom God brings us, especially our children, and to help those who already know Him to grow in His grace and love.

In a way we have got a little ahead of ourselves. We have presented a solution here instead of after we have laid a proper foundation. However, in another way, this is part of the foundation. We all know the importance of love. We sense it in our own lives. How empty and inconsequential we feel when it is missing.

If love is the answer, how and where do we find it when we have a child who is caught up in prostitution, or when our daughter has just found out she is pregnant, or when our son has been swept up in a gang and finds himself intoxicated with its power? Of course, the love is found in Jesus, but who will point to Him? Who will plant the seed, then water and nurture it, then take care that the bloom is not crushed underfoot?

Who will do all this, and how will it be done when our children are under the watchful eyes of the New Slavemasters? How will we even get our children's attention, let alone their trust? Turn to the next chapter, and see how we begin to answer that challenge.

CHAPTER ELEVEN

THE TRUTH

*He who did not spare his own Son, but gave him up for us all—how will he not
also, along with him, graciously give us all things?*
—Romans 8:32

*In 1833, I had some very serious religious impressions,
and there was quite a number of slaves in that neighborhood,
who felt very desirous to be taught to read the Bible. There was a
Miss Davis, a poor white girl, who offered to teach a
Sabbath School for the slaves, notwithstanding
public opinion and the law was opposed to it.*
—Autobiography of Henry Bibb, a former slave[1]

Teri was in her early thirties; had a ten-year-old daughter, Candice;
worked as an administrative assistant; and was married to Collin,
whom she loved. For Teri, life had reached a balance. Not spectacular,
not particularly bad, pretty much where she figured life ought to be. But
then her husband died unexpectedly. At first the doctor called it heart
failure but called her later, even before the full impact of Collin's death
hit her, to suggest she be tested for HIV.

In a frenzied mix of betrayal and grief, Teri tore through all of Collin's
things. What she found gave reason to the doctor's request. For the past
two years, as best as she could figure, Collin had been deeply involved in
homosexuality. He had in actuality died from AIDS-related complications.

When her HIV test came back positive, Teri's sense of betrayal was complete. Collin's funeral was in two days, and frankly, as far as she was concerned, he could bury himself. She hurriedly stashed Candice at her mother's and ran off to find some place where the world could no longer touch her and she could end her own life, alone.

But God had other plans for Teri. While Satan whispered his lies in Teri's ear—bitter lies that tried to maneuver her into a place where she could find no one to help her—God presented the one antidote to these and all lies.

He presented the Truth.

Celia was seventeen and attended our church. A date had turned bad, and after bailing out on the guy, she had called home to get a ride, but her dad was out. "God," she said to the night sky, "You and I need to get that man a cell phone." Her only option was to start walking. After a quick prayer for protection in what seemed like a less-than-perfect neighborhood, she did just that.

Teri, still dazed, wanted to drive toward the ocean, but she wasn't sure where she was going. Although locked in the dungeon of her own rage, she suddenly saw Celia walking alone. Worried for the girl's safety, she stopped. "Would you like a ride somewhere?" Teri called to her. "This is a bad place to be walking alone."

"I'm not alone," Celia said, sliding into the car. "Jesus is with me."

"Jesus?" Teri grunted with a large dose of sarcasm. "Well, I am alone. Very alone."

"Would you like to change that?" Celia asked, slipping her hand into the back pocket of her jeans and pulling out a New Testament and Psalms. "Got something here that'll help you." Leaning back in the seat, Celia began to share from the little book.

"Never will I leave you; never will I forsake you." So we say with confidence, "The Lord is my helper; I will not be afraid. What can man do to me?"   —Hebrews 13:5–6

Then she told Teri how Jesus is always with her.

"Nobody can help me."

"I got one for that, too." Celia thumbed through a few pages. "…
because those who are led by the Spirit of God are sons of God," she
read. "For you did not receive a spirit that makes you a slave again to
fear, but you received the Spirit of sonship. And by him we cry, '*Abba*,
Father.' The Spirit himself testifies with our spirit that we are God's
children (Romans 8:14–16).

"Ask Jesus into your heart, and you're a son—well, daughter—of
God. That makes you an heir with Jesus. Now that doesn't mean everything always goes the way you want it to. But God's with you all the
time. You got kids?"

"One. She's ten."

"You wouldn't just let her roam around alone if you could help it,
right? Neither would God, if you were His child."

Teri started to cry. She realized that was exactly what she had
planned to do to her daughter—leave her alone, an orphan. Teri then
asked a lot of questions, and they all seemed to be answered when Celia
said: "God's gonna be right there with you through it all. And they got
drugs now. It's not the death sentence it used to be. But the big thing is,
you're not alone. You'll never be alone again."

That's the truth we cling to in those moments when, like Teri, we are
alone and in pain. In such moments we can look the Devil right in the
lie and tell him that Jesus is right there by our side and that He will be
forever comforting, guiding, loving. And life is a wonderful thing, in
God's service.

The truth Celia finally presented to Teri is the conclusion to the verse
I placed at the top of this chapter:

For I am convinced that neither death nor life, neither angels nor
demons, neither the present nor the future, nor any powers,
neither height nor depth, nor anything else in all creation, will be

able to separate us from the love of God that is in Christ Jesus
our Lord   —Romans 8:38–39

> *When we have given our lives to Jesus Christ, nothing can separate us from God's love.*

When we have given our lives to Jesus Christ, nothing can separate us from God's love, His companionship and support, or His guiding hand. He is with us always, to the ends of the earth (Matthew 28:20).

THE TRUTH WHEN WE ARE WEAK

When we are weak, lost, or confused, when our instincts tell us to roll ourselves into a fetal position and hope no one trips over us, God's truth commands us to get up, get stretched and prepared, and get busy. There is no sitting on our hands in the Lord's army. My favorite reaffirmation of God's protection is found in Psalm 91:1–2:

He who dwells in the shelter of the Most High will rest in the shadow of the Almighty. I will say of the LORD, "He is my refuge and my fortress, my God, in whom I trust."

God *is* our protection. His plan for us is better than any plan we might forge for ourselves. And it will succeed. Of course, at times we may not *feel* like world-beaters. There are times when I don't even feel like an eggbeater. Not a day goes by that this bishop in one of the largest African American denominations in the world isn't challenged and doesn't end up wondering if he has anywhere near what it takes to lead God's children. Yet this isn't my life I lead; this is the life God created for me to lead. And each time I meet an obstacle that seems just too big for me to handle, I tell myself firmly, "God didn't bring me here to fail. Trust in Him. And move forward confidently." Why? Because of what God's servant penned about Him in verses 3 through 8 of Psalm 91:

Surely he will save you from the fowler's snare and from the deadly pestilence. He will cover you with his feathers, and under his wings you will find refuge; his faithfulness will be your shield and rampart. You will not fear the terror of night, nor the arrow that flies by day, nor the pestilence that stalks in the darkness, nor the plague that destroys at midday. A thousand may fall at your side, ten thousand at your right hand, but it will not come near you. You will only observe with your eyes and see the punishment of the wicked.

Does that mean Christians will never be hurt, persecuted, or abused? Hardly. Listen to the stories from any missionary. We also are told in the first few verses of the book of Job that such horrors and calamities befall all of God's beloved children. But we also see in Job God's strong hand as He remains with and comforts Job during his ordeal and, because of his faithfulness, brings Job and Himself glory in the end.

When we do suffer, we can be assured that our suffering is part of a divine plan. In Ephesians 1:11–12, Paul points out that truth:

In him [Christ] we were also chosen, having been predestined *according to the plan of him who works out everything in conformity with the purpose of his will*, in order that we, who were the first to hope in Christ, might be for the praise of his glory.

Isn't that marvelous comfort in times of weakness? No matter how hopeless our lot may appear, every moment we live is part of God's plan for us.

And it is a marvelous plan, even when we are asked to suffer for our Lord, as Paul tells us in Romans 8:28:

And we know that in all things God works for the good of those who love him, who have been called according to his purpose.

That plan will certainly bring us good. It will reveal God to us as we see Him work within and around us. It will also strengthen, further, and expand His kingdom as we encourage and witness to those He brings to us. And, above all else, it will bring glory and honor to God. Nowhere in His plan is there weakness, confusion, or indecision. And when those elements of our humanity take hold of us, the quickest way to break their hold is to grab onto God and simply ask, "Lord, what step would You have me take now?" Believe me, wherever we are going, He is there before we arrive.

THE TRUTHFUL ANTIDOTE OF RAGE

Teri was profoundly angry. "She was really upset, Bishop," Celia told me later. "Especially about the HIV. 'If God loves me,' she said to me, 'why did I get HIV, and from a man who was supposed to love me?' Wouldn't you ask that question? I know I would. Anyway, she asked me: 'Is that what love is—hurting people? Is that what God does—hurt people?' I told her that sometimes we have to live with bad stuff, and HIV is bad stuff. I sure don't want any part of it. Was that the right thing to say?"

I nodded and thanked her for being there for Teri when she needed her.

"I felt so sorry for her," Celia replied. "I know some girls at school—well, one anyway—who is HIV positive. I pray for her a lot."

I told her to keep praying; then I thanked her for her involvement. After Celia had left, I thought about Teri for a while. Anger can be hugely destructive, and I was sure Teri was experiencing an unhealthy dose of it. That is not to say that her anger wasn't legitimate. I was even angry at her betraying husband and the guy who had given him the infection. *And* those who had enticed her husband into homosexuality in the first place. Although I wasn't angry with God, I knew that Teri was angry with Him for letting all this happen to her, because of the terrible price being demanded of her. But what could I do while sitting alone in my office? I said a little prayer, then turned my attention back to the pile of work on my desk.

But about a week later, things changed. Teri stood before my desk, blurry eyed and intoxicated. She had just finished enrolling her daughter, Candice, in our school. After the fifth-grade teacher had taken Candice to class, an unsteady Teri burst into my office. "I'm Teri, Celia's friend … I guess we're friends. I want to kill somebody, and I want you to stop me. Of course," her voice was low and hateful, "after I tell you everything, maybe you'll loan me the gun."

With my secretary sitting in the corner of my office, I began to listen as Teri told her story. It was pretty much as I had heard it from Celia, except for the last part. After seeking medical help, Teri had told her mother about her infection and, of course, about how she acquired it. Instead of being Teri's comfort and encouragement, her mother had immediately retained an attorney and filed suit to have Candice taken away from her. "She's afraid I'll give Candice AIDS. I just lost my husband, maybe my life—no, I *have* lost my life, certainly the one I had— and she wants to take my daughter? I just want to kill her. You believe in God, right?"

I nodded, a feeble hand coming up to indicate the wall of books to her right and the three different versions of the Bible on my desk.

"Good. Then tell me, why is God doing this to me?"

This question places the blame exactly where Satan wants it—on God. And Satan expects God to buckle beneath the pressure of it. But God doesn't. His Word tells us what we are to do with the anger that is produced by the twists and turns of our lives. In chapter 8 we discussed the New Slavemaster of buried anger and how to detect it in ourselves. We also saw that once it is detected, we must deal with it.

As for Teri, there was nothing buried in her anger. But buried or not, when identified, this is what we must do with it.

A MATTER OF FAITH

What causes anger? A whole cadre of issues, but I believe they all distill down to this: We have been demeaned, treated as less than who we truly are. And rage is our demand to be treated as we should be.

The longer I counsel angry people, the more I believe rage and faith are at the opposite ends of life's spectrum. The more rage flames in the breast, the less faith flowers in the heart. The more faith guides the sight and steps, the less rage gains a foothold. But why?

The writer of the book of Hebrews defines faith this way: Now faith is being sure of what we hope for and certain of what we do not see (Hebrews 11:1).

Faith says that God is in control and that He wants only the best for His people (Romans 8:28). It also says that He possesses the power and ability to bring it about (Ephesians 1:11). Faith is the firm belief that when life turns hostile, even destructive, when the dust clears, we will be better off for it.

If God is in control even the most grievous injustice is merely God taking us where we wouldn't choose to go ourselves.

So where does rage fit? It doesn't. If God is in control, even the most difficult situation, the most grievous injustice, is merely God redirecting our steps, taking us where we wouldn't choose to go ourselves. That was certainly true of Joseph when his brothers pushed him down a cistern and then sold him into slavery to some traveling tradesmen (Genesis 37:23–28). Or when Potiphar's wife lied about him and had him wrongfully imprisoned (Genesis 39:1–23). But that imprisonment eventually got Joseph into Pharaoh's confidence and, as a result, got Israel into a safe place to grow and prosper (Genesis 40–41). Injustice, as painful as it is, can be a friend.

And that's what Teri and I talked about. Could HIV ever be seen as good? What if because of her infection she comes to know Jesus as her personal Lord and Savior? It very well could be seen that way.

"But Mom wants to steal my daughter," she said again. "Shouldn't she be helping me deal with all this? I'm dying, and she's my mother. One thing is sure, she'll never see Candice again. Never."

It was time for another truth: Do not take revenge, my friends, but leave room for God's wrath, for it is written: "It is mine to avenge; I will repay," says the Lord. On the contrary: "If your enemy is hungry, feed him; if he is thirsty, give him something to drink. In doing this, you will heap burning coals on his head." Do not be overcome by evil, but overcome evil with good (Romans 12:19–21).

Revenge doesn't work. It escalates into regrets, particularly toward those close to you. That doesn't mean that if someone treats you unjustly you allow it; it means that

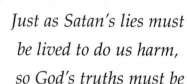

Just as Satan's lies must be lived to do us harm, so God's truths must be lived to do us good.

you should react with measured understanding. Teri's mother had a real concern. In her mind Teri's HIV meant that she had to choose between her daughter's feelings and her granddaughter's life: a terrible trade-off.

"Educate her," I suggested to Teri. "Convince your mother that her granddaughter's life is not at risk."

Revenge drives the person away. And Christians want the opposite. We want to bring difficult people to Christ. The unsaved person thinks differently, which is another reason Teri responded by saying, "I'm so angry, I'm not sure I can even talk to her."

Our time together ended soon after that. I asked someone to drive her home, and I prayed.

When I reconsidered my time with Teri, some thoughts began to jell into a strong belief. Just as Satan's lies must be lived to do us harm, so God's truths must be lived to do us good.

I counsel so many people who, like Teri, have no Christian reference points. To them, God, if He exists at all, is an indifferent force. Christian concepts have no practical meaning, which makes believing and living them pretty tough. This is a profound shame, because Christian truths are the only foundation upon which we human beings can possibly build fulfilling, productive, joyful lives. God is clear: *These truths set us free* (John 8:31–32). And because these truths are so important, they need to be learned, accepted, and lived from infancy. But who has God designated to bring these truths early enough in life that they become part of us, become the guideposts of our lives, the straight and narrow pathway upon which we walk (Matthew 7:14 KJV)? In the next chapter we will find out.

CHAPTER TWELVE

GOD'S TRUTH TELLER:
THE FAMILY

I will remember the deeds of the LORD;
yes, I will remember your miracles of long ago.
I will meditate on all your works
and consider all your mighty deeds.
—Psalm 77:11–12

My mother and I were separated when I was but an infant —
before I knew her as my mother.
—Autobiography of Frederick Douglass, an escaped slave

In the past few chapters we have looked pretty closely at the tragedy and the brutality of slavery, especially its practice of breaking up families.[1] We have seen how the New Slavemasters wreak the same spiritual havoc on the world, particularly on God's people, as did the old slave masters. The New Slavemasters also work to keep us alone, weak, and enraged and to make us increasingly susceptible to Satan's devastating lies. These lies, if believed, help drive a wedge between our beloved Lord and us. How can we reverse what seems to be a relentless, surging tide? How do we break free of these New Slavemasters?

With the *truth*. A thorough, relentless, personalized presentation of the truth, to ourselves, our children, and everyone else who will listen.

Our safe fortress is built from the same building blocks it has always been built—the family.

And to do that, we have to go back to the basics, back to how God planned this life in the beginning. We are engaged in an ancient war (Ephesians 6:10–18), and although the weapons may be newer, our safe fortress is built from the same building blocks it has always been built—the family.

GOD AND THE FAMILY

When the decay of our inner-city neighborhoods plagues us or when the angry grind of rebellious music attacks us or when we are touched by the godless behavior that infects our streets, it is sometimes hard to believe that it hasn't always been that way. But when God created the world, it was beautiful and sinless, a wondrous monument to His love and provision. So much so that He called the place where He placed us a *garden.* And I believe it was a garden in every lush sense of that word—luxuriant, colorful, peaceful—richly alive and wonderfully stimulating to the senses (Genesis 1:26–27).

Here we meet Adam, the first man created by God, and learn about the job God gave him, which was to be the steward of God's creation. He also gave him the authority and intellect to do it, but He didn't give Adam any help. In the second chapter of Genesis we learn how God remedied that situation. "It is not good for the man to be alone," God said. "I will make a helper suitable for him" (Genesis 2:18). But it wasn't enough that God knew Adam needed help; Adam needed to know it, too.

Why? This historic first relationship between man and woman had to be one of mutual reliance and respect. Had God created them simultaneously, without one realizing the need for the other, their relationship might have been immediately torn by jealous rivalry. So God told Adam to name all the animals. By doing so, Adam saw what God saw—only another of Adam's kind would have the wherewithal to be the physical, emotional, and spiritual helper Adam needed (Genesis 2:19–20).

So God did some more creating. Being a God of order and purpose, He set down the first block in His kingdom's firm foundation. But what was it?

He didn't create more men and tell Adam to form a government. Nor did He create a congregation for Adam and tell him to organize a church.

Instead, God created a family.

It is time for a bold assertion: *The family is vital to God's plan for all human cultures, including ours—the family is God's building block.*

The family is vital to God's plan for all human cultures, including ours—the family is God's building block.

GOD CREATED THE FAMILY

So the LORD God caused the man to fall into a deep sleep; and while he was sleeping, he took one of the man's ribs and closed up the place with flesh. Then the LORD God made a woman from the rib he had taken out of the man, and he brought her to the man. The man said, "This is now bone of my bones and flesh of my flesh." —Genesis 2:21–23

This wasn't a secretary God created. God forged Adam a wife: "For this reason a man will leave his father and mother and be united to his wife, and they will become one flesh" (Genesis 2:24). Thus was created a husband and wife—the first family—the first building block. Then, as we read on, other families come about; and just as our families are under attack now, that first family came under attack immediately.

That attack concerned the tree of the knowledge of good and evil. God had commanded Adam and Eve not to eat of the fruit that dangled on that tree, or they would surely die. The serpent, infected by Satan, tempted this first husband and wife. "You will not surely die," he told them. "In fact, if you eat it, you'll be like God" (Genesis 3:4). This was a possibility that Eve, then Adam, found irresistible. And so man fell. Discovered by God to have eaten of the forbidden fruit, man was cursed by God—bitter work for him, excruciating pain in childbirth for her—and the serpent (Satan) was doomed to one day have his head crushed, although he would strike God's heel (Genesis 3:6–19).

At that tragic moment in man's history, God could have dismantled the family, but He didn't. Nor did He when one of Adam and Eve's sons, Cain, murdered his brother, Abel (Genesis 4:1–8). Instead, God showed His commitment to the family when He had Eve present Adam with another godly son, Seth (Genesis 4:25). God continued to uphold this commitment even after man had once again proved himself over-whelmingly vulnerable to sin. In Genesis 6:5–6 we read:

> The LORD saw how great man's wickedness on the earth had become, and that every inclination of the thoughts of his heart was only evil all the time. The LORD was grieved that he had made man on the earth, and his heart was filled with pain.

Hadn't the family failed to keep man from falling into the very depths of moral depravity? But God never went to option two, whatever that might have been. Instead He chose another family—Noah; his wife; his three sons, Shem, Ham, and Japheth; and their wives—to repopulate the earth after God had cleansed it in the flood (Genesis 6–9).

ABRAHAM

It came time for God to build a physical representation of His spiritual kingdom on earth. He called it Israel. Now, put yourself in God's shoes.

If you were building a new nation, wouldn't you start by assembling a group of experts in government, economics, and social engineering? Not God. He started with a family—Abram and his wife, Sarai—setting them apart as Abraham and Sarah, Israel's first family, God's chosen family. Then He structured the entire nation as an offshoot of a family—Abraham's grandson Jacob and his twelve children, the patriarchs of Israel's twelve tribes.

God used Israel to form the universal family—a father, mother, and children—in which the father was the head of the family, the mother was the helper, and both worked to raise their children in the training and instruction of the Lord (Ephesians 6:4). It was to Israel that God wrote in Deuteronomy 6:6–9:

> These commandments that I give you today are to be upon your hearts. Impress them on your children. Talk about them when you sit at home and when you walk along the road, when you lie down and when you get up. Tie them as symbols on your hands and bind them on your foreheads. Write them on the doorframes of your houses and on your gates.

This is the template our families should use to pass God on to our children: one husband, one wife, and their children growing up to know the Lord.

A final bit of evidence that God is wholly committed to the family comes from the words of His own Son Jesus as recorded in Mark 10:5–9:

> "It was because your hearts were hard that Moses wrote you this law," Jesus replied. "But at the beginning of creation God 'made them male and female.' 'For this reason a man will leave his father and mother and be united to his wife, and the two will become one flesh.' So they are no longer two, but one. Therefore what God has joined together, let man not separate."

These verses tell us that God sees the family as sacred and that an attack on His family is an attack on Him.

GOD'S COMMITMENT TO THE FAMILY

Why have I gone to such lengths to establish God's commitment to the family? The next two stories illustrate the answer. In the first story, allow me to introduce my family.

My father was an itinerant preacher and sharecropper with only a third-grade education. Not a man expected to leave much of a footprint—maybe one not even expected to survive. But my father knew God, drew strength from Him, and trusted Him for provision. My mother's commitment to God was every bit as strong as my father's. Her focus, though, was on her family. Her goal was to feed, clothe, guide, and bring up all fourteen of her children to know and love the Lord. I was her ninth child.

We were profoundly poor out there on the farm, but as a very conservative Christian family, our poverty didn't dampen our Christian fervor. If anything, living on the ragged edge of solvency strengthened it. When you are hanging by your fingernails, you grasp at lifelines, and God is the best lifeline of all. From the beginning, God was placed, and thereafter remained, at the very center of our home. But with fourteen children, keeping Him there required thought and discipline and a limitation of the temptations that usually stalked us kids. Deeply suspicious eyes studied all forms of entertainment, which was obviously just the Devil trying to get us to drop our guard and sweep us into something spiritually disastrous. So we didn't dance, didn't play cards, didn't go to movies, and didn't read novels.

We could, however, be in school plays, so when one came along, my brother Rufus and I jumped at it. One particular play was cast when Rufus was about fifteen and I was about thirteen. It was spring, and our little hamlet of Jonesboro was beginning to warm up—which meant that the trees were budding, the birds were singing, and Rufus and I were restless. For teenage boys at such times, temptations get strong; and when those temptations bump up against opportunity, well, the results can put a real strain on those boys' character.

One evening, during one of those play rehearsals, the circus came to town. With wide eyes cast toward clowns and tamed lions, Rufus and I made a break for it.

The circus was sparkling and magical, and we saw it all—so much of it, in fact, that we didn't get home till around midnight. Needless to say, our mother was beside herself. We knew she would be, so before we got home Rufus uttered a phase that, since he later became a lawyer, he has probably said quite often: "I'll take care of it."

The instant our mother confronted us, Rufus told her that the rehearsal had lasted longer than usual and we had gotten home as quickly as we could. Mom gave us one of those "you've got to be kidding" looks, rolled her eyes, and just groaned. To state the obvious, she didn't buy our excuse.

[The rest of this story puts me in a good light, so I want it to go on record.] There was nothing holier-than-thou about me as a child. What I did at that moment I did because over the years my mother had made me just plain scared to lie. So I told her the truth.

And because I did, she exempted me from the punishment that I deserved.

At thirteen, the last thing I wanted to consider were all the snares laying for me out there. I wanted to experience all the fun in life I could, and the fun I sought winked at me from the heart of danger. My mother, though, wanted something different for me. She knew that an undisciplined life, and all the lies that keep it in the air, would eventually lead to catastrophe. She wanted victory for me and all her children. And the active role she took in all our lives, joined with God's commitment to our family, brought that victory.

Where our family was the poster family for God's faithfulness and commitment, and a shining example of how He sustains families through struggle, this next story shows how important it is for all of us to always stay focused on God's commitment to His families.

Tanya counted on it in a wonderful way. Let me tell you how.

Nearing forty, Tanya had a nineteen-year-old daughter, Rayna, who had a precious little boy named Toby. Almost from the moment Toby was born, Tanya took care of him. Rayna wasn't the most responsible mother in the world and spent most nights away from home with the boy's father, who was constantly in trouble with the law. So far these were just minor scrapes, but Tanya feared something bigger was on the way. But all her warnings fell on deaf ears. In fact, it seemed the more concern she expressed, the more often Rayna left Toby with her. It was a mixed blessing. Tanya hated that Rayna showed so little discernment in picking a man, but Tanya adored Toby, and the more time she spent with him, the greater her adoration grew.

When Tanya mentioned all her concerns to her husband, Dave, he grunted something unintelligible and went back to his crossword puzzle. One night, about 1:00 A.M., Tanya awoke to rapid footsteps on the stairs. Rayna was carrying Toby from his bedroom toward the front door. Tanya stood at the top of stairs and called: "Where are you taking little Toby? It's cold out there; he needs a coat or something."

But Rayna didn't get him a coat. She hardly stopped at all. Only long enough to tell her mother that she and Toby had to go away for a while—they would call later. And then Rayna and Toby disappeared out the front door. Tanya ran after them, but by the time she got to the front door, Rayna's car was already squealing around a distant corner.

Frantic with worry that Rayna and her precious grandson were running away with a criminal, Tanya ran upstairs and woke Dave. "Isn't that what you wanted?" he said, barely awake. "You wanted him with his mother. Now he is." Tanya could say nothing more but just sat on the side of the bed frustrated and frightened. Sometime later, though, God moved in her heart.

That Sunday Tanya asked me to pray for Rayna and Toby. I, of course, said I would. But then she said something that I will never forget. "I'm sure it'll be okay though," she told me. "God didn't create my family to fall apart. For all our troubles, God has something in mind for us. We're going to be okay. I know it. I've just got to keep doing the right thing, and we'll be all right. Toby and Rayna will be back; I know they will."

That's why I went to such lengths in this chapter to show you the commitment that God has to the institution of the family, and to your family in particular, whatever form your family may take.

God was faithful to our family, beginning with my great-grandmother Jenny and great-grandfather G. D. They married as slaves, and after the Emancipation, they remained married and faithful to one another. Both Christians, they stressed to their children that the way to escape abject poverty and ignorance was faithfulness to God and the pursuit of excellence in education and life.

Because of that emphasis, God was faithful in return. Of my parents' twelve surviving children, all finished high school, ten achieved college degrees, while the other two finished business colleges. Three are now pastors, two are lawyers, one is a dentist, one is a college administrator, two are professors, and one is an elementary school teacher.

But more than achievement in the world, our warmest, our richest family value is our commitment to one another. In times of hardship and stress, our family is a safe haven, a place of encouragement and safety. My mother helped create such a haven by helping when every grandchild was born and by always writing letters of encouragement and love each time one of her children faced life's challenges. We enjoyed her strong support until her death at age 87 in 1984.

There will be times in your Christian walk when you will be convinced that Satan, in league with the world, is winning in his war against your family and your commitment to build a Christian home. I am sure that Tanya felt that way. Maybe you find yourself in the same place, or someplace worse, and your heart is deeply troubled, so troubled you may want to throw in the towel. That is the time to remember your family holds a special place in God's heart, in His plan for His kingdom, and that He is right there with you. His blessing rests on your family and on you as you fight for it.

God's admonition for times like these, as expressed by the apostle Paul, says it all: "Let us not become weary in doing good, for at the proper time we will reap a harvest if we do not give up" (Galatians 6:9). God's Word never returns to Him void; it accomplishes what it is sent to accomplish (Isaiah 55:11 KJV).

THE NEXT STEP TOWARD FREEDOM

So far in this book, we have met what I believe are the major New Slavemasters. We have seen that God's truth gives us the weapons to use against them and that those weapons are the key to breaking free from their destructive grip. We have examined the family and its role in God's plan to keep His people free and safe from these New Slavemasters.

Now it is time for you to take what I consider to be the most important step—either break free of your current Slavemasters or make sure they never enslave you. This step will help you work within your family to make sure your family, no matter what it looks like at the moment, remains absolutely free from these terrible beasts now and forever.

It is the first big step in a long journey to freedom, freedom for you and your family. Freedom to feel God's power coursing through your veins and burning in your heart. Freedom to know that the God of the universe is working through you and that you are preparing those He has given you to do the same.

It is the freedom to be all God wants you to be, all He has prepared in advance for you.

It is the freedom to be *the real unhindered, unlimited you He has always wanted*.

Let's take that step now.

CHAPTER THIRTEEN

YOUR LEGACY

See he is puffed up; his desires are not upright —
but he righteous will live by his faith.
—Habakkuk 2:4

I gave but little encouragement to this proposition [getting married], *as I was*
determined to make another trial to get my liberty,
and I knew that if I should have a wife, I should not be
willing to leave her behind; and if I should attempt to bring
her with me, the chances would be difficult for success. However,
Eliza was purchased, and brought into the family.
—Autobiography of William Wells Brown, an escaped slave

Remember Sarah and Gerald from chapter 7? Gerald, a slave to porno-graphy, had placed his marriage directly in Satan's crosshairs, and what's worse, he seemed resigned to the coming salvo. Sarah, experiencing that resignation, decided that divorce was her only option.

Of course, sometimes divorce *is* the only option—where there is vio-lence or desertion, for instance. But if there is any hope, the couple should do all they can to reconcile. Marriage is too precious to discard. And Sarah was beginning to believe that Gerald needed saving. But she had been deeply hurt. And Gerald remained resigned to being a slave.

But it was easy to see they still loved each other. If they did break up, their hearts would break with them.

I decided to talk to Gerald. After nearly a week of trying to get him to my office, he finally morosely planted himself like a boulder in the dark leather chair opposite my desk. Some husbands will sit there with an expression that dares me to confront them. They are angry I would even think I could suggest that they are wrong. Not Gerald. He sat like a man defeated, powerless to intervene on his own behalf.

After fifteen minutes of talk, he hadn't changed. "It doesn't matter what you say. I can leave here committed to staying absolutely clean, and the next time I come within a hundred yards of a dirty picture, I'll be right there staring at it. What's the use of trying? Trying doesn't work." He must have repeated that mantra three times, and each time he sank deeper into the chair, his eyes deeper in defeat.

At least he knew himself. Addiction to porn is like addiction to drugs or anything else that emotionally and physically stalks its prey. When we are strong, we can avoid it; when we are weak, we fall. And we are weak quite often.

The challenge is to remain strong. And when we are weak, to call on something that strengthens us. As it turned out, the weakest member of Gerald's family was the one who provided Gerald with the strength he needed. "You have three children, don't you, Gerald?" I asked rhetorically.

"Twin boys and a girl."

"I had five boys," I said. "Other fathers tell me little girls have a way of worming their ways into a father's heart. That true?"

Gerald's face, although still fortressed behind dark clouds, managed a smile. "Jessi ... Jessica," he said. "She's ten. Smart. I wouldn't trade my boys for anything, but Jessi's special. Very special."

"You have a picture?" He fished one out his wallet. I had seen her at the church before, but the picture was particularly cute. "She's a lovely young lady," I told him. "Now, look at the picture." He did, and his eyes widened, and his lips twitched up in appreciative smile. "How would those eyes change if she found those magazines you've stashed away? What would she think about her dad then?"

His expression didn't change much, but I sensed discomfort, an electric charge firing through him. He loved his children. He wanted to be remembered by them as a good father, one who would never put them at risk. Suddenly he realized that his porn addiction was doing just that.

His eyes came up with a frightened look in them, a tear poised to run down his cheek. "Where can I go for help?" he asked.

BREAKING FREE

Breaking free from your New Slavemasters is starting an arduous journey. The same was true for slaves. They made their escape knowing the horror they might encounter along the way and the greater horror if they were apprehended. William Wells Brown writes this of his journey to freedom:

> I walked up and down the road until near midnight, when the clouds disappeared, and I welcomed the sight of my friend, truly the slave's friend, the North Star!
>
> As soon as I saw it, I knew my course, and before daylight I traveled twenty or twenty-five miles. It being in the winter I suffered intensely from the cold; being without an overcoat, and my other clothes rather thin for the season. I was provided with a tinderbox, so that I could make up a fire when necessary. And but for this, I should certainly have frozen to death. ... On the fourth day, my provisions gave out, and then what to do I could not tell. ... On the first night after my food was gone, I went to a barn on the road-side, and there found some ears of corn. I took ten or twelve of them, and kept on my journey. During the next day, while in the woods, I roasted my corn and feasted upon it, thanking God that I was so well provided for.[1]

Like William Brown's escape, ours requires strong commitment and the assurance that we take our Savior with us. I believe our commitment comes when we focus where Gerald did—on our legacy—how we want to be remembered by those who know us best and love us most. Then, to keep the commitment alive as William Brown did, we concentrate on where we are going and the freedom that awaits us there. And through it all, we recognize our Savior is right there with us so that we are never alone.

This wasn't the first time centering on a legacy helped someone keep moving toward freedom. Remember Rufus and me at the circus? I told you that my mother wanted to protect me from the effects of an undisciplined life and the lies that supported it. But I didn't tell you what she said to me as I sat terrified at the kitchen table that night. "Son, who do you want to become? When people say your name—George Dallas McKinney—what do you want them to think about you?"

I was thirteen. Who thinks about something like this at that age? I told her I had never thought about it.

"Well, it's time you started thinking about it. Especially after what you did tonight. Do you want to be known as someone who lies, who betrays the trust of those who trust in you? You love Rufus, right?"

Not to say anything negative about my other twelve siblings, but Rufus and I have always been close. Yes, I loved Rufus. Still do.

"How do you want Rufus to see you? As someone who keeps his word? Or as someone who betrays people? Stop and think now. If you're willing to lie to me, won't he eventually realize you just might lie to him, too, and one day betray his trust? What do you think your relationship will be then?"

The instant she focused on Rufus, I understood. Sure, I wanted us to have fun and goof around together, but I never wanted him to think I would betray him—and if I betrayed my mom, I could betray him.

My legacy suddenly mattered.

Just as it had with Gerald.

Just as it will with all of
us. When how others perceive
us becomes important—even
crucial—then the war with
the New Slavemasters against
which we struggle is instantly
joined. That's not to say we
have quick victory, but it does
allow us to picture what that

When how others perceive us becomes important then the war with the New Slavemasters is instantly joined.

victory holds for us. For Gerald, the image was sweet: love and respect from his children preserved, marital trust reborn, and passions rekindled. When we can describe the future for which we want to be remembered, we can make it our own. But to achieve that future, we then must break the slave shackles so that we might become the persons our future demands.

Gerald quickly entered counseling and worked hard to overcome his addiction. I, too, at thirteen, launched by the vision of the future my mother planted within me, worked hard—and imperfectly—to become a man of honor, one my parents, and Rufus, would never doubt.

But not everyone has that same reaction to this suggestion. "Look to the future? Here I am, not able to get through the day without looking at dirty pictures, and all you can say is *look to the future?* How naïve are you?"

I am not naïve, and that is exactly what I ask you to do. Our future is built on our present. If we want to create strong, vibrant tomorrows, we must create strong, vibrant todays.

And what better way to subdue these beasts that try to demean and destroy us than to take lives of shame and defeat and turn them into lives for which we want to be remembered.

"I suddenly felt like my life had purpose."

William Wells Brown's life had purpose. It wasn't on the plantation. It wasn't to please his masters and mistresses. His purpose was to escape, and earlier in this chapter we saw that he fulfilled that purpose. But we also saw it was this focus on purpose that caused him to delay satisfying the desires of his own heart—marriage—because to marry meant to delay, maybe indefinitely, his escape. He knew he would have to be alone as he threaded his way through the forests, evading dogs and inquisitive strangers, suffering cold and starvation on his way to freedom.[2] Nothing else mattered; he was committed to freedom. Having that purpose changed pain and weakness to strength and endurance; it turned his sense of being alone and fearful into focus and power.

The same transformation occurred to Gerald. Like all addictions, they are seldom about what the addiction is to; more often, they are about what the addiction brings. Pornography is generally rooted in a need to be in control, a need for power in relationships. People have no greater power than they have over a picture; they can look at it when they want, treat it any way they like, discard it when it no longer serves a purpose. And it demands nothing in return: no birthday presents, no "Where you been? How come you're late?" But it is also cold, humorless, heartless, and certainly unloving. Gerald gave up a lot when he sought satisfaction from something slick and glossy.

When he went into counseling and sketched out the legacy he wanted to live and leave, his life, like William Brown's, gained purpose.

"I decided first to be a good Christian, next to be a good husband and father. I suddenly felt like I had a reason to get up in the morning again. Instead of focusing on myself all the time, I was concentrating on Sarah and the kids. Pornography was so far away from that goal. And when it tempted me—and it did now and then—I'd talk back to it. 'I don't want you part of my life anymore,' I'd say. 'My life isn't about that anymore.'"

> *For not only do we gain purpose when we build our legacy, but building it also causes us to be honest with ourselves about ourselves.*

As I write this, I wonder how Edward's life might have changed had he stopped and considered his legacy. If, instead of being remembered as a catalyst to tragedy, he had decided to be remembered as a good son, a good brother, an asset to God and his community. Would such decisions have helped him gain the power and direction to change? I believe they would.

For not only do we gain purpose when we build our legacy, but building it also causes us to be honest *with* ourselves *about* ourselves.

OUR LEGACY KEEPS US HONEST

Since the New Slavemasters pay allegiance to the father of all lies (John 8:44), they are a deceptive bunch. As Gerald discovered, when we begin to break free, we will frequently hear their siren song enticing us back. There may be times when we will find ourselves actually lying to ourselves when tempted to enslave ourselves again. When we live our legacy, it becomes far more difficult to keep such a lie alive.

For instance, about two weeks into counseling, Gerald, feeling freer than he had in years, decided he wanted to be seen as a generous man by his family and community. A few dollars to the church suddenly was not enough, so he began to tithe. Christmas was coming, and he took a hard look at the presents he gave to his family. As a result, the pile around the Christmas tree got bigger, and when opened, it became obvious that the presents were more thoughtful. When Sarah came to him for money for shelves in her sewing room, he gave her more than she asked for, enough for better lighting, too.

He also began to give of his time at church and elsewhere. And he used that time he gave *elsewhere* to witness to those who were giving their time to the same cause. He saw his witness as generosity—giving of what God had so mercifully given him.

When all is said and done, we will be seen for what we are as much as for what we do.

OUR LEGACY KEEPS US FROM BEING HYPOCRITES

Doesn't it make us hypocrites if we behave in a noble way only because we want to be seen as noble? A fair question. After all, aren't we trying to be perceived as someone we are not? When we behave generously when we are really Scrooge at heart, aren't we just acting for the public?

I don't think so. Remember our ultimate goal: to break free of the New Slavemasters, to put real distance between ourselves and the *crack* of their whip. I don't know how many times I have read accounts written by those precious slaves in which they described their escape attempts. Often they would disguise themselves, not their person—it was hard for them to pretend they weren't black—but their intent. While walking in the forest they would carry a horse's halter, so they could explain, if confronted, they were merely searching for a stray horse.

Just as that halter was a slave's way out, Gerald once found that his generosity was also. Those addicted to porn schedule their visits to it. Gerald would make his way to a certain newsstand at lunchtime. One day after counseling he found himself near that same newsstand. It was before lunch, and he had five bucks in his pocket. Just enough for a magazine. He could actually hear the Slavemaster's voice calling to him. "Come on over. Just one look. What can it hurt?" It acted like a magnet pulling him in—until he dropped the money in a Salvation Army kettle set up on the street corner. Was Gerald a hypocrite when he acknowledged the worker's appreciation for his donation? No. He was being generous even when it was hard to be. Gerald was "walking the walk," not just "talking the talk."

But there is another reason we are not hypocrites when we do such things. All Christians are sinners saved by grace (Ephesians 2:8–9); we are always less noble than we want to be. Some days at church I am disappointed or emotionally down and just don't feel like being there. Yet my congregation needs me to be emotionally up, ready to meet their challenges with determination and cheer. Even when emotionally blunted, I crank up a smile and get to work. Does that make me a hypocrite? No. And neither are you when you feel out of sorts on the inside but present a cheerful smile to the world. Would an honest scowl be better?

How often have we, as Christians, been encouraged to be like Jesus, the expression of God's love and provision, His salt and light within a fallen world? Are any of us as wise as Jesus, as loving as Jesus, as perceptive and as giving as Jesus? Yet we want to present ourselves as much like Jesus as we can. Is that hypocrisy, or is it simply our Christian goal? The same is true when we consider our legacy. It is the truly generous people who are generous even when they just don't feel like doing so.

And God may bless you.
When Gerald tossed that money into the Salvation Army kettle, God knew how difficult it was for him. God knew the temptation he had just conquered. And when Gerald gave away that money instead of buying a dirty magazine with it, God blessed him.

"Suddenly the temptation was gone," he said. "All that existed was that guy in the blue uniform with the bell. God took all the temptation away. A moment before I was actually beginning to feel the stripes on my back again; then I was free again. God blessed—He truly blessed."

Whenever we do the right thing, particularly when we have to wage a great battle within us to do so, God blesses. God is our Good Father. He loves us more than we know. And He is the Rewarder of those who diligently seek Him (Hebrews 11:6 KJV). And a good part of the diligence may include negotiating an arduous road.

Our Legacy Helps Us Draw Power and Recommitment from the Journey

William Brown tells us a little more about his escape:

On the fifth or sixth day, it rained very fast, and it froze about as fast as it fell, so that my clothes were one glare of ice. I traveled on at night until I became so chilled and benumbed—the wind blowing into my face—that I found it impossible to go any further, and accordingly took shelter in a barn, where I was obliged to walk about to keep from freezing.[3]

This was a tough journey. But Brown didn't give up. His strength to keep going came from within:

Keep your eyes riveted on the future and the legacy you wish to build.

My escape to a land of freedom now appeared certain, and the prospects of the future occupied a great part of my thoughts.[4]

Just as the vision of a free future motivated William Wells Brown to start his journey, that same vision re-energized him and kept him going.

Now you know what you must do to break free of the New Slavemaster's whip. Keep your eyes riveted on the future and the legacy you wish to build. And, as you build it, keep refining the legacy, so that you become exactly the person God has created you to be.

HOW TO START

Look critically at your life. Are you a slave to any of the Slavemasters we have met? How about any others? How have the New Slavemasters affected how others see you? How do you want people to see you? Be honest and make a list. That's where you start—with this list. May I suggest a few entries?

Honesty

Honesty is more than returning extra change a cashier accidentally gives us. It is how we present ourselves to others; whether we are forthright, trustworthy, and completely without guile; whether our yes means yes and our no means no; whether a promise made is a promise kept.

Courage

Courage is *God's people doing God's work God's way, even when common sense tells us to avoid, to evade, or to escape.*

Courage means using our gifts for God's glory. Do you sing, dance, act? Are you patient, funny, understanding of people and their struggles? These are all gifts from God for use in His service.

Faith

Faith is dependence upon God. The stronger our faith, the stronger our dependence and the less we take matters into our own hands when times get tough.

And there are others for your list: selfless love, enduring patience, and true joy. As life unfolds, identify others and add them to your list; then expand upon them. Understand how they work, how they matter in your life, and what to do to be seen as someone possessing these characteristics. Then determine to "walk the walk."

THE LEGACY OF YOUR CALLING

Each one of us is unique. But when we are in bondage, at the whim of some reckless, vicious Slavemaster, that uniqueness is blurred by the wretchedness of slavery. We are all just field hands, getting up each day to serve the slave master and done only when he says we are done. We are not authors or swimmers or violinists or financial wizards or any number of other gifted souls called by God to work in His kingdom.

Maybe you had a calling before you became a slave, or maybe you only had a desire. In either case, set your eyes on the future. Your slavery is yesterday's news. Today's news is what you have been called to become. And that calling will occupy a large place in your legacy. If you are a nurse, your legacy will be one of healing. If you are a plumber, you legacy will be about hard, meticulous work.

Take a moment now, and describe your legacy in terms of the unique life to which God has called you. For instance, the legacies of African missionaries would include courage in the face of political unrest. If you sense a calling as a teacher, consider the patience you will need, the willingness to never stop learning.

Now that you have your list and probably better understand your calling, I challenge you to do whatever you must to break free of your personal Slavemaster. If that Slavemaster is an addiction, get into counseling and the appropriate rehab program. If it is an emotional issue, find a good Christian counselor. Whatever it is, pray earnestly for guidance and wisdom; then talk to your pastor and loved ones, and weigh heavily their advice. You now know that you are an important part of God's plan. You are needed. Don't allow this opportunity to be all God wants you to be to pass you by. Break free of your Slavemaster, and take your rightful place in God's army.

And, unless you are one of a small minority, you are called to be part of a family. Now that you have begun to break free of your New Slavemaster, an important call to heed is the one that asks you to help your family break free from theirs. The remainder of this book will help you answer that call.

THE FREEDOM FAMILY

"Therefore everyone who hears these words of mine and puts them into practice is

like a wise man who built his house on the rock."

—Matthew 7:24

I went to the jail again the next day, and Mr. Simonds, the keeper,

allowed me to see my sister for the last time.

—Autobiography of William Wells Brown, an escaped slave

C hurches aren't immune to the New Slavemaster's whip. St. Stephen's Church of God in Christ is where I have labored for forty-two years. In the fall of 1984, on the eve of our twenty-second anniversary—just two weeks after we had dedicated our new school to the Lord's service—Satan sent a young man enslaved to rage and bitterness to do his worst against us. The night before was unusually hot and humid for September. That discomfort, mixed with my excitement at the next day's activities, meant I couldn't sleep. I was still awake at 2 A.M. when the phone rang. Seconds later, I rushed out to see angry flames devouring our beloved church. Firefighters worked bravely and feverishly, but St. Stephen's could not be saved. And as the dawn broke over gray eastern hills, all our hopes for the future, all the hopes I had planned to raise up to God in that morning's address to thousands of our faithful, lay before us in smoldering black ash.

I wanted to give up and, I thought, for a very good reason. Hadn't God just told me in the relentless pulse of those hungry flames that all my future plans were of no use to Him? Hadn't He just put out whatever light we had been to the community? Maybe He was telling me to go, too. Maybe I should just oblige.

But then something happened. The Christian community stepped in to assist. That very morning churches around San Diego offered money to help rebuild, gave us facilities in which to meet, and soon we were given a huge tent in which to hold services on our own property again. Then, around the nation, others rose up to help. God wasn't telling me to give up. He was telling me to rebuild and recommit, that it wasn't *our* efforts that would make St. Stephen's a wondrous beacon to the community again, but His. I have come to believe that horrific morning was allowed so we would know that our future, a future much greater than our past, would most assuredly be built on Jesus, by Jesus.

The Lord wants the same for the rest of His kingdom. And to assure that it is, He wants His kingdom constructed from strong building blocks: vibrant, deeply committed Christian families united in their commitment to each other and built on the rock, upon Jesus. Such families have broken free of the New Slavemasters; such families keep the New Slavemasters at bay.

Is yours such a family? Having been ravaged by the New Slavemasters for so long, the vast majority of our families look like targets, peppered with holes, their hearts and souls blown away. Like St. Stephen's that hot September morning, far too many precious Christian families lie in ashes. Perhaps you see your own family that way. Maybe you are a single mother barely able to keep food on the table, juggling work and kids, while you watch the futures of both starting to crumble before your eyes. Or maybe you are a grandparent who hoped for a much-needed retirement, until your grandchildren showed up on your doorstep. Or maybe you are raising a niece or nephew or a younger brother or sister. If so, you may be a family brought together by circumstance and kept together by obligation. Maybe your highest goal is merely to survive. That was my goal as I stared, seemingly defeated, at those ashes.

I am here to offer you hope, real hope.

Just as St. Stephen's rose to be an even greater influence for Christ than ever before, so can your family. And just as you have taken your first steps to free yourself from the New Slavemaster's lash, it is time to help your family take those steps. And as you and your family journey together, you will see yourselves becoming powerful forces within God's kingdom.

FAMILIES DON'T JUST HAPPEN

Whatever your family now looks like, did you plan it? If you are a single parent, did you plan to be one? If you are that grandparent, did you plan to one day raise your grandchildren? Even if your family started the traditional way, didn't you just meet a pair of luscious eyes somewhere that beckoned your way, then—*poof!*—wedding bells? Or, speaking nontraditionally, did a casual moment of sinful pleasure bring a child, and again, a family just happened?

We Christians would like to *think* our lives unfold more deliberately than that. But how can we plan such events, particularly when human emotion is involved? Who can plan an infatuation? Can a woman set out with assurance to meet and marry the man of her dreams? Or can a man leave the house and know for sure he will find the woman who will be his undying support and inspiration? If we could make such a plan, wouldn't some self-help guru have written a best-seller long ago and now be living in the lap of luxury off its royalties, perhaps in a New York penthouse?

Well, a book has been written, and I suppose you could call the writer a self-help guru, although He promises to help *us* as well. And He now lives in the lap of luxury, if sitting at the right hand of God can be called the lap of luxury. Of course, He had to go through death on the

If we build our family His way, our family won't just happen—it will become part of God's kingdom here on earth and part of His plan to nurture and further it.

cross to get there (Hebrews 3:1–3). That book is the Bible; that man is Jesus. And if you are a Christian who happens to live in a New York penthouse, He is right there with you, just as He is with all of us.

What He tells us in this book is that if, from this moment on, we build our family His way, using the blueprint in the Bible, our family won't just happen—it will become part of God's kingdom here on earth and part of His plan to nurture and further it. Our family will be fashioned, supported, and blessed by God and used to His glory. What an exciting prospect!

Which means that building a family is serious stuff, after our relationship with Christ, the most serious activity in our life. On our deathbed, invariably, there will be regrets concerning our family: "I wish I had spent more time with the kids; I wish I had been more giving to my wife, more supportive of my husband." And, unlike our career, hobby, or neighborhood, family lasts a lifetime.

WE HAD NO CONTROL BACK THEN

Time after time we have seen how the old slave masters worked diligently to destroy slave families. They had absolute control over how our families ended up. And that wasn't by accident. I believe it was Satan's way to keep us alone and weak and in pain, to keep us so preoccupied with our own hurt that we would never reach out to God, never avail ourselves of His healing touch. One striking example of this lack of control is illustrated by what happened between William Wells Brown and his sister, whom he loved very much. When William returned to Saint Louis from being hired out for an extended period of time, he discovered his sister had been sold. Her new master was going to take her to Natchez, Mississippi, to the fields of the Deep South. Since his sister had "expressed her determination to die" rather than live that horrific life of blood and toil, she had been thrown in jail to await her journey. After repeated attempts to see her, William was finally allowed to do so:

She was seated with her face towards the door where I entered, yet she did not look up until I walked up to her. As soon as she observed me, she sprung up, threw her arms around my neck, leaned her head upon my breast, and, without uttering a word, burst into tears.[1]

The New Slavemasters work to gain that same control today, but with the power of God on our side, we can thwart them.

After she recovered herself, she urged him to escape slavery, no matter what. "There's no hope for me," she told him, "but there is for you."[2]

Our enslaved ancestors had no control of their families. And if there is a recurring theme in their writings, that is it. It was the slave master's call where the family ended up, and generally they ended up apart.

The New Slavemasters work to gain that same control today, but try as they might, with the power of God on our side, we can thwart them. And it is time to do just that, even if the actions we are called upon to take are at odds with our feelings. Feelings can cause us to behave in less-than-perfect ways, and when we do so, the result will be less than perfect.

However, if we walk in God's path, there will be sweet rewards along the way. There will also be trials, temptations, monumental difficulties, and many disappointments. But as they occur, we will be far better prepared to deal with them. Then, as we build and live our legacy, we will not only assure our own freedom, but also help our mate and our children assure theirs.

In the next chapter we will discuss some important elements of a strong husband-wife relationship, elements that lay the foundation for a strong family legacy and help assure that the fortress walls you and I build to stand against the New Slavemasters remain secure.

CHAPTER FIFTEEN

HUSBANDS AND WIVES: KEEPING THE NEW SLAVEMASTERS AT BAY

Unless the LORD builds the house,

its builders labor in vain.

—Psalm 127:1

Soon after she [Henry's wife, Malinda] *arrived at this place,*

Garrison gave her to understand what he brought her there for, and made a most

disgraceful assault on her virtue, which she promptly repelled; and for which

Garrison punished her with the lash,

threatening her that if she did not submit that he would sell her child.

—Autobiography of Henry Bibb, an escaped slave

Henry Bibb wanted nothing more than to escape slavery, and he had tried several times. One failed attempt landed him in a slave prison in Louisville. Henry describes this jail as "one of the most disagreeable places" he had ever seen. Not only was it filthy beyond description, but also there were bedbugs, fleas, lice, and mosquitoes "in abundance."[1]

Henry Bibb was deeply in love with his wife, Malinda. He and Malinda had a little girl, Frances. Madison Garrison, a "soul driver," bought the three of them and planned to take them to New Orleans for resale. Since Henry Bibb was known for his escape attempts, Garrison removed Malinda and Frances from the Louisville jail to make sure that he didn't remove himself.

The sanctity of marriage meant nothing to the old slave masters, and it certainly meant nothing to Garrison. As the quote at the beginning of the chapter tells us, that brutal, immoral man tried his best to pry Malinda by force and intimidation from her virtue. He repeatedly threatened to sell her child if she didn't submit, and she repeatedly refused.[2] Finally, he took Frances from Malinda and stashed her in another part of town, threatening more emphatically to sell the baby and "swearing by his Maker that she should submit to him or die."[3]

It was several weeks before Henry Bibb saw Malinda again and learned that Garrison had sold neither Malinda nor the baby, nor had Malinda submitted. When finally released, Henry Bibb's desire to escape was even greater.[4]

Henry and Malinda's ties as husband and wife withstood horrific pressures. Their love for one another was the same kind of love that the apostle Paul speaks of:

Husbands, love your wives, just as Christ loved the church and gave himself up for her to make her holy, cleansing her by the washing with water through the word, and to present her to himself as a radiant church, without stain or wrinkle or any other blemish, but holy and blameless. In this same way, husbands ought to love their wives as their own bodies. He who loves his wife loves himself. After all, no one ever hated his own body, but he feeds and cares for it, just as Christ does the church—for we are members of his body. "For this reason a man will leave his father and mother and be united to his wife, and the two will become one flesh." This is a profound mystery—but I am talking about Christ and the church. However, each one of you also must

love his wife as he loves himself, and the wife must respect her
husband.   —Ephesians 5:25–33

Since the fortress we build to keep the New Slavemasters at bay
begins when we build strong families, and since God built the first family from the top down—husband and wife, then children—it is fitting
that we should start where God did.

Respect for One Another

Even fifty years ago, these verses were the cookbook for all marriages. Back then husbands tried to keep their wives' respect. My father
did. There was nothing wealthy about
him; money was about as foreign to him
as France. A man of the soil and the
Book, he labored daily for his wife's
respect.

*It is time to mingle our
hearts' blood with the
blood of our fathers and
reawaken God's blessings
for our families.*

But how does a husband measure
his wife's respect? A man I know was
dying of cancer. Because of the
chemotherapy and the progress of the
disease, he dared not come in contact
with anyone but his wife. She became his only caregiver, a job that was
physically and emotionally brutal. I phoned and asked if one of us
might relieve her for just a little while, so she could rest. Her reply
brought me to tears: "Bishop, I consider it a privilege to take care of this
man." He died a few weeks later, and then she rested. That is respect.

I am not so sure most husbands today work to gain that kind of
respect from their wives. The same is true for the rest of what these
words express. Well, the time has come to breathe life into them again.
It is time to mingle our hearts' blood with the blood of our fathers and
reawaken God's blessings for our families. How much better, stronger,
and more joyous our families would be—how much greater would be

our impact for the Lord—if these few precious words of Ephesians became our life's goal. Let's drink of them again one sip at a time.

"Husbands, love your wives" (Ephesians 5:25).

We have already seen that love is a commitment to our mate's physical; emotional; and, especially, spiritual well-being. Here the Word of God tells husbands to make their wives' well-being their reason for living. Strong words. But strong words are needed. We, as fallen human beings, first look inward to our own needs; then, when those needs are satisfied, we *may* look to the needs of others. This is not the model for our spouse's needs. For husbands, selfishness is out—*selflessness* is definitely in.

When your wife sees and experiences your commitment to her happiness, she will only naturally work for yours.

But what does a wife need?

Of course, the basics: food, shelter, warmth, clothes; but there is far more. The husband's commitment is to help her become all she can be. For instance, what brings her joy and fulfillment? Husband, it is your job to find out. If she enjoys cooking, make sure she has everything a good cook needs. If she sews, help to make her the seamstress of her dreams. If she has a job, support her in it, including helping her around the house.

But what about your needs?

God will fulfill them. When your wife sees and experiences your commitment to her happiness, she will only naturally work for yours. The committed husband is usually a pretty happy, satisfied, well-fed guy.

"Wives, submit to your husbands" (Ephesians 5:22).

The world sees this verse as a license for tyranny; they point at it and us with scorn. Tyranny is the most unlikely result of this command. These men are committed to their wives' joy and fulfillment. The wives' submission only allows for an orderly decision process; in the event of a dispute, the husband is where the buck stops. If he loves his wife as he should, those decisions are made only after thoughtful consideration of what is best for the wife and the rest of the family. Submission becomes support.

"Make her holy, cleansing her by the washing with water through the word" (Ephesians 5:26).
The husband is the spiritual head of the family—not a job to be taken lightly. God certainly doesn't. In Deuteronomy 6:6–9, speaking through His prophet Moses, God tells the fathers:

> These commandments that I give you today are to be upon your hearts. Impress them on your children. Talk about them when you sit at home and when you walk along the road, when you lie down and when you get up. Tie them as symbols on your hands and bind them on your foreheads. Write them on the doorframes of your houses and on your gates.

There is urgency in the Lord's voice. And no wonder, this is His blueprint for passing on eternal life to our children so that they may become His children. So, Dad, learn the Word. Get on a Bible-reading schedule; do it every day and read it all, cover to cover. Find an adviser, someone you trust, to help make the difficult a little more understandable. Even though I have been studying Scripture for nearly sixty years, there are still parts of it I find a mystery. You will, too. As you learn, don't keep what you have learned to yourself. Every opportunity you get, instruct, teach, lead; you are the spiritual point man in your family. Do your job boldly, but also be gentle and respectful. No one likes to be beaten over the head with the Bible.

"The wife must respect her husband" (Ephesians 5:33).
This is a command, isn't it? Husbands must work for their wives' respect, but wives must respect their husbands whether they work for it

or not. Wives are just to do it. Seems curious, doesn't it? Respect is something that is earned, not something given partially.

Therefore, women are to give their husbands something very precious—their respect—whether they deserve it or not. That sure doesn't give a wife much bargaining power, particularly over a husband with severe shortcomings. Why did the Lord ask this of His kingdom wives?

> *Respect says we are equals before God and our contributions within the kingdom are equal.*

Respect acknowledges that a person has characteristics and abilities that we, and the One we serve, value. We, as God's children, should respect all His children. The characteristics and abilities they possess are God's love, God's work in their lives. But there is another reason we respect all God's children. We are all sinners, we all fall short, and we all have grave shortcomings (Romans 3:23; Isaiah 53:6). To respect some and not others is to say that we are better than some and that those we don't respect have less value in God's kingdom than we do. Respect says we are equals before God and our contributions within the kingdom are equal. Wives are supposed to view their husbands, in spite of all their failings and shortcomings, as men with responsibilities that they and God are working out together.

SHAYLA AND JOHN: A GODLY EXAMPLE

Shayla and John married during college. John wasn't a particularly good student, so soon thereafter, over Shayla's protests, he dropped out and got a job as a mechanic. Shayla graduated and worked for a computer software firm. In the first four years they were married, John became a supervisor and was told he would manage the next store the company opened in that area. His salary climbed, but not as high as Shayla's. John began to feel that his place as "the man of the house" was threatened.

Sadly, John's self-image was poor. His father had deserted his family when John was a toddler; his mother had always been distant. Forever worried about money, she was always mad at this or that boss. One reason John left college was that when things got difficult, he just figured it was the beginning of the end. So when Shayla started to go on business trips, when she bought an expensive car because her "image needed some polishing," and when at evening business functions he started feeling like the fifth wheel, John figured the beginning of the end had begun. He stopped going to church and began to plot his way out of the marriage.

Shayla came to me one day. After she described things at home, I asked her to tell me the story of their marriage. It didn't take long to figure out what the problem was. I suggested a course of action.

The next day a limousine rolled up to where John worked. Shayla, sleekly dressed, stepped from the rear door. "John," she called, "want to take a ride?" The other guys stopped work and stared. John stared, too. The store manager, to whom Shayla had spoken earlier, stepped from his office. "It's okay, John," he said.

John went, greasy fingernails and all. They ended up somewhere special, but what Shayla said to John was even more special: "John, I love you. You are the most important person in my life. You're a hard worker; you care about me; and when we have children, I know you'll care about them too. You're the head of our home; you're the one I expect to take us wherever God leads. I respect you for all that you do and all that you are." After giving him a soft kiss, she said, "I want you to know that I respect you. You're all I want."

John's transformation wasn't immediate. Words can be cheap. But over the next few weeks, Shayla behaved as if she had meant them. She asked his opinion, even on elements of her work. Before the next evening business function, John went out and bought a new suit and spent extra time on his nails. He wanted Shayla to be proud of him, which she was.

RESPECT VERSUS CONTEMPT

Respect between mates is a powerful connection; and the opposite, contempt, is poison. Even if your spouse is having true moral difficulty, never allow contempt to creep into your relationship. It will quickly destroy it. Respect is built on love and honor; contempt boils up from superiority and rage. Wife, respect your husband. He's got a big job, and he needs your help.

As we continue to look at building that strong family legacy that keeps the New Slavemasters outside your gates, in the next chapter we will consider the importance of the two-parent family.

CHAPTER SIXTEEN

THE TWO-PARENT FORTRESS

Do not be deceived: God cannot be mocked. A man reaps what
he sows. The one who sows to please his sinful nature,
from that nature will reap destruction; the one who sows to please
the Spirit, from the Spirit will reap eternal life.
—Galatians 6:7–8

Malinda's business was to labor out in the field the greater part of her time, and
there was no one to take care of poor little Frances,
while her mother was toiling in the field.
—Autobiography of Henry Bibb, an escaped slave

Cyndi was a single parent to six-year-old Nathan. He had never met his father. Just as well, Cyndi always had thought. The guy was something of a baby himself, certainly not emotionally prepared to take on adult responsibility. But all that didn't matter anymore. She and Nathan had a nice little family. God had been good to them.

Cyndi worked at our school, which allowed her to be home when Nathan was there. Late one afternoon she had taken him to the park. While she watched Nathan play on the swings, a little girl swung next to him. She was a little bigger than he was, and every now and then she would kid Nathan about how skinny he was. Cyndi complained to the girl's mother, but she only waved an unconcerned hand and mumbled something unintelligible.

A little later Cyndi heard the girl cry, "Help!" When Cyndi turned back, she saw Nathan poke the girl in the nose. The little girl immediately started crying and ran frantically to her mother. Cyndi just as immediately ran to Nathan and grabbed him by the shoulder and scolded him. "You should never hit. Never. Hitting never solves anything." But her heart wasn't in it. A strong part of her was glad her son had shown that little vixen whom not to pick on. When she finished correcting Nathan, she actually gave him a supportive pat on the back.

"I know it's none of my business," came a man's voice, gentle but purposeful.

Cyndi saw a man about her own age with his son who was a little older than Nathan. She remembered them playing catch on the nearby grass. "What?" she challenged. "I have this situation under control."

"I know you do," he nodded. "But just a suggestion. There are times when boys need to defend themselves. To tell him never to hit may not be what you really mean."

"I know what I meant," she fired back, but more from pride.

"But this wasn't one of those times," he went on. "I always like to tell Joshua that little boys are supposed to protect little girls, even when they give us a hard time. It's what men are supposed to do."

"Oh," she managed.

Cyndi, as she worked to build a strong family, came to grips with an important issue that afternoon: A two-parent family provides children with *consistent, but very different, role models—the perspectives of women and men.* Created differently, men and women play different roles within the family. As you can imagine, these roles often overlap, and they may differ depending on the individual's physical and emotional strengths, but in most cases, each perspective creates a much stronger, more balanced family. Often when a particular perspective and influence is missing, children must learn these missing lessons and understandings later in life. And sometimes these lessons come at a huge cost. A friend once confided that his father was an alcoholic and was seldom around. "There were times I did things simply because I was sure real men did them. I risked my life in Vietnam because I thought that's what real

Two perspectives wrapped around a common course of action make the worst moments manageable.

men would do. I gave up a career for which I was truly suited in favor of another I found manlier—and I hated it. Not having a good male role model in the home cost me a great deal."

And it is not just the children who suffer where there is a perspective deficiency. The parents suffer, too. For instance, wouldn't it have been easier for Cyndi had her husband been there, someone who knew Nathan intimately, someone who could have given Nathan firm correction the instant the transgression occurred or, better still, just before? Having a husband with her would have made Cyndi's time in the park with Nathan far less stressful. This, of course, is a trivial example. Wouldn't it be easier for both parents to have two very thoughtful perspectives if they should find a "joint" of marijuana in their son's or daughter's bureau drawer? Two perspectives wrapped around a common course of action make the worst moments manageable.

There are many other benefits to a two-parent family. And like the first one, they are just as easy to describe and just as profound in their benefit to the family. They also help keep the New Slavemasters at bay.

CHILDREN ARE A FULL-TIME JOB

Children are a full-time job, as they were years ago. Henry Bibb was married to Malinda. After a few months of living on separate farms, Henry was sold to Malinda's master. This was a bittersweet time for him. It was good to be with his beloved, "but to live where I must be eye witness to her insults, scourgings, and abuses, such as are common to be inflicted upon slaves, was more than I could bear."[1]

The two-parent family affords you the greatest opportunity to guard yourself, your spouse, and your children against these merciless attacks.

Even more bitter, though, was how the old slave masters treated their daughter. Because Henry Bibb had to leave his wife and daughter for a "season," and Malinda had to work out in the fields, little Frances was left at the slaveholder's house, "to creep under the feet of an unmerciful old mistress, whom I have known to slap with her hand the face of little Frances, for crying after her mother, until her little face was left black and blue."[2] He went on to describe the situation: "I recollect ... poor little Frances came creeping to her mother smiling, but with large tear drops standing in her dear little eyes, sobbing and trying to tell her mother that she had been abused, but was not able to utter a word. Her little face was bruised black with the whole print of Mrs. Gatewood's hand."[3]

His deep, profound helplessness forced him to come face to face with the fact that he, his wife, and his vulnerable little daughter were merely property, powerless to deal with those who whipped and tortured their infant daughter.[4]

The New Slavemasters want to do the same to your family. They want you to one day look at your children and be helpless to protect them from what they have in mind for them: drugs, pregnancy, abortion, alcohol, anything that locks them into emotional and physical slavery.

ADVANTAGES OF THE TWO-PARENT FAMILY

The two-parent family affords you the greatest opportunity to guard yourself, your spouse, and your children against these merciless attacks. We have seen one reason why that is true: the fact that two parents provide consistent, but very different, role models—the perspectives of both women and men. Let's look at a few more advantages of a two-parent family over a one-parent family.

Two parents provide more energy for loving parenting.

Good parenting is exhausting. You deal with adult issues—jobs, home, church—and you make sure the kids are fed, clothed, kept from harm, disciplined, and sincerely loved. Single parents run themselves ragged in an attempt to do all that. Invariably, time set aside to display tenderness and understanding and simply to "hang out" with the kids suffers. Two parents have four hands to keep all the balls in the air, four hands to keep any from being dropped. They relieve each other when overwhelmed, have fun with one another to relieve the tension, and provide a united front when firmness is required.

Two parents are more able to handle family emergencies.

An auto accident lands one parent in the hospital. A child is suddenly sent home from school with a malady that requires weeks of recovery. The maternal grandmother falls seriously ill and must be attended to around the clock. When the emergency strikes, the family reels under the blow, but when there are two parents, one can deal with the emergency while the other keeps the family going.

Family emergencies often tear at the emotions as well. In a two-parent family, husbands and wives are there to support each other. I see it all the time in my own marriage. When I am down, my wife, Jean, sees it and, with her sweet sense of humor, gets me back up again. And when she is a little down, which only happens rarely, I am right there for her. And since we genuinely care how situations affect each other, and because we know each other so thoroughly, our support of one another is absolutely sincere. In a single-parent family, both schedules and emotions can end up in tatters.

Two parents provide a more consistent financial footing.

A single parent juggles both job and parenting and often must be two places at once. It is common for a single parent to leave work to take care of an errant child at school or even bring the child to work when childcare falters. Both situations make the single parent a less-desirable employee.

When there are two parents, generally one has the time and energy to develop a good paying career while the other is free to focus on home and children. That doesn't necessarily mean that this parent stays at home, but can take a less stressful, less time-critical job, one that affords the needed flexibility to keep the kids top priority. This division of labor allows career-oriented parents to advance further, make more, and bring a stability of income that single parents cannot attain. The children then benefit in a whole host of ways, not to mention more parental supervision and involvement in their growing up and the choices they make.

Family and parenting decisions have the benefit of two-person deliberation.

The old adage "Two heads are better than one" is generally true. As family situations arise, the two parents discuss, pray together, and apply their collective wisdom and perspective. And, in my experience, when God brings a husband and wife together, each will have complementary strengths.

Deliberations also are less rushed, which allows more information to be considered, more "what ifs" to be explored, and the strengths and weaknesses of each course of action pondered. In the end, the decisions and solutions are simply better and more creative and the unintended consequences fewer. And those that do occur have two minds ready to deal with them. Single parents face life and parenting alone; for them, time is always running out, decisions often are made from sheer desperation. A busy signal to a single parent might be the backbreaking straw; in a two-parent family it means the parent simply calls upon the other partner for assistance.

MORE REASONS TO STRESS TWO-PARENT FAMILIES

I stress the idea of having two parents at the head of the freedom family for several reasons. First, as we have seen, two parents are simply better than one. If you are looking to start a family, make sure the family you establish has two parents—a man and a woman. If you are married and either have children already or plan to have them soon, make sure you and your mate do everything you can to stay together. If you are a single parent, like Cyndi, realize that your children need the influence of the opposite gender.

I also stress the value of a two-parent family because it is better for the child and for the parents. If you or someone over whom you exert influence should have a baby outside marriage, particularly if the father will be uninvolved, I strongly suggest that you consider the child be adopted into a two-parent Christian family.

Usually when I suggest this to an unmarried, pregnant mother, her first reaction is to look down at her expanding middle, stroke it lovingly, and say: "No, I love my baby. How could I possibly give it up?"

I know it is a hard choice to make, but we just have seen how much better off a child within a two-parent home will be, which means that you are not giving away your baby—you are loving your baby with a selfless, godly love. Just as the Bible says that all things will work together for your good if you are loving and serving God (Romans 8:28), so you need to make a decision that will work for the good of your child. God builds into Mom and Dad a realization that sacrifices may be needed to raise a godly child. Putting your child up for adoption is such a sacrifice. It is a huge sacrifice to be sure, but if you are not prepared to be the best parent possible for your children, true love dictates you find the best possible situation for them.

But to put up your child for adoption is not done just for the child. You want your family, when it does come together, to have the best

> *The New Slavemasters want nothing more than to tear down the fortress that you have built to protect your family.*

opportunity for success. *Adoption gives you a second chance.* It allows you, as a future parent, a second chance at a more traditional, more successful family, which gives you the opportunity to start over and do it God's way next time.

WHY NOT JUST LIVE TOGETHER?

There is no denying that I have stressed marriage as the foundation of a united family. But large elements of today's society discount marriage. Their point is, if you can get everything you want outside marriage—the sexual experience, the companionship, the blissful connection—why marry? Why not just live together? What's the harm in it?

The New Slavemasters want nothing more than to tear down the fortress that you have built to protect your family. This fortress must be made of strong brick and mortar. And living together has neither. Both partners can leave anytime they want, and though it may sound romantic to proclaim that it is love that keeps them in the same bed, in fact, it is their lack of love that keeps them from a commitment. The New Slavemasters will have a much easier time breaking through those flimsy, superficial barriers of convenience and self-interest than through sturdy walls cemented together by sincere, heartfelt promise and commitment.

The most important harm spiritually is that by living together outside of marriage, you are mocking God. And God will not be mocked (Galatians 6:7). When you do, *harm* results. You probably won't foresee the form that harm will take, but you can bet that one day you will regret your decision to build your family your own way. God created marriage to be beautiful. When you hijack it for your own purposes, you tell God that His purposes don't matter. How do you think God is going to react to that attitude?

On the other hand, if you build your family God's way, He has every incentive to bless that godly commitment and reward your patience and obedience. He also has a huge stake in your marriage's success. You are His witness. He wants to reveal Himself to others through your witness to work for your success. He will be right there with you as you work to keep the New Slavemasters away.

And the closer you walk with Him, the more diligently you work to rid yourself of the sin that separates you from Him; the more committed to Him you appear to your relatives, friends, and neighbors; the greater God's interest in smoothing the rough times within your married life, and the greater His interest in keeping the New Slavemasters away.

ALLOW THE SEXUAL EXPERIENCE TO BLOSSOM WITHIN MARRIAGE

After marriage, allow the sexual experience to mean everything God has ordained it to mean. Make it the sign of your commitment and everlasting love to one another. Be together often, any and every time the spirit moves. And don't deny one another (1 Corinthians 7:5). Of course, there may be times when one may have a legitimate reason to say no, but don't say no very often. Then, with a crystal-clear conscience, have fun with it. Only within marriage can the sexual experience be as much fun as people unsuccessfully try to make it be outside marriage.

EVERYTHING YOU DO INFLUENCES HOW YOU DEVELOP AS PARENTS

Have you ever asked people you would characterize as good parents what in life prepared them to become such good parents? The list might be shorter if you asked them what didn't. In fact, the moment you decide to build a strong, Christ-centered family—whether you are fifteen or fifty—consciously take from them whatever you can that will help you become a more godly parent and build a strong, free family.

I certainly learned a lot from this principle. When I started out in ministry, I earned a "tent-maker's" living as a shoe repairman. More often than I would like to admit, when I held those small brass nails between my meaty thumb and forefinger, I hammered my thumb instead of the nail. And it hurt! But in all that time, in six or seven years, never once did my left hand tell my right hand: "Don't you touch me. You hit me. You hurt me. I don't trust you anymore." This is an example of *unity in the body* and the definition of the strong, freedom family to which I have referred. My left and right hands worked together even though one occasionally hurts the other.

But what is the practical meaning of all this? The immediate family is sown together by iron threads of love—honest, no-nonsense, practical love—and love means forgiveness. This kind of love makes the family a safe harbor in times of distress, the perfect classroom in times of confusion and doubt, the reservoir of understanding in times of need. No one knows you better than your family; no one loves you more than your family. And just as your family keeps your best interests at heart, you need to keep your family's best interests at heart as well. No family is more consistently strong enough to keep each member supported, loved, nurtured, and focused than the family with two parents.

MARY AND MARTHA'S PLACE

There is another benefit to a stable, two-parent family. If you have created a safe harbor for your family, you have created a safe harbor for others. When others are weary, when their burdens weigh them down, your family will be there as a place of rest, refreshment, direction, truth, and love.

Haven't you experienced a home like that, a warm place that accepts you when life beats you down? There is always a cool soda in the fridge, easy music on the stereo, a soft place to "crash," an open ear to listen.

The people in that home give you what you need, not necessarily what you came to find. They give you what godly wisdom tells them is best for you. It is Mary and Martha's place, where our Lord Jesus took refreshment (Luke 10:38–42). The freedom family is also free to support the kingdom.

But for all the value we see in the two-parent family, it is becoming increasingly rare. It is still the ideal and creates the greatest fortress against the enemy, but families come in so many other forms now, each facing the war to keep the New Slavemasters outside the gate. And each family form has its own special challenges within that war. In the next chapter, we will consider one that currently seems to need the greatest help: the one headed by a single parent. Whether that is your family or not, read about it; there are elements of its struggle that exist in all families.

CHAPTER SEVENTEEN

THE SINGLE PARENT

For I am not seeking my own good but the good of many,

so that they may be saved.

—1 Corinthians 10:33

She [his mother] *made her journeys to see me in the night,*

traveling the whole distance [twelve miles] *on foot, after the*

performance of her day's work. She was a field hand,

and a whipping is the penalty for not being in the field at sunrise.

—Autobiography of Frederick Douglass, an escaped slave

An image returns to me now and again. I am not sure when I first saw her, but it was early in my ministry: a single mother standing between her two young children, a hand on each of their shoulders. Her posture says that she is tired. I can't see her face very well; it's hidden in shadow, while golden sunlight streams in from an unseen window and illuminates her children. She is presenting them to me and to the world; her children are *her world*.

Today, that image is not politically correct. There is nothing in it about self-actualization, or being all you can be, or about single women having it all. But no matter, these many years later, my heart still goes out to her—and my respect. She sacrificed to put her children first and was understandably proud of them; they *were*, and still *are*, her life. Whether she thought in these terms or not, the New Slavemasters were not part of her children's lives and are not likely to be in the future.

She has many sisters who raise their children on their own. She also is beginning to have many brothers, men who do the same. This chapter is for both. As you, my brother in Christ, read this chapter, remember that I am speaking to you, too. The issues that both the male and the female single parents face as they build godly legacies are much the same.

> *Successful parents have a narrow focus; a firm commitment; courage; and, above all else, reliance on a powerful, yet tender, loving God.*

And those issues are enormous, the task all-consuming, but the compensation immeasurable: to watch your children grow into godly adults. It is an eventuality I wish for all single parents. But that exciting moment is not automatic. Successful parents have a narrow focus; a firm commitment; courage; and, above all else, reliance on a powerful, yet tender, loving God.

But just in case you think it requires more focus and energy than you possess, consider for a moment Frederick Douglass's mother. Often before slave children reached their first birthday, their mothers were sold off to a distant farm and the children put in the care of another female slave too old for fieldwork. Frederick Douglass speculates that dividing mother from child at this early age blunts the development of the "natural affections" between them, a goal of the old slave masters. But even though he saw his mother only four or five times in his life, her affection for him didn't diminish. In order to see him, she walked twelve miles at night after working in the fields all day, spent but a few hours with him in her arms, then returned the twelve miles to work the following day in those same fields—a story of remarkable love, courage, energy, and commitment.[1]

Your children deserve no less.

And it doesn't matter how you became a single parent, or if you have the kids full time or part time, the issues are the same.

Whatever your marital or family situation, you must focus on the children.

YOUR FOCUS

Whatever your marital or family situation, you must focus on the children. The New Slavemasters are devious. Like their master, Satan, they lurk about, seeking whom they may devour (1 Peter 5:8 KJV). Your focus, along with your prayers, is needed to keep these enemies at bay. But keeping a focus on your children doesn't mean you wear rags. Or that they have Christmas presents while you scrub floors to make it possible. The focus on the children is sacrificial, not masochistic. You are allowed a life, but your children's physical, emotional, and spiritual welfare must always be top priority. It is time for you to make a commitment to keep that focus, and this commitment should be both to yourself and to God. Be accountable to Him.

But issues may actually stand in the way of such a commitment. If any do, deal with them. When you do so, there will be two huge benefits: You will have taken a number of steps toward your legacy, and your children will be that much closer to being inoculated against ever feeling the New Slavemaster's whip. Let's identify a few of those issues.

Resentment

Life was going along just fine; then the kids came and everything soured. You may resent them, perhaps not openly, but the seeds have been sown and covered up. In time, they will germinate, and the weeds that result will hurt your kids. In fact, they may be hurting them now.

The time has come to dig up those weeds.

First, take responsibility for your children. What you did made them, birth control or not; nothing but abstinence is 100 percent effective. But more important, see your children as gifts from God.

The apostle Paul tells us in Romans 8:28: "And we know that in all things God works for the good of those who love him, who have been called according to his purpose." Even though your children may have come at what you see as an inconvenient time, they came in God's time and for God's purpose. You have been given a great opportunity in God's kingdom, an opportunity to raise up children to know Him. That is a great honor He will help you fulfill. So don't resent the kids; thank God for them. As you put them first in your life, you will see God revealed in ways you can't even imagine.

Anger toward the other parent

You may be furious with the other parent, who just won't go away because every time you look at the kids, you see their father or mother.

Vanquish this anger. Anger will keep you from being the parent you need to be and the other parent from having the relationship with the children he or she ought to have.

Forgive. Release the pride and the desire to get even. You are both sinners, and if there is any "even" to get, God will get it (Romans 12:19). Remember, these injustices you suffer are preparation for service in His army, for some future good work in His kingdom. Instead of rage, you should give thanks for the opportunity to serve God at the Ground Zero of your spiritual war.

Anger with God

Being angry with God is something like kicking a boulder: nothing results but a hurt foot. But the fact remains, God *is* all-powerful, and with a flick of His finger He could have made your life far better, from your vantage point anyway. Yet He didn't. And maybe you resent Him for not doing so. Well, God is big enough to absorb your anger.

Habakkuk, a prophet of old, was angry with God. It seemed to him that God had allowed Israel to fall further and further away from Him, and He was doing nothing about it. In Habakkuk 2:1, after raising an angry voice to God, he said:

> I will stand at my watch and station myself on the ramparts; I will look to see what he will say to me, and what answer I am to give to this complaint.

In the next verse, God came back and calmly, yet firmly, told Habakkuk that he hadn't seen anything yet. God wants you to talk things out with Him. So confess your anger to Him. Be specific. Then, after you have vented, stop and realize that God only brings us good. Even what you now suffer will end up for your good. Ask Him to take your anger away. Then, as your life unfolds, see how it deepens as you grow closer to Him. If your anger persists, get help, particularly if it prevents you from putting your children first. Don't miss out on the blessings that await you because your anger stands in the way.

If other issues keep you from putting the children first, work with your pastor or counselor to identify them and deal with them.

IDENTIFY THE FAMILY ROLES YOU MUST PLAY

Single parents generally try to be both father and mother. But you really can't be both. As a single custodial mother, you can *do* what a father does—for instance, provide spiritual leadership—but you can't do it in the *way* a man would, just as a father with children will never provide all that a mother would. Men and women are just wired differently. But when you consider the issue of gender differences, the result is positive. First, it causes you to take a critical look at your children's physical, emotional, and spiritual needs. Second, it forces you to determine how you can realistically provide for them and what you might need to have supplied by someone else. What are some of the essential parenting tasks involved in building a stable home life?

BUILD A STABLE HOME LIFE

Children need stability. They need to know they will be safe and secure when tomorrow arrives. Children can adapt to change, of course; but, like all of us, the more gradual change is, the less threatening it is. A parent's job is to build physical, emotional, and spiritual stability. We will examine two of these in this chapter and the third in the following chapter.

Physical stability

Physical stability starts with sound finances, making sure that outgo does not exceed income. So, if you don't already have a job, you need to get one. There are welfare agencies to help, if need be, but welfare is temporary. A job, even if it ends one day, usually leads to another, which leads to a career and all the stability and self-respect that a career generates.

To get a job, you need to identify and capitalize on marketable skills—typing or sales proficiency, for instance. If you have no skills, find something for which you have an aptitude, and develop a skill based on it. Again, there are places to go for help. But in the meantime, get a job that uses your current abilities. And whether it's a new job or one you already possess, be cheerful, helpful, easy to get along with, quick to train, and committed to excellence and your boss' goals. You will be surprised how far those qualities will take you.

Be disciplined with your money; forge a realistic budget. Take pencil to paper and plan your income and spending. Figure in everything. If you need help, get it. Churches know all about budgets; your parents may be able to help as well. If you find yourself spending more than you earn, cut something. Whatever you do, don't resort to credit cards. Debt is not a saddle you want to wear. Resist the temptation to borrow to make ends meet. God will provide (Philippians 4:19). Often He reveals Himself most wonderfully through His acts of provision.

Physical stability also means having a pleasant place to live, which *can* fit into a lean budget. Try picking up furniture at garage sales, using slipcovers, or just making do; in this throw-away society, bargains are everywhere. It's not the cost of the furniture that matters; it's the clean, neat room in which it is placed. And keeping it that way allows you to divvy up responsibilities among the kids. My mother ran our home on very little money, yet she managed quite well. All of us kids had our jobs to do, and doing them gave us a sense of belonging and accomplishment. And not doing them gave us other sensations—like discipline.

But kids also need freedom to develop into who they are. One way to teach creativity along with necessary discipline and responsibility is to give children their own individual space. If space is too limited to provide their own room, make it part of a room or a few square feet on a wall or the refrigerator. Make it a place they can call their own, a place they can decorate, keep clean and in order, and, if it's large enough, a place they can go to avoid everything but responsibility.

Speaking of places to go, children need a safe, stimulating place to go while you work, which makes age-appropriate childcare a huge issue with single parents. If the children have suitable grandparents, use them; grandparents are second only to parents when it comes to being there for children. But if grandparents aren't the answer for you, find warm, stable childcare. If your church doesn't provide it, find a facility near your home. And be choosy. Even if your church is a provider, evaluate its childcare services: talk to references, come unannounced during the day to see what happens, check out the backgrounds and credentials of those who actually care for your little ones. Even after you have placed your children in childcare, ask them about their day. If you ever regret your choice, make another one—quickly.

Emotional stability

Then, as your physical environment "gels," you will also be pouring the foundation for your family's emotional stability. A solid physical world minimizes the source of most emotional upset. But there are a few other issues that concern emotional stability that you will want to address. One of them concerned Janet and her two young children.

Her husband came home a little late from work one night and was caught in the crossfire of a drive-by shooting. Although she did her best to comfort the children, less than an hour after the funeral Janet began to believe that life had become too burdensome to endure. She sank into deep depression, one that sent her to an overstuffed chair near the window in her front room. There she sat, hoping God would bury her as well.

Tommy, her oldest, was six. The loss of his daddy hit him hard, while Kelly, the four-year-old, became instantly withdrawn. Janet was about to crawl the rest of the way inside herself when Tommy pushed himself into her lap, tears running down his cheeks. "You won't leave us like Daddy did, will you?" he asked. Just then Kelly, who stood behind him, pushed out her lower lip in an anxious pout and asked, "Are you going to leave us, too, Mommy?"

Janet used a deep breath to push the sudden emotional darkness away and then gave both her children huge hugs. "We'll be okay, guys. I'm not going anywhere. What say we put on a *Veggie Tales* video? I bet we could all use a dancing tomato or two." That night, after the kids were in bed, Janet had a good cry; then she called a few friends, and slowly, in the quiet of her room, she grieved for the lives she had lost—her husband's and her own—and prepared herself for the life to come.

Emotional stability starts with you. Like Janet, if you are chronically depressed, angry, or anxious, or if your emotions bounce from highs to lows, then back again, get help. Contact your pastor or counselor and make every effort to deal with whatever roller coaster you are on. I can't overstate how important this is. You may have just sailed some turbulent seas—gone through a difficult divorce, been through a violent relationship—and you may feel that you have earned your breakdown. But you have the emotional well-being of your children to consider, and seeing you chronically upset or depressed does them no good. Kids need the confidence that you can handle any eventuality. You may have doubts, as Janet did, but the kids shouldn't see them. That doesn't mean that you have to be an unemotional zombie, but it does mean your emotions should be appropriate. There were a few times when the kids found Janet crying. Instantly concerned, they asked her what was wrong. "I'm just sad because I miss your daddy." They would nod and wrap consoling arms around her, their worry gone. They understood these particular tears of sadness. They had shed a few of their own.

Stressful changes may produce a few tears in children, too. Emotional stability is helped when you keep them away from those changes. Like a new man in your life, who becomes a new man in their lives. If you do date, keep your dates away from the children until you are sure you have found Mr. Right. And even then, be very careful. Children form attachments easily, and they don't need to have relationships torn away from them as often as you may find someone new. They have fragile hearts and egos, and even though you may not have a permanent relationship for a long while, they need to know that relationships *can* be permanent.

Another word about dating: It should be a distant second to *living for your children.* In fact, anyone watching should think your children are your steady date. Then, if you date, date God's way.

THE OTHER PARENT

Another issue to resolve God's way concerns the absent parent, and resolving it contributes a lot to your home's emotional stability.

If the other parent is involved …

The other parent usually sparks strong emotions. You may have been betrayed, dumped, cheated on, even abused. You may prefer flaming bamboo strips under your fingernails to spending fifteen minutes in the same room with your ex-spouse. If you or the children have been abused—verbally, physically, or sexually—you are right to feel that way. Keep your distance. But in most cases, even if the breakup was ugly, it is appropriate that the children be allowed, even encouraged, to develop and maintain the best relationship they can with the other parent.

That means that you must deal with or suppress all those savage emotions and work with your ex-spouse to coordinate and make that relationship as rewarding for the children as you can. This may take a lot of prayer and patience, particularly if there are moral differences between the two of you; however, in the end, your children grow into kids who know they are loved by you and by God.

I do have a few experience-tested suggestions concerning communications with the other parent. First, *never speak from anger.* Inevitably, the other parent will push your buttons, and you will want to explode. *Don't.* If rage erupts, stop; take all the time you need to let the anger subside; then reply as dispassionately as you can. It is also a help to *preplan responses to likely volatile situations.* Ask yourself: "Okay, what's likely to happen in this situation?" Suppose, for example, the kids are brought home late from his weekend with new bad habits. Or when the kids return from their weekend with her, you learn from them that she has taken a live-in boyfriend. Sit down with the Lord and a trusted adviser, and preplan your response. Then, if it happens, respond as planned. And every time you respond, take the Lord into the conversation with you. See Him standing there, and ask Him for wisdom and guidance; then listen as He leads.

Finally, just talk to your ex-spouse like a casual friend. Care about him, what he's doing, how he's feeling, how he's coping, what his hopes are for the future and his regrets for the past. Don't manipulate, and don't assign guilt—just talk and listen. As you do, you may sense the barriers begin to dissolve. As they do, you will find it easier to come to agreement on issues that have divided you before, particularly those involving the kids.

If the other parent is not involved ...

In that case, you have a different set of issues to address. Your children know they have been deserted, traded for a thousand other places the other parent may spend time, money, and energy. The children will be deeply hurt, and their view of themselves and others will be scarred.

Don't avoid this issue; talk to them about it. Reassure them—fervently and often—that what the other parent did had nothing to do with them, that they are not the reason for what happened. Build them up every chance you get; tell them they are wonderful kids, lovable and sweet. Let them know that it is the other parent who is missing out, not them.

But all that reassurance doesn't negate their need for the gender influence of the missing parent. If Daddy is gone, they need someone to provide a male perspective, a man who can build a close relationship with them—which is the ultimate proof that *they are not* the problem. Grandparents can help here. But if they can't, find someone at church. Of course, no one will be as faithful as the original parent should have been, but if the children's expectations are properly managed, their experience can be positive.

To build a quick bridge to the issues of spiritual stability, which we will cover in the next chapter, remember God is the true faithful parent. When you mirror that love and faithfulness while parenting your children, regardless of whether you are their mother or their father, you will help them understand the depth and sacrifice of God's love and faithfulness. And by putting them first, you will confirm their worth as people, which gives them the strength and confidence to reject what the New Slavemasters offer.

CHAPTER EIGHTEEN

THE SINGLE PARENT:
SPIRITUAL STABILITY

We have this hope as an anchor for the soul, firm and secure.
—Hebrews 6:19

The same gentleman, but a short time previous, tied up a woman of his, by the name of Delphia, and whipped her nearly to death; yet he was a deacon in the Baptist church, in good and regular standing. Poor Delphia! I was well acquainted with her, and called to see her while upon her sick bed; and I shall never forget her appearance. She was a member of the same church with her master.
—Autobiography of William Wells Brown, an escaped slave

LEARN THE THINGS OF THE LORD

Frederick Douglass, while still a slave, once taught a "Sabbath School" at the home of a free "colored man."[1] At times he taught forty students of all ages, but mostly men and women. "I look back to those Sundays with an amount of pleasure not to be expressed. They were great days to my soul,"[2] he later wrote. He went on to call those days of instructing his "dear fellow slaves" as the sweetest engagement with which he was ever blessed. Over the course of the year he and his students became very close. He loved them.

And after he had escaped and looked back on this wondrous time of teaching God's Word and realized that most of those dear friends were still "shut up in the prison-house of slavery," those feelings would overcome him, and he would be tempted to ask, "Does a righteous God govern the universe? And for what does he hold the thunders in his right hand, if not to smite the oppressor, and deliver the spoiled out of the hand of the spoiler?"[3] For his students didn't come to "Sabbath School" on a whim. If caught, they would have been blessed with thirty-nine lashes. "They came because they wished to learn."[4]

It is a parent's responsibility to make sure the children place Jesus as their firm foundation.

In the last chapter we discussed physical and emotional stability. Both are important, but they mean very little if not accompanied by spiritual stability. Children, like all of us, need the Lord. Otherwise, they and we may have a life here on earth that may appear healthy and prosperous, but when that life fades, we may all face a lost eternity. As the Lord put it:

> "What good will it be for a man if he gains the whole world, yet forfeits his soul? Or what can a man give in exchange for his soul?"   —Matthew 16:26

It is a parent's responsibility to make sure the children place Jesus as their firm foundation. When they do, spiritual stability has come to their home. Vital to that stability, like for those in Frederick Douglass's Sunday school, is keeping the desire to learn and live God's Word fanned into hot flame.

As the spiritual leader in your home, just as those subjected to the cruelty of the old slave masters put themselves at painful risk to learn about the Lord, you need to keep yourself focused in that same direction. Read your Bible every day, at least two or three chapters; read every word of it—even difficult books like Numbers and Deuteronomy. Get up early if you have to. And if it means that you miss your favorite TV programs, you miss them.

Then, pray about and meditate on what you read. Ask God to interpret it for you and help you to apply it to your heart. Ask Him also to provide companion material to read to help you understand it.

Cultivate a mentor, someone to answer your questions, someone you trust and understand, someone who will keep your best interests at heart. Then, as situations present themselves, apply biblical principles to them. Where faith is needed, keep it; where honesty is needed, be it; where love is needed, give it. And as you do so, learn to see God at work in what results.

When you make mistakes, confess them and make amends. Your knowledge of God will increase, and you will grow nearer to Him as it does. And, to strengthen your hand against the New Slavemasters, you will be an example to your children.

LET THE WHOLE OF SCRIPTURE MINISTER TO YOU

William Wells Brown tells us that it was not uncommon to walk by a slave auction in Saint Louis and hear the auctioneer cry out, "How much is offered for this woman? She is a good cook, good washer, a good, obedient servant. She has got religion!"[5] Why did it matter to the one doing the buying that the slave had "religion"? In Missouri—and Brown figured in the other slave states as well—the old slave masters taught that religious slaves would never strike a white man; that God made the black person for a slave; and that when whipped, he or she should not find fault with the one holding the whip. Slaves were told that the Bible taught: "He that knoweth the master's will, and doeth it not, shall be beaten with many stripes!" (Luke 12:47 KJV).

This narrow, ignorant focus also resulted in William Wells Brown witnessing what he describes in the quotation that heads this chapter.[6] That quotation concerns a brother and sister in Christ, two of God's people

We want to make sure that we, as children of the Word, do not fall into the same trap that those old slave masters did.

who belonged to the same church; one a deacon, one not; one free, one a slave. Then the story delved into the unbelievable: the deacon, fully justified by what he believed he found in God's Holy Word, beat his sister in Christ nearly to death. How could this be? Yet it occurred, and we want to make sure that we, as children of the Word, do not fall into the same trap that those old slave masters did. Those cruel men, intoxicated by arrogance and power, were passionate enough to believe that God sanctioned their evil barbarity.

How do we keep from falling into the same pit? By allowing the whole of Scripture to minister to us. Read the Bible in its entirety. Leave nothing out. And as you do, take in the individual verses, certainly, but also be aware of the big picture—the full tapestry of history over which God reigns. Had the old slave masters done that, they would have seen that God treats His people with love and honor and expects us to treat each other in the same way. They would have taken a paraphrased verse like Luke 12:47 KJV and would have balanced it off with this verse found in Ephesians 6:9:

And masters, treat your slaves in the same way [with respect]. Do not threaten them, since you know that he who is both their Master and yours is in heaven, and there is no favoritism with him.

From the perspective of our poor enslaved ancestor, another verse, Proverbs 22:3, needed to be factored in:

A prudent man sees danger and takes refuge, but the simple keep going and suffer for it.

Had this verse been considered, when our brothers and sisters were subjected to such cruelty, escape would have been justified. It wasn't justified in the law because these evil slaveholders were blinded to Scripture that disagreed with the depravity of their hearts.

Of course, slavery is only mentioned in Scripture because it existed in biblical times as well, and slaves, like all Christians, are to work within the world where God has placed them—unless that world becomes threatening. Then their duty is to escape. Although mentioned and dealt with, slavery was never a godly practice.

ATTEND CHURCH SERVICES REGULARLY

Although the old slave masters wanted slaves infected with their kind of religion, the kind that caused slaves to merely take the brutality their masters wanted to inflict, they also feared slaves being taught to read and write. Knowledge made slaves "restless," made them yearn for the freedom that knowledge said existed. Obviously fearing the knowledge the slaves would gain over the benefit that religion would bring, the slave masters took pains to keep their slaves away from Sunday services. Henry Bibb tells us about the Sunday practices of the old slave masters.[7]

For the slave masters, the Lord's Day became a time to use and abuse for their own amusement.

Since the slaves had no schools to attend and no moral or religious instruction on Sundays, few regarded it as a day of rest. Since they had nothing else to do, they would engage in various amusements. They would head in large numbers to "the woods," then hide among the trees to gamble, fight, and drink. Actually, they didn't need to hide. Often the slaveholders encouraged them. For them, this was sport. They enjoyed plying the slaves with whiskey to see them dance, sing, and play on their banjos—then, when they were drunk enough, watch them wrestle, fight, and butt each other like sheep. Bets were laid down, and money won and lost. For the slave masters, the Lord's Day became a time to use and abuse for their own amusement.

Spiritual stability comes when a firm spiritual foundation is laid. And that foundation is largely laid at the local church. Attend with your children. Become involved in those elements of the church that are there for your benefit: worship services, Bible studies, singles groups, church-sponsored activities, support groups. Become an asset to your church. Pray for it every opportunity you have.

Get the children involved in age-appropriate ministries. From nursery to youth groups to college and career, urge them to go, and support them when they do. Help the youth leaders when you are able, and pray for them daily. You are living for your children, and your success in being a good parent to them rests largely on your church's contribution to their lives.

PRAY

William Wells Brown tells of prayer within his master's family. His master held services both morning and night. At night the slaves were brought in to participate, but in the morning the slaves were at work in the fields, and only the master's family and the house slaves attended. The master was fond of mint julep, an alcoholic drink, and in the morning, before worship, it was William's job to help pour the pitcher. Then, while feeling the effects of the alcohol, the group went into worship.[8] The master did all the praying. Once, before the service ended, William accidentally knocked over the pitcher of mint julep and, after the service, was severely "chastised."

The idea of a family worship, certainly of a family prayer time, is good. This particular slave master, although the method was terrible, was right in having it. To make yours far more significant and productive, remove all distractions—and that definitely means no mint julep. And no television, radio, cassette or CD players. No telephone calls, no friends at the door, no animals interrupting. Make it a time between only you and the children.

Then ask your children to behave as if they are going into a king's throne room—which they are. They are not to be afraid of this King, but they are to behave reverently in His presence. He also loves them, so they are not to worry about choosing their words or saying something wrong; He will understand. Anyway, He already knows the desires of their hearts before they ask (Matthew 6:8). Encourage them to speak for themselves, to tell God what they want and how they feel. And, above all, be honest. God knows the truth anyway.

Also encourage them to pray for their friends. Tell them that good friends pray for what their friends really need, so they should talk with their friends to find out what their needs are. Have them keep a prayer journal to help them remember what they have asked for and see how God answers. Over time they will see God revealed time and again within the pages of that journal.

READ BIBLE STORIES TOGETHER

What young child can resist the drama of David and Goliath, Joseph and the coat of many colors, Daniel in the lions' den, the Hebrew children in the fiery furnace, Jonah and the great fish, and Job and his tribulations? And finally, Jesus Himself. Help them, again through their prayer journal, to see God at work in their lives just as He worked in the lives of those Bible story heroes.

INCLUDE CHILDREN IN DECISION MAKING

Henry Bibb found himself in the middle of the slavery management process (which makes it sound a bit

Even when you include the Lord at every turn, at times you will feel desperately alone.

173

more legitimate than it was) when he was unexpectedly made an over-seer. His story goes like this.

Henry, his wife, and child were about to end up on the auction block. Fearing that the family would be irreversibly split, Henry decided to find a slaveholder willing to buy his family intact. Armed with a note from his master, he started to look for a buyer. Since Henry was a Christian, he thought that life would be better if a fellow believer bought them. Hearing about a church deacon who was in the market for slaves, and seeing that the man was well dressed and likable, Henry rested easier when the man consented to Henry's proposal. Henry's family would stay together, and he could serve a fellow Christian.

What he failed to realize was that the deacon was "one of the basest hypocrites" that Henry had ever seen. When he reached the man's farm in Tennessee, he found the other slaves ill fed and poorly clothed. But that revelation paled in the light of this horrific episode:

Next a mulatto girl who waited about the house, on her mistress, displeased her, for which the Deacon stripped and tied her up. He then handed me the lash and ordered me to put it on—but I told him I never had done the like, and hoped he would not com-pel me to do it. He then informed me that I was to be his over-seer, and that he had bought me for that purpose. He was paying a man $800 a year to oversee, and he believed I was competent to do the same business, and if I would do it up right he would put nothing harder on me to do; and if I knew not how to flog a slave, he would set me an example by which I might be gov-erned. He then commenced on this poor girl, and gave her two hundred lashes before he had her untied.[9]

But that wasn't the worst of the narrative. Henry described how after fifty lashes, the deacon stopped and lectured the girl a while, ask-ing her if she planned to perform her duties more diligently next time.

She, in turn, begged him to stop beating her, promising that she would, from that moment on, obey her mistress religiously. But he refused to have mercy on her. After his lecture was finished, he gave her the rest of her punishment.

> ... and this flogging was carried on in the most inhuman manner until she had received two hundred stripes on her naked quivering flesh, tied up and exposed to the public gaze of all. And this was the example that I was to copy after.
>
> He then compelled me to wash her back off with strong salt brine, before she was untied.[10]

This experience was so gut wrenching for Henry that he could only perform this heinous duty in tears.

The deacon brought Henry Bibb into the nasty process of overseeing slaves unwittingly. You, on the other hand, bring your children into the process of overseeing your family gently and deliberately. During these special times of prayer and reflection with your children, but also during dinner, and when you are out shopping, or at the park—in fact, anytime it makes sense—bring them into your family decision-making process. Allow them to be a part of the way your family meets its daily challenges.

Finally, at appropriate intervals, bring someone of your opposite gender, perhaps someone from your church, into your family Bible time. This will provide the kids, and you, a missing perspective. If that missing gender is the same as your children, it will help them better understand their spiritual role within the family.

A CALL FOR PATIENCE

Single parenthood can become overwhelming. In fact, if it hasn't done so already, it will one day. Even when you include the Lord at every turn, at times you will feel desperately alone, dangling out there at the end of your rope. As your knuckles grow white, and you feel your fingertips grow raw and slip, you will instinctively grab for help. The worst possible hand to grab is one that belongs to an available mate.

People you have dated who, when life was under reasonable control, had real faults, can suddenly look very good when you are desperate. You can easily say to yourself: "So he drinks; doesn't everyone? What if he doesn't like kids now; he'll learn to love them." And suddenly you think you should marry that person, so he can save you. Bad idea! When you feel overwhelmed, seek help from family, church, friends—and, especially, the Lord.

The best way I have found to do that is to meditate on this Bible verse: "He who did not spare his own Son, but gave him up for us all—how will he not also, along with him, graciously give us all things?" (Romans 8:32).

That sense of being overwhelmed *doesn't* come from God. Read that verse again.

The God described by the apostle Paul in these words doesn't overwhelm us. He is with us every step, to help and guide us toward an abundant life in Him (John 10:10; Jeremiah 29:11). Your sense of desperation comes from the New Slavemasters, those who want to enslave you as the old slave masters enslaved Henry Bibb and his family. They want you to feel like that poor girl Henry watched beaten and abused—that you can't go on, that God has forsaken you, that your hope lies somewhere other than in Jesus.

Just let that verse minister to you. Hear God's soothing voice whisper it to you: "I who did not spare My own Son, but gave Him up for you— how will I not also, along with Him, graciously give you all things?" Hear Him tell you again and again how important you are to Him. How could He possibly abandon you now? He will see you through this. All you have to do is take the next step in faith—whatever that step is—and He will be beside you to help you take the next and the next. As you mature in your relationship with Him, it will become easier to set the desperation aside and live in the calm of His promises.

Being a single parent is difficult. Within your family you are provider, disciplinarian, supporter, nurturer, guide, and so much more. To fulfill all these roles is more than a full-time job, a job the New Slavemasters would prefer you do poorly. The easiest way they know to assure that you do it poorly is by throwing some strong temptations your way. In the next chapter we will examine what I believe is the strongest of these temptations.

CHAPTER NINETEEN

THE SINGLE PARENT:
THE SEXUAL PREDATOR SEEKING WHOM HE MAY DEVOUR

When Judah saw her, he thought she was a prostitute,

for she had covered her face. Not realizing that she was

his daughter-in-law, he went over to her by the roadside

and said, "Come now, let me sleep with you."

—Genesis 38:15–16

He took her back to St. Louis, established her as his mistress

and housekeeper at his farm, and before I left, he had two children

by her. But, mark the end! Since I have been at the North,

I have been credibly informed that Walker has been married,

and, as a previous measure, sold poor Cynthia and her four children (she have had

two more since I came away) into hopeless bondage.

—Autobiography of William Wells Brown, an escaped slave

Trisha had a beautiful voice. Some might add "for her age." But I never did. She had a beautiful voice for any age. We just came to realize it when she was only fifteen. This was before *American Idol* and Simon's barrage of insults. Had that TV show been around then, Trisha would have undoubtedly begged her mother, Joanna, to let her try out. And Joanna would have undoubtedly refused to let her. She had had experiences she wanted Trisha to avoid.

Joanna had a good voice, too, and there was a time when she turned professional for a while. After singing at some local clubs, she joined a band and cut a few demo records. When on the verge of a recording contract, she was noticed by a talent agent who convinced her that she needed his help. After gaining her confidence, he tried to lure her into bed. Tired of her rejections, he tried coercion. "You know, I've got two other singers like you. Neither of them has your talent, but they're cooperating with me. You're not. Do you want the good jobs or not? You know, fame has a price."

Joanna was unwilling to pay it. Disillusioned, she decided to return to a more modest but glorious career singing in church.

Now her fifteen-year-old daughter was pulling at that same tether; she wanted to soar on her voice's wings. "Trisha, you're not ready," Joanna told her flatly. "The temptations are strong out there, and you're not able to handle them right now. Do what you can here, and when you're ready, we'll ease you into it."

Of course, Trisha didn't want to be eased into it, but she was a good kid. Not yet born again, but searching and willing to be led. Although she struggled, she eventually listened to her mother.

Soon after Trisha's sixteenth birthday though, everything changed. Joanna met Cadence, the single father of Trisha's best friend. Trisha's father had left them nearly ten years earlier, and since then Joanna had remained focused only on Trisha. But her gaze shifted when Cadence stepped through her front door. Tall with a chiseled muscularity, he commanded her full attention. Her sexual attraction to him was palpable.

No more than a month later, Trisha caught Joanna and Cadence in bed together. From then on, Trisha made it her mission to ride her voice out of that house. Within a year she was lying about her age and singing in clubs. Within two years, for the sake of what she perceived a growing career, she had had two abortions. Now I have lost track of her, as has Joanna. If Trisha has a professional career, it is not on any radar screens. Joanna hasn't seen Cadence in at least two years and now lives with a heart hardened by guilt and loneliness.

It seems that when the New Slavemasters hit our thick walls of spiritual resolve, they often bring out the big guns—they become sexual predators. Of course, some might say, so what? After all, they argue, there may be a few casualties like Trisha, but by and large children benefit from sexually active single parents. When you are a single parent and have obviously had your sexual desires fulfilled in the past, trying to give up those desires only leads to frustration and bitterness. And what child wants a frustrated, bitter parent?

Actually, the opposite is true, and by the time you turn the last page of this chapter, I hope you will agree. Frankly, those who argue that sexual experience outside of marriage is good—whether children are involved or not—are unconsciously supporting the New Slavemasters in their drive to enslave us or if we haven't broken free yet, to keep us enslaved.

When misused, the sexual experience causes deep, overwhelming pain to those foolish enough to engage in it.

This big gun is truly big!

SEX AND SLAVERY

No other human behavior provides such profound beauty as sex when experienced appropriately. It is the zenith of intimacy, the conduit of a thousand physical and emotional threads that connect those in love; it is the voice of oneness that God plants within those lovers He unites. But, when misused, the sexual experience causes deep, overwhelming pain to those foolish enough to engage in it.

Satan knew this fact. He used two elements of the slaveholders' fallen character to corrupt them and keep them in spiritual chains: the acquisition of more and more power and the gratification of their sordid lusts—through sex.

The escaped slaves wrote extensively about the way slave women were treated—as pawns in Satan's war to keep the slaveholders slaves to satisfying their sinful hungers. Frederick Douglass, for instance, believed he had a white father, perhaps even his master.[1] Linda Brent, whom we met in chapter 10, experienced the horror of being a beautiful slave blossoming into womanhood.[2] Cynthia, the woman described in the earlier quotation,[3] was also beautiful. In fact, William Brown described her as the most beautiful woman he had ever seen. And even though he knew Cynthia as a woman who "bore an irreproachable character for virtue and propriety of conduct," he also knew the instant he laid eyes on her that she would be cursed to a life of being sordidly used. This terrible sexual enslavement of both slaves and slaveholders sometimes led to catastrophically bizarre behaviors.

When sex is positive, it is truly positive, because God created it for very positive reasons.

Again, it is William Brown who tells Patsey's story. Patsey was a slave who belonged to a Mr. Colburn. Colburn had feelings for Patsey, but she was engaged to John, a slave who belonged to a Major William Christy who had a farm down the road. John and Patsey "went to meeting" one evening, and John walked her home. Colburn had decided to flog John when they arrived, but John got away from him before Colburn could lay the whip to him. Frustrated, Colburn tied Patsey up and whipped her—whipped her so ferociously that some of his boarders came out and pleaded with him to stop.[4] Can you imagine cruelly whipping someone for whom you have strong feelings? The old slave masters were as emotionally deceptive as the New.

God reserves the sexual experience for marriage, and if our hearts are inclined in God's direction, we will keep it there.

And if you are a single parent—any kind of parent, really—those masters of deception are after you right now. They are eager to throw the chains of slavery on you again or tighten the chains that enslave you now so that you will never break free.

You can have victory over them, however. And the rest of this chapter tells you how.

THE IMPLICATIONS OF SEX

First, there is no such thing as *safe* or *recreational sex*. Not only do most sexual experiences potentially lead to both wanted and unwanted children, but sex in *all* its forms has heavy emotional, psychological, and spiritual implications. Only within the committed marriage relationship do any of them become positive. When sex is positive, it is truly *positive*, because God created it for very positive reasons.

Physically, it is a powerful internal drive designed to keep mankind as a vital presence here on earth; simply stated, it makes babies. *Emotionally*, within the marriage bond, it is the purest, most beautiful, and most exclusive joining of husband and wife, the grandest, most intimate expression of love and caring between them. And *spiritually*, it is divinely created and instituted. God reserves the sexual experience for marriage, and if our hearts are inclined in God's direction, we will keep it there. When we do, God blesses the experience; it becomes all that He created it to be.

But when we engage in the sexual experience outside the marriage bond, much that is negative replaces the beautiful blessing that God intended it to be.

For instance, illicit sex *cheapens the woman; she becomes little more than merchandise.* When a man is unwilling to commit his life to a woman in marriage yet wants what he should only get within marriage, he is telling her, "You're just not worth it." If told that often enough, she may begin to believe it.

Illicit sex severely betrays a woman's trust. When a man whispers words of love and commitment into a woman's ear, even when they both believe them, but he then changes his mind, the woman's trust is severely shaken. Who can she believe? If she is treated this way repeatedly, she may even begin to doubt that God can be trusted. *After all,* she may think, *didn't God send me these guys?*

And what are "these guys" now? *They have been turned into a liars, predators, and manipulators.* When a man realizes that all he has to do is buy a few dinners, purchase a few gifts, whisper a few sweet nothings in a woman's ear, and she becomes his for a time, that sort of power is hard to keep under ethical wraps. He quickly becomes the grand manipulator. Soon he loses respect for women in general; he begins to see all women as gullible, as intellectually challenged. Contempt naturally follows.

Illicit sex makes the woman become a manipulator, too. There is a lot to frighten women these days. Since feelings are all that compel a man to stay, and since feelings wane, how much trust can a woman have in her sex partner? A man can usually get what he wants anywhere. Fear of losing him may turn the woman into a manipulator. She may go so far as to try to chain him to her by having his child.

With all that manipulation going on, *trust between marriage partners is weakened:* If the sexual experience occurred before the wedding, what guarantee does either mate have that it will be confined to marriage afterward? If it was recreational before, what assurance does either have that it will not become recreational again?

As each manipulates the other, *the sexual experience is cheapened*. Its deep, soul-touching meaning that God intended is lost. It becomes nothing more than recreation, like television or a movie and a burger. And if cheapened outside marriage, how can it again be that profoundly meaningful communication between married partners that God wants within the marriage? Which means that the deep expression of love and commitment reserved for the sexual experience may no longer have a voice. That is a terrible loss to a relationship as sacred as marriage.

It also means that marriage is not quite so sacred anymore. *Marriage has been cheapened*. If what couples once married for occurs without marriage, marriage is worthless. It is not as important as it once was. Sadly, too, just as marriage loses value, *the sexual partners themselves may lose tenderness and sweet understanding*. The sexual experience, because of its intimacy and its overwhelming emotional power, can become the measure of a relationship's health rather than the true measures: heart-caressing tenderness *to* one another and sweet understanding *of* one another.

Consider Millie.

Millie loved Raggles, a beagle that could be a handful. Her father had given Raggles to her as a puppy just before his death when Millie was still a young teen. That was nearly fourteen years ago, and Millie still missed her father very much.

Millie also thought she loved Eric. Millie was a Christian, Eric was not, but soon after they met they began a strong sexual relationship. Although they had a few things in common, when they came together in the bedroom, some strong emotions were kindled.

One Saturday morning Millie and Eric got up to what they figured would be a normal Saturday. Millie would work around the house, and Eric would take a quick shower and head out to shoot some hoops. All that changed when Millie went to feed Raggles. Her heart froze. Raggles lay half in and half out of his bed, his tongue lolling lifelessly, its tip cold on the linoleum. "Eric," she cried out. "Raggles is …"

Eric was quickly beside her. "He's dead," he said almost off-handedly. "Never did like that mutt."

Millie's jaw dropped; she could only look at him dumbly. Had he really said that? "Raggles is ..." she said again, still choking off the name. "It's Raggles," she said, pleading to be understood. But Eric never did understand. A few minutes later, after he had refused to help her move Raggles, he left to shoot those hoops.

Help did come to her, however, from the guy who lived next door. He was a little older than she was, and she spied him mowing his lawn from the kitchen window. "I'm sorry about your dog," he said gently after they got Raggles to the garage. "I think you told me once your dad had given him to you," he said. "Just before he died."

"I told you that?"

"Raggles is probably all wrapped up in memories of your dad. Losing the little guy brings all that back, doesn't it? Makes it pretty hard for you, I'll bet."

Do everything you can to prepare yourself to enter into a marriage that is stable, strong, holy.

Millie could only bury her face in her neighbor's shoulder and weep. Soon thereafter, Millie said good-bye to Eric, and she and the guy next door started seeing more of one another—God's way. *Tenderness, understanding, support*—all synonymous with someone who truly loves you—are all synonymous with Jesus.

KEEP SEX IN MARRIAGE

The final reason to keep the sexual experience within the marriage bond is that *sex makes kids, and kids need real families.* No contraception, except for abstinence, is 100 percent foolproof. Eventually pregnancy occurs, and if it occurs outside marriage, real harm to children and parents follows. We will talk about some of what happens a little later.

"But society, peer pressure, and my own desires won't let me wait!" Beating off the New Slavemasters by forging a sound Christian legacy won't be easy. And keeping the sexual experience within marriage may be the most difficult part of that. But there are ways. First, give your sex life over to the Lord. Go to Him openly, and commit it to Him and His glory. Sound a little strange? Is it like going to your dad and talking to him about sex? Yes, it's just like that. Only this "daddy" is the God of the universe and knows all about your sex life anyway. Keep in mind, though, that sex, when kept to marriage, is wonderful to God. So commit your behavior to Him, and ask Him for His keeping, His guidance, and His wisdom.

Then live a committed life. If need be, redefine your dating process. Make dates for what God intended. Have fun. Learn about one another: ask questions, share each other's hopes for the future, experience each other's reactions to situations, take each other's advice and see what results. When someone doesn't measure up, go on to the next, or just be with yourself for a while. You will find relationships a lot easier. There won't be the reservoir of hurt that usually accompanies a sexually active relationship.

A Final Note

If you are engaged in a premarital sexual relationship that doesn't lead to marriage, you are messing around with a person who will become someone else's spouse. Repent and abstain from sexual sin! (Exodus 20:14; 1 Corinthians 6:18). You are definitely planting your seeds in someone else's garden. So do everything you can to prepare yourself to enter into a marriage that is stable, strong, holy—one that honors God, one you can look at with spiritual pride, one that God is sure to bless.

This kind of maturity, however, doesn't exist for some single parents, for those who are hardly more than children themselves. Although every word in this chapter applies to them, their youth makes them particularly vulnerable to the New Slavemasters, and it presents a special challenge to them and to their parents, their children's grandparents. We will take on these issues in the next chapter.

CHAPTER TWENTY

FAMILIES WITHIN FAMILIES:
PARENTS OF YOUNG PARENTS

For wisdom is more precious than rubies,
and nothing you desire can compare with her.
—Proverbs 8:11

Even the little child, who is accustomed to wait on her mistress and her
children, will learn, before she is twelve years old, why it is that her mistress
hates such and such a one among the slaves. Perhaps the child's own
mother is among those hated ones.
—Autobiography of Linda Brent, a former slave

We met Linda Brent when we discussed the war against children. We meet her again in the quotation above as we explore another front in that war.[1] Linda's merciless slave masters weakened her as they kept her fear-ravaged senses searching for her much older, much stronger master's approach and in pain as she suffered his terrible abuse and the futility of escape. The New Slavemasters enslave our young girls the same way. They keep them weak by making them mere sexual objects often of men who are much older and, in our view, little more than predators. They keep them confused and painfully aware of their inescapable lot in life by stealing their childhood with the responsibility of raising a child.

They did that to Shauna, and at fourteen she nearly killed that baby. She attended our youth group for a time, and although she remained on the fringe of group activities, she came often, usually as the guest of a Christian friend. Sometime before her fourteenth birthday she got pregnant. Loose clothing kept her secret until she was about six months along. When her condition became obvious, even though the friend kept inviting her, she abandoned youth group altogether. Her mother, Carol, didn't attend church.

I first became aware of them during the investigation that followed. Two months after her little boy was born, Shauna stuffed the infant in a large plastic trash bag and placed him in a trash bin about a block from her house. Then she returned home to wait for her mother to get home from work. When Carol returned, Shauna told her that someone had snatched the baby away from her in the park. "Some guy in a gang shirt. Probably going to raise him to be a killer or something."

Carol was understandably upset. She had raised the child as her own and had nurtured a mother's attachment to the little guy. She didn't believe her daughter for a second; not only was the story unbelievable, but Shauna's calm demeanor contradicted it. Instinctively, Carol knew that something had happened to her grandson and that time *had* to be working against him. Frantically, she called the police. The moment they answered, she told them what Shauna had said. And moments later, they reassured her they had the baby. Fortunately, there had been a small hole in the bag that allowed the baby to breathe and his cries to be heard.

Why had Shauna done this terrible thing? The investigators quickly determined that Shauna was jealous of her own baby. She had been the only child for fourteen years, and now she had to share the stage with someone else. But later both Carol and Shauna told me there was more to it than that. Not to excuse Shauna's behavior, but her mother's anger had made Shauna's life difficult.

Before the baby came, Carol had looked forward to more freedom, but now all those hopes had evaporated. Shauna was a typical young teen—all music, dancing, parties, and boys. She could hardly remember to clean her room once a week, so how could she be trusted to take care of another human being? Carol immediately inserted herself between Shauna and the care of the baby, essentially becoming the mother of an infant once again. And every opportunity she had, she let Shauna know how much she resented it. Shauna, not mature enough to deal with this complex tangle of emotions, and profoundly susceptible to the lies told by the New Slavemasters, grew to hate her child. And at age fourteen, what is hated is disposed of.

> *"Right and best" starts with each member of the family coming to a saving knowledge of Jesus Christ.*

How did the New Slavemasters work to destroy this family? Of course, they are too wily an enemy to provide us with any easy answers. And just because they worked their terrible magic on Carol and Shauna doesn't mean they will be successful in your family. But for a time—a very important time—they were able to get Carol and Shauna to forget their family legacy and the fact that a family's first goal is to come together: Carol, Shauna, and the baby. In fact, they forgot they were a family at all.

At the time of this incident they were not a Christian family. If they had been, they would have known that a family, in times of difficulty, does what is right and best for each of its members. "Right and best" starts with each member of the family coming to a saving knowledge of Jesus Christ. Of course, God knows that, and we can be assured that He is still at work in that family.

WHAT ABOUT YOUR FAMILY?

But let's focus on *your* family. If you have a family like Carol's—a family within a family—in which the new mother is seventeen or younger, you need to take the natural dynamics of this overall family structure very seriously. If you don't, it can, as Carol's did, become a tangle of strong forces, forces that intersect, conflict, and compete. And when they do, it's like the New Slavemasters violently rubbing two very dry sticks together: the forces spark, ignite, and ultimately consume and destroy. Some of these forces are:

◆ Babies need specific and relentless care, yet the new parent is inexperienced; prideful; and a cauldron of natural emotions, many now being felt for the first time. At this age, these feelings can be overwhelming and misunderstood.

◆ There is the need for older parents to still exercise authority yet somehow balance their authority with the God-given authority of a new, inexperienced parent.

◆ A young parent finds herself thrown into a world of adult responsibilities yet wants to go back; or a young parent is consumed with the desire to be a parent but lacks the temperament and skill, often knowing just enough to get herself and her child into trouble.

◆ Older parents wrestle with precious grandparents' feelings yet find their futures yanked out from under them as they are "forced" to be parents to an infant again. This situation fosters resentment and frustration, which propels their attempt to hurry the young parent into adulthood so the young parent can take up her rightful responsibilities, which will ultimately get them off the hook.

And that's just to name a few. Do you see any of these dynamics at work in your family? Whether or not you do, it is easy to see how the New Slavemasters can help these forces collide and cause damage—*if* we take our spiritual eyes and ears off Christ even for a moment.

Fortunately in Carol and Shauna's case, the episode didn't end in tragedy. Shauna got some needed emotional help; the mother got some needed counseling; and the baby was placed in a two-parent home, at least for the time being. Both Shauna and Carol have been open to spiritual help as well, and our prayers are with them—and to all families like them.

Let's put it in a single sentence. If you are a Christian family, in order to keep the New Slavemasters at bay and live your legacy as a family builder, your goal is simple: to stay far enough ahead of those forces in order to turn them into positive influences that bring your family closer together, closer to Christ, and help you grow and mature into an even mightier Christian family.

Pretty easy to say, isn't it? But how is it accomplished?

It starts with real, honest, tough, no-holds-barred love.
Nearly 70 percent of African American children are born outside of marriage, and many of those babies are born to girls who, by any rational measure, are still children themselves. Shauna was a prime example. That is a lot of children, and I am talking about the parents here. Some are still in elementary school, and they are having babies of their own. Statistically, it is a terrible problem. But the child-parent in your family is far more than a

Our admonition is to offer these unfortunate babies for adoption into traditional two-parent families.

statistic. She is *your* child, or she is *you*—in either case, she is a real human being with real troubles and a real future, all of which can be made far worse by the New Slavemasters. May I suggest a way to quickly avoid them and improve all your futures? Create a future of pure, unselfish love. Give up the baby for adoption into a traditional two-parent family.

ADOPTION IS DOUBLY IMPORTANT

In chapter 16 we discussed the value of a traditional two-parent family. It goes without saying then that if we love our children, we believe that all children born outside of such a stable, loving family should have the opportunity to experience the benefits and protection it affords. Our admonition, then, is to offer these unfortunate babies for adoption into traditional two-parent families.

With our younger parents, this admonition is doubly important. That is not to say that young single parents *can't* raise children. They can. Youth, health, strength, and the ability to work hard without much sleep are all on their side. But our parental goal is to be more than just caretakers. We are to raise our children to be all they can be. We are to bring them up in "the nurture and admonition of the Lord" (Ephesians 6:4 KJV), so they will one day take their position in God's spiritual army. The question is can a young single parent do that, especially in this world haunted by the old slave masters and stalked by the New, the truly hostile world into which God has placed her?

In my fifty-some-odd years of Christian service, I have seen repeatedly that no matter how strong the intentions, the commitment to Christ, or the emotional stability, a teenager is simply unprepared to be a mother in this society. Both mother and child will suffer. The greatest love a teenage parent can show her child is to place the child where he or she will have the best opportunity to live an abundant, God-glorifying life, in a stable, two-parent Christian home.

However, if the young parent decides against adoption, it is time for the biological family to pull together and do what is best for everyone involved, particularly the baby. To this end, I have found it helpful to review the family structure that helps the *family within a family* to do just that. Let's start from the top.

THE HEAD OF THE HOUSE: THE FATHER ROLE

Terri always wanted a second child. But since her husband abandoned her and her daughter, Brenda, several years ago, and other men kept their distance, it didn't look like she would ever have another child. Brenda was fifteen, and her lively brown eyes lost much of their luster after her dad left, a luster that hadn't returned. The light in Terri's eyes died that day, too, but then Brenda announced that she was pregnant, and a spark in Terri's eyes ignited. Ordinarily Brenda's condition would be bad news. Both Terri and Brenda considered themselves Christians, and both knew that Brenda's behavior had been wrong. But Terri saw this bad news as answered prayer. Not only did the pregnancy compel Brenda to vow to live a more God-honoring life, but it also meant that Terri could raise the child as her own.

Brenda thought the logic a little strained, but it did solve the problem. Brenda would have the child, and her mother would carry the rest of the burden: a solution right out of Solomon's court.

The house bubbled with true joy when Brenda went into labor. As Terri stood in the delivery room clad in green scrubs anticipating the painless birth of *her* child, she was genuinely excited. But the instant she held the newly cleaned little girl in her arms, something unexpected occurred. As Terri explained it to me, clarity broke over her like a bright, very clear dawn. This was not *her* baby. This was Brenda's baby; even though Brenda was ill prepared to raise a child, God had given this little girl to her. God wanted Brenda to be the ultimate parent. And whatever that meant for the family, Terri knew that she and Brenda had to work it out.

If you are the head of your household, and God is about to embed, or has already embedded, a young family into it, understand this: That baby is God's gift to your child, not to you. But God also wants your family to work through and learn from the issues this baby brings.

Some of these issues are ...

Your daughter, the new baby's parent, is *still* under your authority. Brenda was still Terri's daughter; Terri was still the spiritual head of the house. She still set all the rules, still meted out all the discipline, and still maintained her God-given position as head of household. Don't let the fact your child now has some of the same responsibilities you do confuse you. She still needs your guidance, wisdom, maturity, and tough parental love.

> *Although not fully prepared, she needs to be the spiritual head of her little family—and you are there to help her.*

Something has changed, however. Your daughter has become a *head of the house in training*. Although not fully prepared, she needs to be the spiritual head of her little family—and you are there to help her. Encourage her to pray for her child, read Bible stories, and have devotions; it is her turn to teach her child about the Lord the same way you taught her—and still do.

She must also learn how to guide and discipline her child, a delicate requirement because a toddler needs to be disciplined firmly, yet gently, with a smack on the bottom or hand, a firm word, time-outs, and so forth. This discipline needs to be child specific and should never be administered from anger. It should always be "bookended" by hugs; kisses; and all other forms of deep, abiding love. To achieve this balance requires maturity, a maturity that is also needed when the child tests parental authority, as your daughter probably did with you. When that happens, buttons get pushed, rage flares, and discipline can become an ugly power struggle. Until your child displays maturity enough to cope, you should supervise all discipline; your daughter should still perform it, but you should approve, encourage, and guide.

The head of the house also handles *the family finances*. Help your daughter come up with a budget *for her family*—what her family needs and how much it costs. Depending on her age and ability, make her responsible for at least a portion of it. Maybe she earns enough to buy the diapers, the baby's food or bedding, and pay a portion of her rent. One man in our church showed his daughter from the classified ads that the room she and her child lived in would rent for nearly $600 a month. He requested that she pay $50 of it. "And while you go to school, including college, that's what it will be. The moment you quit, it's $600." The incentive was clear.

As you encourage your daughter, negotiate the house rules. Act respectfully but firmly, as one Christian head of the household to another. You both have common goals now, the welfare of your respective families. And you have similar responsibilities: to make sure you do all you can, with God's help, to fulfill your God-given role.

I am not naïve; I realize that for some families the negotiation will be relatively easy, while for others it will be a nightmare. But if you explain why you require what you require, and how the young parent and her child will benefit from it, then back up the requirement with firm leadership and discipline, even the most difficult child *may* come around eventually.

THE CAREGIVER: THE MOTHER ROLE

Your child needs the nurture and care this role emphasizes, as does the baby. Your child needs a place to go for advice, encouragement, counsel, and love. The baby has needs—food, baths, clothing, sleep, play, fresh air, protection—in fact, babies are lavish in their needs. Your child, the young parent, is lavish in her needs, too, but she can do a lot for herself. One of your tasks is to realistically assess what she can do alone, what she can do with your help, and what she can't do at all. Then you and she have to work together to make sure that what needs to be done for all members of your family gets done.

As your lives together unfold, keep a gentle hand on your daughter's pulse; make sure you know how she is coping and what help she needs. She is still your child, which makes it your primary parental duty to help her come to know Jesus as her personal Lord and Savior, if she doesn't already. If she does, help her grow in His grace. This situation is filled with opportunities for both of you.

Boundaries
Children are masters of manipulation, and with all the emotions that swirl around these pivotal events, you may become vulnerable to your

daughter's clever wiles. Don't let yourself be manipulated. Set down firm, well-considered, well-understood rules and boundaries; then violate them only when you have an extremely good reason.

If you have other children, some of those boundaries should protect them. Even though you will spend considerable time helping the young parent, don't neglect your other children. They shouldn't be made to suffer for their good choices. They need love and nurture, too. Make sure they get all they need.

Money

You won't let either your daughter or her baby starve. Your daughter knows this. Nor will the little guy or gal ever go without diapers or warmth or protection. So what incentive does your daughter have to work and pay that rent or buy those supplies all babies need? The man who came up with the $50 rent told his daughter that if she didn't have the rent to him by the fifth of every month, until it did come in, she lost electricity—no television, radio, lights—and worst of all, no hair dryer. She tested him only once.

Baby-sitting

Your child, no matter how committed she is to *her* child, wants a childhood. She wants fun, parties, long talks with acquaintances, connections to best friends. And a smattering of that is healthy for her. But her child is her main responsibility now. One of your jobs is to help her maintain a good balance. To limit the baby-sitting hours available to her is one way to do that. Make it four hours a week, for instance, and two evenings a month. You decide, but make it reasonable and firm. Another option is to give the young parent unlimited baby-sitting; it would just cost her so much an hour.

THE YOUNG PARENT'S BROTHER OR SISTER

The sibling of a young parent still has the same responsibilities. He still needs to continue walking humbly with his Lord and help the family every way possible to fulfill the plan God has for it. But in another way, this role is extremely difficult and requires a selfless heart. This brother must give other family members all the help he can and give it knowing that there will be less family time available to satisfy his needs.

That will hurt.

"Here she gets pregnant," one youth group member told me, angry that his parents hadn't shown up for a play in which he acted. "She has a kid, and instead of grounding her for the rest of her life, everybody fawns all over her. They should have kicked her into the street."

This just isn't the time to envy his sister; it is time to make sure he doesn't follow in her footsteps. Remind these siblings to keep their sexual activity in check, reserved for marriage where God will bless it and turn it into something wonderful and fulfilling. And as they deal with injustices and inequities—and believe me, there will be many of them—encourage them to resist the temptation to get even. As they do, God will reveal Himself in many exciting ways. Just as Mary, the sister of Martha, did, encourage them to live the sibling life at the feet of Jesus (Luke 10:38–39).

In the previous two chapters we discussed the unmarried parent with children—usually the single mother. In the next chapter we will discuss the unmarried parent without children—usually the single father.

THE UNMARRIED FATHER:
THE MALE FORTRESS

Fathers, do not exasperate your children; instead,
bring them up in the training and instruction of the Lord.
—Ephesians 6:4

And unfortunately for me, I am the father of a slave,
a word too obnoxious to be spoken by a fugitive slave.
It calls fresh to my mind the separation of husband and wife;
of stripping, tying up and flogging; of tearing children
from their parents, and selling them on the auction block.
—Autobiography of Henry Bibb, an escaped slave

O ne evening as I got out of my car at a convenience store, I overheard a twenty-something male bragging to two others. "No, you
only wish you're a man. I got four babies on the way. And all from different ladies." He laughed haughtily. "I'm the real man." While one of
the others started bragging about having twins on the way, they slid
into a primer-smudged car and drove off.

I had heard this kind of talk before. It's all too common. A friend
who sells life insurance signed up a man for coverage who put down

The logic of some men is simple: If women love them enough to bear their children, the men must be really something.

four women and ten children as his beneficiaries. "I've never done anything for them, so I probably should do this," he commented when he was about halfway down the list.

THE OPPOSITE IS TRUE

The logic of some men is simple: If women love them enough to bear their children, the men must be really something—they must possess a powerful, manly spirit. To get a woman dreamy eyed is like the conquest of a tall mountain. To get her pregnant is like scaling its peak. And each conquest makes the victory summit that much higher. All that remains is to find more wombs to fill.

The New Slavemasters are delighted when men see themselves as little more than sperm donors, willing to casually separate themselves from the children they spawn. That is certainly what the old slave masters wanted. Separating children from their fathers separates them from the strength and guidance fathers provide.

Henry Bibb resisted them for as long as he could. His wife, Malinda, and his child, little Frances, were precious to him:

> ... for it was sometimes a pleasure to be with my little family even in slavery. I loved them as my wife and child. Little Frances was a pretty child; she was quiet, playful, bright, and interesting. She had a keen black eye, and the very image of her mother was stamped upon her cheek.[1]

Yet, as the opening quotation to this chapter tells us, he looked on them both with deep sorrow.[2] They were slaves subject to the evil whims of the slave masters. What pleasure could a man take in bringing a child into the world to suffer that terrible fate?

Centuries later, you have the same choice.

You, too, can choose to abandon your children to the whims of the New Slavemasters, to the influence of drugs, sexual gratification, and the like; or you can choose to be part of the fortress that protects them. After all, of the four children fathered by that man I overheard outside the convenience store, I hope all of them will end up loving and calling some other man "Daddy." I hope, all of them will look at some other man and see him as the manlier man, the more powerful man, the real man. Don't you want to be the one your children call "Daddy"?

Be a real man to your children, because …

THEY ARE *YOUR* CHILDREN

Custody or not, they are your responsibility.

Even if you were tricked into fatherhood—even if their mother lied about using birth control, for instance, when you engaged in a sexual relationship with her—you signed a contract; if a baby results, you are the father. Admit it to the mother, the children (if appropriate), and to God. "These are my children; I am responsible for them. I want to do what's right, and, God, I want Your help."

Those responsibilities can be divided into two categories: legal and moral. Legal translates into child support, spousal support, visitation requirements, and other judgments. I am not qualified to comment on these issues, and they vary from state to state. I am, however, eminently qualified to discuss moral responsibilities—and they are serious.

How important is it to you if your children's mother can't afford warm winter coats for your kids?

THIS IS SERIOUS BUSINESS

Some men live and die by what happens in the NBA. Others can think of nothing but the stock market. To the guy out in front of the convenience store, looking good to his buddies was important. What's important to you? For instance, how important is it to you if your children's mother can't afford warm winter coats for your kids, or your son never knows what it is to be a godly man, or your daughter decides to start her own family

If your son joins that gang, your not being there for him might end up killing him.

because you tore the heart out of yours? How important is it if your son, unable to make the male connection he needs, joins a gang to get it? Being a father is serious business. How serious? If your son joins that gang, your not being there for him might end up killing him.

YOUR MORAL RESPONSIBILITY

It is your moral responsibility to address your children's needs, whenever possible, as if you lived in the home. This is a bold requirement that demands bold action, but being a good father is worth the effort. And if need be, you should focus some of that effort on your children's mother. To help the children, you need to build a sound, helpful relationship with their mother. Here's how. First, lose your pride; stash all hidden agendas; and commit to selflessly addressing your children's physical, emotional, and spiritual needs. Then, support their mother as she does the same.

THEIR PHYSICAL NEEDS

Danny and Donna dated only a few times. But when Donna began attending church, Danny dumped her. Then, through mutual friends, he heard she was pregnant. Not completely heartless, he went to see her. Standing outside her apartment door, he asked if he could possibly be the father. She never answered him. After a tortured silence, she just shut the door in his face.

He didn't think about her again. Not for two years, anyway, until the day he was visited by child-support services from the DA's office. He was told that he owed Donna back child support. Of course, he denied everything, but his denial didn't matter. Donna had received a judgment for nearly $5,000, and $200 a month ongoing. "If it was just for me, I wouldn't care," she had stated. "But little Michelle needs what that money can buy."

Angry, Danny decided that paying was better than going to jail and made out Donna's first check to "Ms. Bloodsucker." Donna asked him to rewrite the check, and when he delivered it, he saw Michelle for the first time sitting on the living-room floor at the center of a whole herd of stuffed animals. Danny's heart went to mush, and he took a quick step toward her. Donna grabbed his arm.

"I want to see my kid," Danny said, but Donna shook her head and reminded him pointedly that he had never asked for visitation. "I wouldn't give it to you anyway. What kind of man won't support his kid? I don't want her around someone like that."

Donna, of course, was right. If your child is no more important to you than a few bucks, what kind of father will you be? Your children are *the* major part of your life; be generous with your support.

Understand your children's physical needs.

Whenever possible, help their mother provide what they need, *what would come from a loving God.*

Danny decided he had to see Michelle again. But Donna was right; he hadn't asked for visitation. In fact, he had scoffed at the idea. A few days later, though, he knocked on Donna's door. "I want to help," he told her.

"No more 'Bloodsucker' checks?"

"I promise. I can help you store Michelle's stuffed animals." And he pulled from his jacket pocket a large kite-string fishnet. "Give me a minute." That's all it took him. He quickly screwed three hooks into the wall in the corner over Michelle's bed and then stretched the net between them. He had made a hammock for her stuffed animals; then he watched enthralled while Donna and Michelle made a game of tossing the animals into it. He had solved a problem. And for his trouble, he was invited to stay to play with Michelle, although the little girl hadn't yet been told who he was.

Include education in their needs.

The hammock satisfied a current need, but physical needs also include preparation for the future—and education tops that list. At-home fathers help with schoolwork or provide tutors when needed. You should do the same. But don't push the kids off onto a tutor just because you can't be bothered. Time with them is too important to toss away. Any second a "math" session might morph into a discussion about drugs or dating or God.

Real fathers also encourage their children's talents and gifts. All God's children have them, and we give our children a great gift when we help identify and develop theirs. When we do, we help prepare them for the future, and we help fulfill God's plan for them.

Danny quickly saw that Michelle enjoyed using her stuffed animals to make up stories. To encourage her imagination, he expanded on the stories as they played together. Soon she started picking up the stories where he would leave off. She would even pick up a story where he had left it a few days before. Donna hadn't realized how fertile Michelle's imagination was; she saw the stuffed animals as just soft little baby-sitters. After Danny mentioned it, Donna looked for evidence. She found it at the end of Michelle's bedtime story that night when the two-year-old made up a clever alternative ending.

Provide for your children's protection.

A man protects his household. With their mother's concurrence, teach your children how to defend themselves. Your son shouldn't be a bully, but neither should he be the school's punching bag. Your daughter should be feminine, but she shouldn't be an easy mark for some guy with muscles. Teach them how to avoid trouble, about inappropriate touching, but also teach them that in this violent world, self-defense is essential. You can help with it all.

THEIR EMOTIONAL NEEDS

Children need to know that Daddy cares about them. As you see to their physical needs, you show them that you care. Although only two years old, Michelle was deeply affected when Donna finally told her who Danny was. Although Donna wasn't sure Michelle completely understood, when Danny said good-bye that evening, she did something unusual. She wrapped her little arms around his neck and gave him a sweet little kiss on his cheek. "Good night, Daddy," she whispered, unsure of the words but eager to try them out.

However, if you still don't support your children physically, realize that you are hurting them emotionally. Far too many children know their fathers only from what Mom tells them, which generally isn't much. As your children grow, a part of them is always searching—is never satisfied—and as that void gains power, it shapes what they believe about themselves and about others. *After all*, they say to themselves, *what kind of a person could I be if my own father doesn't want me?* Do you ever want your children to ask themselves that question?

No? Then, with their mother's approval, care *for* them. Show them they are important to you and minimize their self-doubts. Show them they are valued and help clear their pathway of self-imposed hurdles.

Another way you can make their pathway a little smoother is by bringing a male perspective to the issues they face. It helps sons understand their manhood, helps them determine who real men are. And it helps daughters understand how men think, how they see the world, and how they see women. Such knowledge helps them forge stronger male relationships and, since Daddy loves them, forge them with the knowledge that they can form and maintain healthy relationships with men.

They also will benefit from your experiences. God gave you a life filled with insights, unique ideas and discoveries, and loads of mis-takes—all of which can now be used to help your children. Through your guidance, their circumstances become less troublesome, their fears of new situations diminish, their confidence in the future grows, and they are freer to express and try new ideas. This assurance brings them a greater sense of peace and joy and positively affects their sense of emo-tional well-being. Their daddy loves them; how great is that? And the New Slavemasters have no place to gain an emotional foothold.

THEIR SPIRITUAL NEEDS

To help your children with their spiritual needs, you first must tend to your own. On this subject, I am going to be blunt.

You have fathered a child outside the bonds of marriage. You have committed sexual sin, and you need to drop to your knees before God and repent of that sin. First, sincerely regret your sin, regret that you hurt your child's mother and hurt your child, and regret that you sinned against God. Second, promise never to do it again.

But before you repent, determine something very important about yourself: Are you saved? (Acts 2:21). Are you a child of God? (Romans 8:16). Have you gone before God's throne of grace with a broken and contrite heart and asked Him for His mercy and forgiveness for this and all your sins? (Hebrews 4:16; Psalm 51:17; 1 John 1:9). Have you then asked His Son Jesus to come into your heart, confessing Him as your Lord and Savior? (Revelation 3:20; Romans 10:9–10). Have you committed your life to Jesus and promised to live a life that honors God? (1 Peter 2:23 KJV; 2 Timothy 2:21 KJV). And are you now work-ing out your salvation with fear and trembling as you grow daily in God's grace? (Philippians 2:12; 2 Peter 3:18.). If you answer no to any of these questions, find whatever spiritual help you need to turn that no into a yes. Trade an eternity spent where there is weeping and gnashing of teeth for an eternity spent in fellowship with a loving God (Matthew 13:40–43).

Be a spiritual example.

Be a spiritual example to your children. Be a good Christian man. Go to church *every* Sunday, not just when you have the kids for the weekend, and help your church have a thriving youth group. Read Scripture with your kids; pray and trust God to answer them in His good time; finally, be kind, giving, ethical, and loving to others; and above all else, love your children by doing what's best for them.

This sounds easy, but it's not. Absentee fathers want their kids to like them. Since they see their kids only a few times a week or a couple of weekends a month, they don't want a minute with them marred by disruption or anger. So, instead of making the kids toe the line, they let them do things they would never allow under ordinary circumstances. For example, they may let their teenage daughters date guys with skull and crossbones tattoos. They even buy them tickets to Friday's heavy-metal concert. Not good. Love your children by being consistent, concerned, and committed to taking the tough stands—and the heat that follows.

When your children are with you, give them your undivided attention. No ESPN when your daughter wants you to play Barbies with her or when your son wants you to teach him to ride his new bike. Make their time your time; it is all an opportunity to be the best father and life witness you can.

Love their mother.

Often the relationship between the absentee father and the children's mother lies somewhere between strained and "one more step toward me and you're dead." Whatever your relationship with their mother was, now help her raise your children. Start by being friendly. She may be abrasive, even hostile; she may call you names and belittle you in front of the kids. Don't let her get to you. Always respond with respect, cheer, and flexibility. And when you are with the children, build her up in the children's eyes. When you do, the kids will be more likely to respect her and obey her. Their lives will be better for it.

Also, follow her lead with discipline and rewards. It is vital that the kids have the same rules in both homes—same bedtimes, same television restrictions. Children need consistency. Tensions are minimized, and it is more difficult for children to play one parent off the other; it also tells the children that the rules are well thought out and made for their benefit. Even if you think their mother is purposely restricting the children to limit your options with them, that's okay. As your relationship with her improves, the games between you will stop, and the cooperation between you will go a long way toward helping you both build stable, love-filled lives for the kids. It will also help you smooth out the inevitable rough spots that develop among all of you. Everything you do will work together to help you be of real value to your children.

However, no matter how effective you are as an absentee father, you will never be as effective as a live-in father. If you are free to marry your children's mother, work toward doing just that. Talk to her, court her, and be the man she and God would want you to be. Give up only if she turns you down. Either way, continue to shoulder your responsibilities lovingly, cooperatively, and with flexibility. When your children are finally grown, you will be glad you were the father they needed. Your legacy will be firm; you will be a man who possessed a powerful spirit, a real man, a man who kept the New Slavemasters from enslaving his family.

In the next chapter we will examine another breed of family, one no less able to carry God's banner, but one that usually springs from the ashes of other families already decimated by the New Slavemasters. We will call it the jumbled family, and, like all families, we will see that we can learn a great deal from the issues it faces.

CHAPTER TWENTY-TWO

THE JUMBLED FAMILY:
THE FORTRESS OF
DECISION

"Whoever listens to me will live in safety
and be at ease, without fear of harm."
—Proverbs 1:33

"I tell you what, Dr. Flint," said she [Linda Brent's grandmother],
"you ain't got many more years to live, and you'd better be saying
your prayers. It will take 'em all, and more too,
to wash the dirt off your soul."

"Do you know whom you are talking to?" he exclaimed.

She replied, "Yes, I know very well who I am talking to."

He left the house in a great rage. I looked at my grandmother.
Our eyes met. Their angry expression had passed away,
but she looked sorrowful and weary—weary of incessant strife.
—Autobiography of Linda Brent, a former slave

Both in their mid-sixties, Bryan and Martha planned to retire soon.
They had raised their three children long ago, and although they
had six grandchildren, five of whom were already in high school, they
only saw them occasionally. In a year or so it would be off to a quiet

> *"Somebody kicked the track and derailed our train—the cars that carried our future got all jumbled up."*

valley in the hills east of San Diego to enjoy what years God still had planned for them.

Their life was on track.

"But then," Martha observed, "somebody kicked the track and derailed our train—the cars that carried our future got all jumbled up."

Their middle daughter, who had been difficult from the beginning, was arrested for dealing drugs, and her live-in boyfriend bolted and disappeared. Her daughters were fourteen, thirteen, and twelve years old, respectively; and since Bryan and Martha were their nearest relatives, the police brought them over early one Saturday. After dragging himself to the door, Bryan found himself staring down at three sets of tired, very angry female eyes.

Bryan's brows knit tightly as one of the officers forced a stiff smile. "If you want them, they're yours for a while," he said.

"Surprise," the oldest one groaned.

THE JUMBLED FAMILY

The New Slavemasters of drugs and violence, aided by the deep decay of our nation's moral fiber, have wreaked havoc on this and many other families. It is as if each member of the family was a piece from very different puzzles and was suddenly thrown onto a table and forced to fit together. Like Bryan and Martha, grandparents and even great-grandparents now find themselves raising MTV-generation teens. Or older children who have planned limitless futures are now anchored in the present as the "parents" of younger siblings. Everyone battles confusion, anger, and bitterness—while those who fill the parental role do their best to learn new skills, often overnight. And these new "kids" often bring some pretty weighty baggage along with them. These are our *jumbled families*. In spite of what may appear, these are families God has brought together from confused and broken places so that all can be raised up and nurtured— and that He may be glorified.

Jumbled families aren't new. Slaves of old often took haven from the storms of violence, humiliation, and need in jumbled families. Linda Brent certainly took such haven.

We met Linda before, the tragic victim of sexual abuse by her master, Dr. Flint, which began when she was little more than a child. At age fifteen, she had a child and another when she was nineteen. Although she understood the immorality of her actions, she asked for understanding. She told her readers that she was driven by the hope of freedom, the flattery of being cared for by a kindly widowed white man, and the hope of having revenge on her evil master. Her second child was a little girl, and Linda feared that she would one day be abused as well.

> *These are families God has brought together from confused and broken places so that all can be raised up and nurtured.*

"Slavery is terrible for men," she wrote, "but it is far more terrible for women. Superadded to the burden common to all, they have wrongs, and sufferings, and mortifications peculiarly their own."[1] Her mother had died several years earlier, so when Dr. Flint's jealous wife threw her from the house, Linda took haven in her grandmother's home. The slave of a kindlier mistress, her grandmother was allowed a bit of freedom since she could earn her own way baking and selling crackers, cakes, and preserves. She hoped this enterprise would one day allow her to purchase her five children, but it never did.

Whether you are the safe haven, or the one seeking protection, there are several steps you should take together as a family. But before we discuss them, if your family has a more traditional look, keep reading. I am sure you know a jumbled family somewhere who needs your prayers, support, and encouragement, and what follows can help you provide all three.

Bring calm to the whirlwind.

Several forces in Linda Brent's life converged. She got pregnant by the "kindly" white widower, Dr. Flint began to build a cottage where he hoped to install her as his mistress, and her resolve not to be his mistress solidified to iron rebellion. The moment he finished the cottage and ordered her there, she refused and revealed she was pregnant by another white man. Shocked, Dr. Flint stared at her dumbly, then left. The instant she saw his back, the sweet revenge for which she had hoped dissolved to dread. How would her family, and particularly her grandmother, react to her immoral behavior?

Linda's prize possession was her mother's wedding ring which Linda had worn faithfully since her mom's death. When Linda told her family about her pregnancy, her grandmother, unaware of the tragic abuse Linda had experienced over the years, wrenched the ring from her hand, declared her granddaughter a disgrace to her mother's name, and threw her from the house. Devastated, Linda slumped to the home of friend, a woman who had been a friend of her mother's. Her secret finally too heavy to carry alone, Linda told her everything.

After listening in horror, she suggested that Linda confide in her grandmother. So Linda sent for her, but her grandmother was slow to respond. For Linda, the waiting was agony. When her grandmother did come, Linda spilled her heart before her and told her the whole sordid story, everything that had led her to motherhood.

If your family situation turns chaotic seek God's help, guidance, and peace.

"I begged of her to pity me," she wrote, "for my dead mother's sake. And she did pity me. She did not say, 'I forgive you'; but she looked at me lovingly, with her eyes full of tears. She laid her old hand gently on my head, and murmured, 'Poor child! Poor child!'"[2]

If your life mirrors Bryan and Martha's, or if, like Linda and her grandmother, the New Slavemasters have prodded you into a hopeless corner, go humbly and calmly to the Lord and ask His help. If your family situation turns chaotic, if your life plans abruptly change, if you find yourself encircled by the unfair and unjust, seek God's help, guidance, and peace.

> "When calamity overtakes you like a storm, when disaster sweeps over you like a whirlwind, when distress and trouble overwhelm you. ... Whoever listens to me will live in safety and be at ease, without fear of harm."   —Proverbs 1:27, 33

Go to God through Jesus and bring calm to the whirlwind.

Don't commit to your new role too lightly.

Bryan and Martha—after a quick, though sincere, "Lord, please help me"—made sure the three kids had breakfast, showered, and rested before they sat down at the kitchen table to decide what to do. Being a parent is an awesome task that takes focus, energy, and tears. Approach the genesis of a jumbled family with eyes wide open. Bryan and Martha did. They loved all their grandchildren, but they knew these three would take work. And they had hoped that their *working* life was about to end. But after a check with the church and county family-support services, they realized they were all that stood between their granddaughters and foster homes. They made the only decision possible—they would raise the children. After that, there was nothing left to do but to love and keep safe those caught in the jumble.

Linda's grandmother faced far different decisions. Both slaves, she and Linda had few options. She did speak with Mr. Sands, the father of Linda's baby, and secured his promise to support the child.[3] This was a major concession in this land of slavery where the child's societal position followed the mother, not the father; "thus taking care that licentiousness shall not interfere with avarice."[4] All that remained was to love Linda and, while Linda remained in her home, encourage her to act with godly honor and wisdom.

As for Linda, now a disgrace and having to face Dr. Flint's ongoing rage and insults, within the next few years she had her second child with the "kindly" Mr. Sands. Her grandmother, although filled with sorrow at her granddaughter's decisions, still gave her all the love, protection, and support her limited means allowed. And as the quotation at the beginning of this chapter illustrates,[5] that support could be perilous. Linda, however, knew she had to do more than just mince words with Flint—she had to escape. Her children were still slaves, and Dr. Flint, when the time was right, would sell them.[6] So she planned her escape—and it was a clever and risky plan that revealed her family reached far beyond the confines of her grandmother's humble home.

As your jumbled family comes together, do as our examples did. The moment the dust clears and you have sought the Lord's support, commit yourself to the task ahead of you. And as each situation presents itself, commit to the right course of action and take it. Otherwise, chaos will take hold—and God is not a God of chaos but of order (1 Corinthians 14:33, 40).

See God's hand in all of it.

God brings jumbled families together.

God brought the three granddaughters to Bryan and Martha. God brought Linda Brent to her grandmother. And God brought your family together, whatever it looks like.

But did God really assemble it? Didn't the New Slavemasters forge it from sin, panic, and desperation? To a large extent they did. But remember Joseph and the coat of many colors? Joseph's brothers hated him for it and threw him into a cistern from which they later retrieved him and sold him into slavery in Egypt. But God used their sin for good—to save many lives and to provide Egypt as a womb in which the nation of Israel was born (Genesis 50:19–21).

God will use the sin that brought your jumbled family together for good as well. For instance, this may be the first time the members of your new family

God will use the sin that brought your jumbled family together for good as well.

have lived with someone who knows the Lord. That was true of Bryan and Martha's granddaughters. "We're going through this," they told each other, "to show them Jesus—His love, understanding, discipline, and joy—and especially His salvation."

Understand your role.

Linda Brent knew her role. Just as her grandmother loved her as one of her own and did her best to protect her, Linda had her own children to love and protect, which dictated that she escape. Her children were slaves to a man who hated her, and although she had hoped he would sell her because of her repeated indiscretions, he hadn't done so. In fact, he had vowed never to sell her, which meant that the man who had fathered her children would never be able to buy her and the children to set them free. And if she didn't consent to accept Dr. Flint's "kindly offer" to be his mistress, he had vowed to make her life and the lives of her children a living hell. He could "break her in," as the slave masters had done to the other mothers on the plantation. When their children were beaten mercilessly in front of them, their spirit was so "crushed by the lash, that they stood by, without courage to protest."[7]

Linda couldn't let that happen to her. But she couldn't just grab her children and run either. Circumstances had taken her to the plantation of Dr. Flint's son, while her children remained with Dr. Flint. They were his assurance that she wouldn't bolt. But, she suddenly realized, they were also the key to her escape. One night, after putting her affairs in order, she "shut all the windows, locked all the doors, and went up to the third story, to wait till midnight." It was time to make her break.

"How long those hours seemed, and how fervently I prayed that God would not forsake me in this hour of utmost need! I was about to risk everything on the throw of a die; and if I failed, O what would become of me and my poor children? They would be made to suffer for my fault."8 She was ready to work her plan and risk everything to be the right kind of mother to her children.

It took Bryan and Martha about six months to don the parental robes. Up to that point, they figured that God was working only in the children's lives. However, Martha read one morning that an Indian casino was going up right next to the property to which they had planned to retire. "The parking lot would have been our front yard. The girls coming spared us all that." Armed with the realization that God was at work in their lives, too, they brought the girls together and voiced their firm commitment to them.

Be sensitive to issues that require consent.

Twelve-year-old Meg liked Grandma Martha and Grandpa Bryan as her new mom and dad. But Candy, thirteen, and Beth, fourteen, already had parents, and they were just going to be away for a while. They resisted every parental move Bryan and Martha made.

That may happen to you. Parental respect and obedience may take some work. A child may need a father but not want one; a sibling may need a mother but not want you to be that to her. If that occurs, do what Martha did. "Listen, girls," she told them toward the end of that meeting, "I know nobody can take your mom's place. And when she's able, I'm sure she'll be back with you. But until then, we're going to love you, care for you, discipline you—" That's when the fourteen-year-old exploded, but Bryan calmed her down. He told her that if they couldn't lovingly discipline her—not beat her or tie her to a bed—but discipline her in love, "Then we'll have to put you in a foster home. Do you want that?"

She didn't.

Then, as Bryan and Martha did the job they were required to do, they were patient. Whenever they were acting in the parental role, they explained that they were making decisions as a "good father/mother would." As time went by, the older children began to respond positively to them as parents.

Linda Brent had to deal with a consent issue the moment her escape plan began to unfold. Her plan was simple, but risky. Since her children were being held as hostages, she decided to escape to a hiding place in a nearby friend's house and stay there until Dr. Flint believed that she had left the South altogether. With her gone, Dr. Flint would then sell her children to Mr. Sands, their father, and he would allow her to take her children to safety. Making sure not to tell her grandmother any of this, at midnight, wrapped in darkness and rain, she first went to steal a kiss from her children; then she headed to her hiding place. The moment Linda got there, her jumbled family increased by one—the woman who hid her, facing the risk of 500 lashes for doing so, became her sister.

Whenever possible obtain legal sanction for your new role.

If possible, get the court to sanction your role in the family. Then only the court can change it, which adds to your credibility as a family and increases family stability. After getting help to navigate the legal labyrinth, work with the appropriate governmental services to get what you need. That is what Bryan and Martha did, and as a result they became their grandchildren's legal guardians.

If you meet firm resistance, get help.

If the children refuse to obey you, or worse, if they become disruptive, after bringing the Lord into it, get professional help quickly. But if, after exhausting all emotional and spiritual counsel, a child remains intractable, particularly if there are other children in the family, cut the disruptive child loose.

Linda Brent met resistance. Dr. Flint didn't give up the search for her; instead, he intensified it. In fact, one night he got so close to the house in which she hid that she was sure he was coming for her.[9]

Panicked, she darted out the back and concealed herself in a dark thicket. Terrified, she huddled there for at least two hours and would have stayed all night had not a poisonous snake bitten her. With her leg swelling painfully, she gave up the thicket and groped her way back through the darkness to the house. With Dr. Flint gone, Linda's new sister was free to nurse her as best she could. But the vicious pain, coupled with the fact that her hiding place may have been compromised, motivated Linda to decide she needed a new sanctuary, one with greater support. God brought her one. One of her grandmother's white friends—the sympathetic wife of a slaveholder—gave Linda a new hiding place, a place where her dearest friend could help her regain her strength.

If the real parents return, use godly wisdom in your reaction.
When the real parents return, usually the children are returned to them. It is important that the return be orderly. This is when Bryan and Martha's legal guardianship came in handy. After two years, when the grandchildren's mother was paroled, the family counselors and the judge listened to them. To make sure the children's interests were always central, they were given custody of the kids while the mother remained on parole.

If, however, the real parents return unexpectedly, or for whatever reason the glue that holds your family together dissolves and your jumbled family flies apart, no matter how difficult this time is for you, console yourself. Realize that God gave you this family for just the right period of time. In that time, God's goals were accomplished. You said everything He wanted you to say—you gave all the love, all the counsel, all the discipline, all the direction He wanted you to give. And now He is there to comfort you through the transition, no matter how difficult it may be. Finally, go to the Lord, thank Him for the time your family had together.

Linda, on the other hand, still hoped her family *would* come together. After several days in her new hideout, her children were still in Dr.

Flint's hands, and he still searched for her and still got close—very close. Dr. Flint actually came to the house in which she hid. But this time when he left, her hostess gave her good news.[10] The doctor just *knew* that Linda had fled to New York, and he wanted to borrow money to pursue her. When he returned a few days later, Linda got what should have been terrible news. Dr. Flint, now sure that Linda had made good her escape, consented to sell the children to a slave trader. But the slave trader had been sent by Mr. Sands, and after he got the children safely out of town, they were spirited back to Linda's grandmother, where Linda, after another day of grueling suspense, was reunited with them. Although still a fugitive, she knew her children would be safe.

When Families Jumble Together

Families are pressured in other ways as well. Rising inner-city rents, coupled with the influx of legal and illegal aliens, may cause two or three families to crowd into one house or apartment. Families with different backgrounds, spiritual needs, even cultures, are forced to bump elbows. These arrangements are annoying, confining, emotionally and spiritually taxing, and may even be dangerous. And they create families with profoundly unique spiritual needs. Time and space force me to be brief, but I don't recommend multifamily arrangements at all. However, if your family finds itself tangled in one, don't hesitate to seek help from the counselors at your church the instant concerns arise.

Over the past few chapters we have discussed how God assembles families to make them, among other things, fortresses against the New Slavemasters. In the next chapter we will discuss what the New Slavemasters do to tear down those families.

FOOTHOLDS

"Anyone who divorces his wife and marries another woman
commits adultery, and the man who marries
a divorced woman commits adultery."
—Luke 16:18

Dear Sir: By your direction, I have given your boy twenty lashes.
He is a very saucy boy, and tried to make me believe that he did
not belong to you, and I put it on to him well for lying to me.
I remain, Your obedient servant.
—Autobiography of William Wells Brown, an escaped slave

Teresa had a condition that made having children more dangerous for her than for other women. She and Daniel knew it when they got married, but like many in love, they didn't want to discuss the hard issues. That might uncover problems better left buried for the moment. It was only after they got married that Daniel started lobbying for children. He didn't demand anything. He just started talking about them: how neat it would be to have a son to play football with or a daughter to take to father-daughter dances.

Of course, it wasn't a tough sell. Teresa wanted kids, too. In fact, she probably wanted them more than Daniel did. The fact that Daniel was talking about it all gave her ammunition to lob at her mom when she voiced concern. "Having babies," Teresa countered, "has *always* been dangerous for all women. It's just a little more dangerous for me. Doctors take care of everything nowadays."

"But," her mom said, "don't you think it's a little selfish of Daniel?"

"Mom," Teresa protested, "what a thing to say! We both want kids."

"But you're the one at risk."

The instant Teresa saw the truth in what her mother was saying, she began to look at her husband differently. Suddenly he wasn't that cuddly little fuzz-ball anymore, that loving person who would supply all her needs. He was simply selfish, putting his wants ahead of her health, maybe even her life.

SELFISHNESS

In Ephesians 5:25–33 the apostle Paul tells men how to love their wives; it's how Christ loves His Church, and He went to the cross for her. Today, few men die for their women, at least not literally, but they are asked to *live* for their wives. In turn, wives should live for their husbands. Although it may sound like each one sacrifices *unreasonably* for the other, marriages thrive when partners make their spouses' lives rewarding and fulfilling. As a result, wives feel loved, safe, and free to be all that God has called them to be; husbands feel appreciated and free to be strong, resourceful, and creative, so they can provide for and help their families grow closer to the Lord.

Selfishness erodes all that. I am not talking about the little times of give-and-take, but the big things of life, the ones that really matter. As we saw with Teresa, the instant a wife senses that her husband is taking advantage of her, she is forced to watch out for herself. Otherwise, her needs will go unmet. As she focuses on those needs, she may appear selfish to her husband, which forces him to see even more to his own needs. Soon husbands and wives live for themselves, competing for the family's valuable time and resources. The strength God builds into the relationship when there is "one flesh" weakens, and the New Slavemasters have a foothold they can take advantage of.

In 1 Peter 5:8 the Bible tells us:

Be self-controlled and alert. Your enemy the devil prowls around like a roaring lion looking for someone to devour.

And which families is he most likely to sink his teeth into? The weak ones. In this chapter we are going to discuss what weakens God's families. We have just discussed selfishness. The next behavior that tears at the family bond and makes it more vulnerable to attack is ...

INSENSITIVITY

Terrance fathered a little boy outside marriage. A few years later he married another woman, and they were saved not long afterward. When his eyes opened to see Christ, he also saw his responsibilities to his son and committed himself to becoming a good absentee father. The child's mother welcomed this new attitude, but Terrance's wife wasn't so sure. She developed a jealous streak and complained each time he scheduled time to be with his son. The complaints became even sharper when she became pregnant. Instead of being proud that she had chosen a man with honor and a sense of responsibility, she was insensitive to his godly desire to fulfill that previous role.

Insensitivity is a selfish lack of awareness. Partners are so focused on their own needs, they fail to wisely sense and lovingly respond to their spouses' needs. The jealous wife was so overwhelmed by her own insecurities, she failed to understand how important her husband's desires were. Insensitivity hurts doubly. The husband, already in emotional pain about how he had treated his son, is told by his wife's complaints that how he feels doesn't matter. Now he has two raw wounds that produce anger and tear at the fabric of marriage. The marriage is weaker, and the fortress walls become just that much easier for the New Slavemasters to breach.

BETRAYAL

William Wells Brown participated in a betrayal of another "colored" man. "This incident shows how it is that slavery makes its victims lying and mean,"[1] he later wrote of this event. We met Mr. Walker, William Brown's master, in chapter 5. He was the slave trader who snatched the crying baby from its mother's arms and gave it to a friend, just so he wouldn't have to listen to it cry anymore. William Brown found himself on the wrong side of Walker one day and was handed a note and a dollar and told to take both to the city jail. William Brown sensed something was wrong, and so, instead of walking directly to the jail, he went to the docks where he asked a sailor to read the note to him. "They are going to give you hell," the sailor told him. "Why?" William asked. The sailor told him, "This is a note to have you whipped, and says that you have a dollar to pay for it."[2]

With the note back in hand, William Brown continued walking toward the jail. But when he reached it, he veered off, stopped a little way away, and thought things over. He knew he had to go. He couldn't get away with not going. But he also knew he didn't want to be whipped. At that moment he saw another "colored" man approaching and had a thought. He told the man that he had a trunk to collect in the jail but was too busy to do it. He made the man a proposition: "This note will release the trunk ... and here's a dollar for your troubles."[3] Glad to make such an easy dollar, the man grabbed the money and the note and disappeared inside the jail.

William stationed himself just outside to wait for the man's reappearance. A little while later the other man reappeared and upon seeing William complained to him angrily. Assuring him that he hadn't tricked him, William asked him what had happened, "They whipped me and took my dollar, and gave me this note."

That note was the quotation at the top of this chapter.[4] William avoided a beating, but slavery had soiled his soul, and he knew it. "This incident," he wrote, "shows how it is that slavery makes its victims lying and mean; for which vices it afterwards reproaches them, and uses them as arguments to prove that they deserve no better fate."[5] He never met the man again and was never able to make amends for deceiving him and causing him undeserved pain.

Trust is the glue that holds relationships together.

Had that man known what William Brown did to him, do you think he would have ever trusted him again? Not likely. The same is true of a spouse. Trust is the glue that holds relationships together. Trust allows us to be ourselves, to make plans, to make mistakes, and to know that our mistakes won't hurt us. Trust is the belief that our partners will fulfill our expectations, including our most *sacred* expectation—like faithfulness, our need to be nurtured, understood, and treated honorably. The greater the betrayal, the greater the damage to the relationship. Once connections break, intimacy dies. When that happens to us, we seek intimacy elsewhere, and the instant we do, the New Slavemasters have gained their foothold.

INDIFFERENCE

Some might argue that hate is the opposite of love, but there are other things connected with hate, like lots of misdirected rage and focus. Indifference says, "You go your way; I'll go mine," which is emotional disconnection. When indifference invades the home, the *one flesh* God brought together becomes two—both on completely different paths—and at least one of them just doesn't care.

Generally the result of prolonged hurt, the accumulation of deep scars brought on by lingering abuse, occurs when one partner can take the pain no longer and simply shuts down. An alcoholic may one day wake up to an indifferent spouse; a person released from prison may return home to an indifferent mate. If you feel yourself lapsing into indifference, as hard as it may be to begin to care again, do so. It is the caring, as hurtful as it may seem, that may keep the New Slavemasters at bay and save your marriage.

Violence

Violence destroys families. I can say it no plainer. If you perpetrate verbal, physical, or emotional violence—excessive shouting, hitting, or intimidating—get help! Go to your pastor or a counseling professional, or turn yourself into the police. Do whatever you have to do to get help. And do it now. Even before you finish this paragraph.

Violence doesn't include giving your children a well-deserved swat on their back end to get their attention or to mete out needed discipline. I am talking about violence—wife or child beating, bar fighting—induced by rage, pride, jealousy, or other strong emotions or just because you feel like doing it. And, frankly, if you are wondering if I mean you personally, I probably do. Get help!

If you or your children are the targets of violence, get to a safe house and stay there until those who can look dispassionately on your situation determine whether it is safe to return.

Violence in our precious Christian homes is increasing; the New Slavemasters are making real inroads. However, violence can result from treatable emotional issues. The violent partner can become nonviolent, so even these marriages can be saved. But the restoration process is long and often difficult. Violent partners must make a real commitment to emotional wellness, must follow through on their treatment faithfully, must be kept away from their families except when supervised. And even after the issues that caused the violence are resolved, it takes a long time for trust to be renewed—if ever.

Divorce

I hate to say it …

When homes reverberate with prolonged insensitivity and indifference, deep betrayal, and violence, the continued quakes often cause them to crumble. And when they do, I hate to say it … but *sometimes divorce is the only reasonable answer.* A point of no return for warring partners often exists and is reached. You may not want to hear this truth, but if a couple is tempted to stay together through unforgiveness and the tidal surge of rank bitterness that results—if they are frequently tempted to throw hot grits in each other's face—as heartbreaking as the decision may be, it's better for them to separate.

But divorce need not be inevitable.

That coin has another side. Even when a marriage is battered, its heartbeat weak and irregular, even when it has been shredded by adultery, *divorce is not inevitable.*

But when the heart is hurting, or, worse yet, when the heart has given up, the fact that divorce need not follow means nothing. It certainly meant nothing to Sarah.

Remember Sarah and Gerald from chapter 7? Gerald betrayed his marriage with pornography, and there came a moment when Sarah decided divorce was her only option. That night, as she cried herself to sleep, she was firmly convinced there was nothing Gerald could possibly do to repair the damage he had done to their marriage. His Slavemaster, instant gratification, had driven her over the edge. Had anyone said to her, "You don't have to get divorced," she would have laughed very loudly and very bitterly. "This isn't about anyone dragging me into divorce court," she would have said. "This is about *just try to keep me out of it.*"

But one night, after the kids were asleep, she allowed herself to long for the life she and Gerald had once had together. They had been a team at one time. They had understood one another perfectly and had known precisely what the other needed and how to provide it.

At that moment, she realized that God meant them for one another. And the more she relived those shared moments, the more she knew her marriage was worth saving. Perhaps if she worked to get over her hurt, and if Gerald was willing to solve his problem, together they could reawaken trust and salvage it.

And that's why divorce isn't inevitable. God brings marriages and families together for a purpose, and He has a stake in their success. It is beyond the scope of our discussion to go into how a couple like Sarah and Gerald rebuild their marriage. The road is narrow and goes uphill, and a number of perils lurk at its edges, but suffice it to say, if both partners humbly and vulnerably come to God with repentant and contrite hearts, God *will* honor their request. Then, with the help of trained Christian counselors, they will see their love resurrected, their marriage and family restored, and themselves reconciled to each other and to God. No psychiatrist or psychologist can heal such a marriage. Only God can do that. And the instant He does, the fortress walls that stand against the New Slavemasters will be rebuilt.

There are reasons to stay married.
Marriage was created to be permanent. In Mark 10:6–9 Jesus put it this way:

> "But at the beginning of creation God 'made them male and female.' 'For this reason a man will leave his father and mother and be united to his wife, and the two will become one flesh.' So they are no longer two, but one. Therefore what God has joined together, let man not separate."

Divorce just may not be the answer.
Dr. Judith Wallerstein and Sandra Blakeslee, in their book *Second Chances: Men, Women and Children a Decade after Divorce*, write:

> Whatever the reasons behind the decision, most people ending a marriage hope to improve the quality of life for themselves and for their children. ... People want to believe that divorce will relieve all their stresses—back we go to square one and begin our lives anew. But divorce does not wipe the slate clean ... few adults anticipate accurately what lies ahead when they decide to

divorce. Life is almost always more arduous and more complicated than they expect.[6]

In his book *Before a Bad Goodbye: How to Turn Your Marriage Around*,
Dr. Timothy Clinton, president of the American Association of
Christian Counselors, identifies what makes the divorce process so
arduous and complicated: "One family expert characterized the
process of divorce negotiations as 'one of the more demanding tasks
that rational beings are expected to perform....'[7] And based on what
I've seen, he's right. And there's little wonder why. In some forms or
another, the battle over the things of divorce brings together a rush of
boiling emotions—including abandonment, anxiety, betrayal, inadequacy, loneliness, rage."[8]

Aren't these the emotions we hope divorce will help us avoid? The
point Dr. Clinton and I are making is simply this: In most cases it is better to work on your marriage. Although you may still walk through an
emotional minefield, at least when you're through it, you will have an
intact marriage and often a better one than before.

If, however, you divorce, believing it will be worth a stroll through a
minefield to be finished with "the bum" or "the ball and chain," think
again. Dr. Wallerstein points out:

Incredibly, one-half of the women and one-third of the men are
still intensely angry at their former spouses, despite the passage
of ... ten and fifteen years. ... A third of the women and a quar-
ter of the men feel that life is unfair, disappointing, and lonely ...
even I was surprised at the staying power of feelings after
divorce. ... There is no evidence that time automatically dimin-
ishes feelings or memories; that hurt and depression are overcome; or that jealousy, anger, and outrage will vanish. ... People
go on living, but just because they have lived ten more years
does not mean they have recovered from the hurt.[9]

But what about the kids? Child psychologist Dr. Lee Salk believes that "the trauma of divorce is second only to death" and that "children sense a deep loss and feel they are suddenly vulnerable to forces beyond their control."[10]

After doing a fifteen-year follow-up with 130 children of divorce, Dr. Wallerstein put it this way: "The first reaction is one of pure terror."[11] Suddenly thrust into a disintegrating world, children suffer intense fear, depression, loneliness, and abandonment. Withdrawal and self-preservation become the words of the day. Every path they walk now leads to a muddle of problems and troubles.

And to make matters worse, children invariably blame themselves for the family disintegration. We can only imagine the guilt they carry and the emotional damage that guilt brings with it.

"But surely children recover. After all, that which doesn't kill us makes us stronger, right?"

Dr. Tom Whiteman, president of Fresh Start Ministries, has made his life's work helping children of broken homes. He defines recovery from divorce this way: "It is the point where divorce no longer has a daily impact on how children affected by it view or live their lives."[12] His research shows nearly one-third recover within two years, one-third recover at some point in their lives, while the remaining one-third never recover—a dismal statistic, one that parents must take to heart.

And if what the children will suffer isn't enough, divorce isn't cheap. Divorce lawyers bill from $250 to $500 an hour, which means that middle-income families will spend $2,500 to $25,000 to separate themselves from one another. But the legal bills are only the start of the costs in money, time, and energy.

And what about starting over? How does a divorced person get back into circulation? Do you *really* want to date again? Some married people I counsel tell me that once they are single again, all they want is be alone. A few cardless Valentine's Days changes that. After all, God built us for relationships. Someday you will want to meet someone again. But who?

When you dated before, you may have been in high school or college. The odds there were pretty good that you would find someone stable, committed, and available. But now you are older. Prospects who are faithful, of good temperament, loving and giving—well, they're already married. Those who are splashing around in the dating pool now are often those who couldn't make marriage work the first time and may not be able to make it work the next.

If divorce is your only option—if your spouse is violent, incurably unfaithful, or in some other way impossible to build an abundant life with—then do what you must. But even though you may have biblical grounds for divorce, neither Moses nor Jesus said that the offended spouse *had* to divorce the offender. Divine forgiveness is always a possibility. So if work—either as a couple or as individuals—can bring you to a place where both of you can see a future for yourselves, then do the work. Create a new future in Christ as you resolve your conflicts and build yourselves a safe haven. This work will be hard. You will have to make yourself vulnerable; allow yourself to forgive; and maybe bring yourself to tolerate and live for a person who has hurt you in the past, someone with whom you have to rebuild trust.

It is not the kind of work you can do alone. You will need help—good sound Christian counsel—and a strong commitment to remake your marriage into one pleasing to God. Through prayer and commitment, tap into God's capacity to give strength, courage, and comfort; request His help to get you through the difficult times on your way to reconciliation.

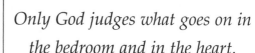

Only God judges what goes on in the bedroom and in the heart.

But if your marriage does crumble, God may grant what only God can: your freedom from that brother or that sister. Only God judges what goes on in the bedroom and in the heart. Only He is able to release you—set you free to live a new life.

Divorce is not the unpardonable sin.

The shame is that more often than we would like to admit, divorces happen to God's people. In fact, the rate of divorce inside the Church has reached the same rate as outside the Church. This is not a statistic to esteem. But I must quickly add, nowhere in Scripture is divorce, even when blatantly ungodly, called the unpardonable sin. Even if we have gone through the most rancorous divorce imaginable, even if our sins have been on display for all to see and we have done little more than shrug them away, God does not wash His hands of us. He is faithful, even when we are not (2 Timothy 2:13).

Of course, we shouldn't tolerate unrepentant sin. But if divorced Christians repent and deal with their failings, they should be welcomed back into the fellowship. Their ministry is not over. In fact, everyone who is divorced should spend time in church. That's where the spiritual and emotional healing is.

ENOUGH THAT'S NEGATIVE

Enough that's negative. Marriages and families succeed because those involved are honestly optimistic about their success. It is the optimism that keeps them from giving up when their marriage and family falter. But optimism alone is not enough. In the next chapter we are going to take a look at what else strengthens families—what puts iron in the fortress wall.

IRON IN THE
FORTRESS WALLS

*After I looked things over, I stood up and said to the nobles, the
officials and the rest of the people, "Don't be afraid of them.
Remember the Lord, who is great and awesome, and fight for your brothers, your
sons and your daughters, your wives and your homes."*
—Nehemiah 4:14

*I had just been telling mother how I should try to get employment
as soon as we reached Canada, and how I intended to purchase us a little farm,
and how I would earn money enough to buy sister and brothers,
and how happy we would be in our FREE HOME—
when three men came up on horseback, and ordered us to stop.*
—Autobiography William Wells Brown, an escaped slave

Mandy's story starts when she was sixteen and came to know Jesus as her personal Lord and Savior. It was a relationship born out of deep tragedy. Her father dealt drugs, and both her parents used. On a single night, her mother overdosed and died, and her father ended up arrested for having provided her the lethal drugs. When the police arrived, Mandy ran off and eventually found her way to our church. Over the next week, we ministered to her, and before she left us to become part of a foster family, Mandy had found peace in the arms of her Savior.

Salvation doesn't automatically heal all emotional scars, nor does it instantly make right the instincts that helped us survive poorly functioning families. Mandy had been largely neglected as a child and had grown up expecting the worst from the world. Although she warmed to a few people at church, she remained largely a loner.

I was encouraged that Mandy was finally getting a little more comfortable around people when, after graduation from high school, she decided to work toward a nursing degree at the University of California at San Diego; it is hard to be nurse and hermit at the same time. But her hermit's heart officially opened when her older brother, Del, showed up with his eighteen-month-old son, Bradley.

"Clean him up," her brother barked. "His mother's who-knows-where, and he and I gotta get out of here tonight, or we'll end up dead. While you're doing that, I'll scare up something." He roughly pushed Bradley at her, then started banging cupboard doors. For the next half-hour, Mandy bathed Bradley, washed his clothes; then, while her brother wolfed down at least four hot dogs, she fed Bradley macaroni and cheese.

Through it all, a conviction grew in her heart. Bradley needed her, perhaps the first human being who ever had. He seemed so lost and fragile, so confused, even fearful. She recognized the feelings from her own childhood. He, as she had then, needed an injection of stability in his life. She just couldn't let Bradley go with her brother. She felt her heart swell with an overpowering sense of love—what she could imagine as a mother's love. With a few beats of that newly transformed heart, she vowed: Bradley stays. But when she put it to her brother, he didn't see it that way. He resisted, but Mandy resisted right back, and at times their discussion—battle, really—became heated. It finally ended though, when he insisted: "He's my kid. I don't leave my kid."

"By dragging him all over the countryside, that's exactly what you're doing."

For some reason those words mattered to him, and the fight left him. Less than ten minutes later, he was gone. Bradley didn't like to see his father leave, but after only a few minutes he snuggled up to Mandy on the couch, as if he belonged.

Mandy's life convulsed; it morphed from independent student with an unlimited future, to mother, father, and aunt with adult roles and responsibilities. Remarkably, as she felt the weight of those new roles and responsibilities take up residence on her shoulders, she took the perfect first step. She took Bradley's hand, bowed her head, and asked the Lord for help.

FIGHT FOR THE FAMILY

Our families are precious. They guard us from loneliness and multiply our wisdom and our ability to deal with the blows, temptations, and the New Slavemasters of this world. Our families love us for who we are, just as Christ does. And above all else, our families, like Mandy's new one, create a place for children to grow and learn, a place where God can work to shape our hearts for salvation and His glory. This chapter is about those behaviors that strengthen our families, that build our families up and make them even more resilient, more able to absorb the bumps and bruises the world metes out, and more able to support each of their members when the world takes aim at them individually. Our families are worth fighting for. Nehemiah told us to fight for them, and Mandy did just that.

William Wells Brown did, too.

Fight by flight

Unable to save his sister from being sold into the horror of the Deep South, William Brown decided it was time to escape, a treacherous course if taken alone, nearly impossible when accompanied by a mother. But William's mother was the only member of his family who remained, and he was not going to leave her. So the two conspired to escape together.

Any trip starts with cash, and he had a little he had tucked away from doing occasional errands for people. With it, he bought a few meager provisions that he put in a bag. One night, at the stroke of nine, they took their first steps toward freedom—and arduous steps they were. Son and mother commandeered a rowboat and made it across the Mississippi River into Illinois, then through a nearby village just as the sun was rising. The next few days were spent hiding by day in the woods and making their way stealthily along dark roads and fields by night. On the eighth day they were battered by rain, and on the tenth their provisions ran out. But God was with them. Feeling that escape was all but assured, they were suddenly stopped by three men on horseback carrying a warrant for their arrest and returned to slavery. At least they had tried.[1]

Even when the odds are stacked against us, we must fight the evil that enslaves.

Even when the odds are stacked against us, we must fight the evil that enslaves. We must confront it and, with God's power and help, win over it. Mandy did, William Brown eventually did, and you and I will, too.

RECOGNIZE EVIL

To fight evil though, we first need to identify it. Gangs, drug dealers, and prostitutes are easy to point a finger at. But other evils aren't. Identifying them takes *discernment*. Some, like cults, masquerade as angels of light and lure us from God with sentiments that only *appear* to be godly (2 Corinthians 11:14–15). While the world's philosophies draw us to them with words that promise peace, inevitably they foment conflict and bitterness.

A friend's wife enjoyed reading her horoscope every morning; it was harmless entertainment, she said. Then for three days running, her horoscope seemed accurate. Suddenly harmless entertainment became a spiritual obsession—the Bible and church drifted to irrelevancy. To keep evils at bay, practice discernment, which comes with knowledge and experience, a combination we have already identified as wisdom. Discernment means recognizing and choosing what God would choose for us.

Such choices don't come by accident. They come when we study God's Word through personal reading and reputable commen-

To keep evils at bay, practice discernment, which comes with knowledge and experience.

taries and Bible classes. Then experience comes when we apply God's Word to our daily lives. Knowledge follows when we see how God works and rewards us when we do apply it. And discernment becomes our way of life when we use that knowledge and experience to select right paths. My friend's wife, had she studied God's Word, would have known what God thought about astrologers and fortune-tellers and would have also known how Satan uses them to draw us into sin. That newspaper would have lined the birdcage before she reached those horoscopes.

In Genesis 3:24 we are told that after God expelled Adam and Eve from the Garden of Eden, He placed "cherubim and a flaming sword flashing back and forth to guard the way to the tree of life." When evil stalks your family, be like the cherubim. Place yourself firmly at the gate and fight off evil as it attacks. Sometimes, as Mandy did, you will have to meet it head-on.

HUMBLE YOURSELF BEFORE GOD

In 2 Chronicles 7:14, God told King Solomon:

> "If my people, who are called by my name, will humble themselves and pray and seek my face and turn from their wicked ways, then will I hear from heaven and will forgive their sin and will heal their land."

There are days when I look out over my flock, and all I see is worry and fret. Mothers wring their hands and talk anxiously about their troubles. Men wax frustrated about their kids acting up and their wives being more than they can handle. Either way, both just wish God would fall into line and see things their way. Seeds of worry and grumbling are sown and watered by arrogance.

But the New Slavemasters aren't kept out when we build a legacy of worry and fretting, grumbling and complaining. We slam the door in their faces when our legacy is that of *family builder*. And to enrich that legacy, we need to sweep our hearts clean of all destructive pride, of everything that says our judgment has greater weight than God's.

When we face something as complex as a family believing that we can handle it on our own, that is just plain folly. God knows best.

Mandy had to come to grips with that truth. Even though the moment she saw Bradley she scooped him up and made him a part of the family, after a week or so the reality of the situation hit her. God was asking her to give up college. And for Mandy that wasn't just giving up an education. Her plan to become a nurse also included a plan to find a nice, successful doctor to marry. Even a nice, successful male nurse wouldn't have been a bad compromise. College was also her ticket out of the inner city and into what she saw as the American dream. And Bradley—with God as his accomplice—had flushed all those hopes down the drain. In the back of her mind, she began to wish her brother would show up and reclaim the little guy.

But he didn't.

After a few weeks, childcare began to run into money, money she didn't have. It was time to get a permanent job, a career. The moment that realization dawned, the truth of God's betrayal took hold. She began to resent Bradley. "I wanted to slap the sweet little smile of his right off his face." And maybe she eventually would have, if something unexpected hadn't happened. After her second day as a cashier trainee at a local Home Depot, she picked up Bradley from the sitter, and he handed her a book the sitter had given him. He wanted her to read it to him. It was the story of David and Goliath. Up to then, she had felt despair and rage taking over. But immediately she saw what God wanted her to see. Her life wasn't about escape. Nor was it about attaining the lifestyle she wanted. Her life was about doing what needed to be done. Her life was about triumph and, at least for now, the love of a little boy.

Which bring us to the next behavior that builds up the family and keeps us free.

PRAY

We have discussed prayer already, yet there is more to say, particularly on prayer as a way to expand and deepen our relationship with God into a *spiritual partnership*.

Partnerships unite people around common goals. Partners sometimes work together, sometimes apart, but always closely, to achieve their shared objectives. Now, see your relationship with God as a spiritual partnership. You and God are united to make your family physically and spiritually healthy—to transform it into a godly family. This partnership compels you to see God right there with you. Every step you take, He takes. Every hurt you suffer, He suffers. And every triumph you experience, He is there to be appreciated and thanked for it.

You and God are united to make your family physically and spiritually healthy.

Paul tells us to pray without ceasing (1 Thessalonians 5:17 KJV), and since God is walking right there with us, *partnership prayer* allows us to do just that. Instead of isolated moments when we fall to our knees and ask God for something, prayer becomes ongoing, a time when God and we discuss in depth the life He has given us. I am not suggesting that we hear an audible voice when we pray to God, but I am suggesting that we talk to Him as if we expected to hear His voice audibly. We should discuss with Him every feeling and concern we experience, every surprise as it occurs, and every sin we uncover within us—even every misstep we take. As we do so, we learn to avoid those missteps and take the steps we should take—moving ever closer to God as our lives unfold. Oh, how the blessings will flow to our family and us.

But prayer isn't all about receiving blessings. It's about knowing God—a privilege reserved only for His people. As we see our sins displayed, we confess them as they occur and turn in a different direction. Since this often stops our sins before we put feet to them, it frequently gives us opportunities to see God at work in our lives.

Usually doing right is more difficult. Otherwise, we wouldn't have such a hard time doing it. By redirecting a misstep mid-stride, we will see the almost immediate fruit of our right choices; we will see God smooth out a rough path, the one we are now on with Him.

But He does more than just make things easier for us; He gives us the desires of our hearts (Psalm 37:1–4). When we continually lay our hearts before the cross, open and vulnerable, we will more often see our hearts' desires fulfilled, and we will more often see the God who fulfills them.

Partnership prayer also provides immediate guidance and comfort from the One who knows the beginning, the end, and all that lies between, the One who has only the best in view for us (Isaiah 46:9–10; Jeremiah 29:11). Mandy certainly needed the comfort of knowing that God was aware of what was happening in her life and was at work in it for her good.

Mandy, who was distrustful of authority, never petitioned the court to be Bradley's legal guardian. She merely took on the role. After two years of faithfully acting as Bradley's surrogate mother, the last problem she thought she had was her brother's return. Bradley was nearly four years old and going to preschool. Like any little boy, he burned energy like a rocket and spent most of the day bouncing off the walls. But he was happy, and largely because Mandy loved him. He had become hers.

She was filled with a mother's pride when he did well and a mother's disappointment when he didn't. He called her Mommy; she called him her Little Sweetie. One Christmas she bought him a complete Hot Wheels set, one she had saved for three months to afford. And he bought her a little doll, dressed like a nurse. Next year he would start kindergarten; she would petition the court then, she decided.

She shouldn't have waited.

One rainy evening, without a knock at the door, her brother burst in. He mumbled something to Mandy about everything being "cool now;" then he scooped up Bradley, who had fallen asleep on the couch. Shocked, Mandy asked him what he was doing.

"I'm taking my son. Thanks for baby-sitting."

"Baby-sitting?" she said, at a loss for words. "I—"

"Well, whatever you did, thanks. Gotta go." And with that her brother and Bradley were gone. A large piece of her heart went with Bradley, and for a long while it felt like it had been ripped out of her.

Prayer is about knowing God.

We have talked about jumbled families, and they can disintegrate as quickly as they are formed, so that lives are seriously disrupted and hearts are broken. Mandy's heart was so tortured she came to the church the next morning in a storm of tears and spent a long while with a counselor who told her: "I know you wonder why God brought him to you only to take him away. But Bradley was with you for just the right period of time. You prayed with him just enough, told him about Jesus as many times as you were supposed to. I know it hurts. But God's grace is there for you." It was her relationship with God, a relationship borne and strengthened by prayer, that allowed her to finally calm down and recognize the truth in what her counselor told her. After a few weeks, and many more tears, Mandy enrolled at UC–San Diego, intent on becoming a nurse.

A FEW MORE
FORTRESS-STRENGTHENING SUGGESTIONS

Whatever your role in the family—father, mother, child, disciple, discipler—*realistically assess the spiritual state of the members of your family*. Of course, none of us can know for sure the condition of someone else's heart, no matter how close we are. But God has given us discernment, not so we can accuse and point a finger, but so we can pray, encourage, and support others in our family—particularly if we are the mom or dad.

If you are married, *always build up your partner*. Compliment, encourage, praise, work with, and help your mate. If your partner clearly acts in ways he or she will later regret, discuss the situation gently, lovingly, and never condescendingly.

Husband, cherish your wife. Date her for no particular reason; surprise her with a candlelit meal; and, above all, remember that you are the family's spiritual leader, protector, and provider.

Wife, support your husband, as imperfect as his efforts may be. Remember, both of you are in this situation together and are doing the best you can.

Connect with your children, even the difficult ones. Whenever you discipline or reward them, do it in love, never out of anger or expedience. Be willing to make tough choices and stick to them. Be consistent. And every chance you get, have fun with your kids. Rules work best when tied to relationships.

As your family members mature and change, do whatever is necessary to keep them vital, spiritually productive members of God's kingdom. And remember, the kingdom and the spiritual war that claws at it are larger than just your family; that larger kingdom needs your prayers and the prayers of all our brothers and sisters in Christ. Form community-, city-, state-, and nationwide networks of prayer. God-sized problems need God-sized answers. As you pray, remember that if God doesn't build the house, the workers labor in vain (Psalm 127:1). If God isn't woven into the fabric of the fortress walls, the New Slavemasters will eventually break through and enslave you again. Ask for God's wisdom, power, direction, and forgiveness. And He will be right there for your family—always.

A Prayer for Our Families

Allow me to end this chapter with a prayer for all of us:

"We confess, O God, that the battle is not ours; the battle is Yours. But You have chosen to use these frail human vessels. We bring to You, O God, all our brokenness. We bring to You, Lord, all that we are; and we ask You to cleanse us, to forgive us, and then to fill us with Your Spirit. Use us in the fight for the recovery of a godly family life. This is our prayer, in Jesus' name. Amen!"

THE SPIRITUAL FAMILY:
THE FAMILY OF GOD

Because those who are led by the Spirit of God are sons of God. For you did not receive a spirit that makes you a slave again to fear, but you received the Spirit of sonship. And by him we cry, "Abba, Father."
—Romans 8:14–15

After being by the fire awhile, I found that my feet had been very much frozen. I was seized with a fever which threatened to confine me to my bed. But my Thompsonian [Quaker] *friends soon raised me, treating me as kindly as if I had been one of their own children.*
—Autobiography of William Wells Brown, an escaped slave

A lice works in the office of one of our local elementary schools. In her mid-thirties and single, she can't have children of her own, the result of an abortion she had as a teen. But all seems well with her. She generally possesses a calm smile and often helps in our church nursery. However, when she came to see me one day, her smile was replaced by a genuine sadness.

"I want children so much. When I hold the babies in the nursery, I imagine they're mine. But they aren't," she said, her eyes misty, "and Christian guys want lots of children." Her voice became hoarse. My heart developed soft fissures as she told me how guys "go out with me for a few months, until I tell them I can't have children—and then they're gone. I never hear from them again."

I leaned forward. "So you met another guy, and you want to know if you have to tell him?"

She shook her head. "No, it's about John. He's a ten-year-old student. I met him on *Death Row*."

I swallowed hard. "Where?"

Seems that Alice's desk in the school office faces "Death Row," three black vinyl chairs that sit beside the office door of the vice principal—the students call him "the Hangman."

"Some kid called John an orphan," Alice went on to explain, "and John punched his lights out. I know he should have turned the other cheek, but that kid's a bully." Alice's eyes glowed with a certain parental pride. "John has no mother. His father's in jail—armed robbery. John is in a foster home. He and I got acquainted as he sat on 'Death Row' every afternoon for two weeks thereafter. 'The Hangman' gave him detention."

Suddenly her face twisted with an even deeper, more tortured sadness. Had John been hit by a car or something? "I brought him to Jesus last night," she managed.

"But why are you so sad?" I asked.

It took her a long time to answer. "I feel like he's my child. But he's not mine."

"How does John feel?" I asked.

"He's just a child; what does he know about feelings?" Bitterness soured her tone. "When he prayed, he asked God to make me his mother." Her eyes were suddenly large and pleading. "But I'm not. I'm not—" and then her words collapsed into what for her was a harrowing reality. "No," she said, as if resigned to sin. "On some strange level I *am* his mother. And I'm so afraid. So terribly afraid. I feel like his mother, and I know both of us are going to get hurt."

I smiled gently. "It's okay. God's in control of all this." I leaned back, relieved. "There are two families in this world," I said. "You're experiencing the second—I believe the most important, and I also believe the most enduring—John has become part of your spiritual family."

We will return to Alice and John in a moment, but first let's consider the *spiritual family*.

BLOOD*LINES* AND BLOOD-*VINES*

We have spent page after page examining the biological family, people bound together by blood*lines* that flow from parents to children. This is a broad category to say the least; everyone since Adam has been a member of a biological family. But there is another family that is also bound by blood—not blood flowing through human veins, but through a blood-*vine*; blood that flows from the fount of grace, from Jesus Christ, from the wounds He suffered on the cross. This is the spiritual family, the family of God. And only some are members of this family, as John and Alice illustrate.

When we come to Him with sincere confession and belief, we become sons and daughters of God.

In Romans 10:9, the apostle Paul tells us "that if you confess with your mouth, 'Jesus is Lord,' and believe in your heart that God raised him from the dead, you will be saved." When we come to Him with sincere confession and belief, we become sons and daughters of God and at the same time spiritually make His family our own.

God never creates casually. Both families have a divine purpose. God created the biological family as an antidote to man's physical loneliness. After the fall of man, the physical family became the crucible in which we see our need for a savior, are pointed to Jesus, and work out our salvation—our sanctification—with "fear and trembling" (Philippians 2:12).

God uses the spiritual family, too. Let's take a look at how He does so.

The spiritual family brings people of different ethnicities together.
Fredrick Douglass, whom we have met often in this book, saw this statement to be true. He wrote about a minister named Mr. Cookman. The
slaves believed him to be a good man, a man who never failed to express
his sympathy for their plight. But more than just express it, he did something about it. The slaves all believed him to be responsible for convincing Samuel Harrison, a "very rich slaveholder," to emancipate his slaves
and also believed him to be working for the freedom of all slaves.
Douglass went on to tell about a Mr. Wilson, a white man who started a
"Sabbath School" for the slaves but quickly had it shut down when his
neighbors found that he was teaching the slaves to read.[1]

William Wells Brown, known then only as William (or Sandford, if
he didn't want to get beaten), also found that his spiritual family
embraced a white family. He was twenty in 1834, and after a number of
failed escape attempts, on New Year's Day evening, the night black and
brutally cold, he broke again for freedom. As he headed north from
Cincinnati toward Cleveland and Canada beyond, the icy temperatures
soon worked their way into his lungs, and he found it difficult even to
walk. As he put it: "Nothing but the prospect of enjoying liberty could
have induced me to undergo such trials, for 'Behind I left the whips and
chains, before me were sweet Freedom's plains!'"[2]

But he knew, in spite of his passion for the freedom, he had to seek
shelter or freeze to death. Because he was sure he could spot a slaveholder "as far as I could see him," and he hoped to find a "colored" man
walking by who would help him, he decided to hide alongside a road
behind a pile of logs and wait.

The second passerby was an old man leading a horse. Obviously
walking for exercise, he wore a broad-brimmed hat and long coat—
and William knew immediately he was the man to ask for help. And
he was. But it wasn't immediately evident that he was the right one.
When William approached him, and the man discerned that William
was a slave, the old man told him that he "was in a very pro-slavery

neighborhood," and if he would wait, the old man would go home and get a covered wagon to take William to his home.

The one thing William feared more than freezing to death was being captured and returned to slavery. As he waited for the man to return, he began to worry the man would return with the authorities to place William again in chains. But soon the covered wagon appeared, and William found himself the guest of Mr. and Mrs. Wells Brown, two Quakers. For the next twelve to fifteen days, William was treated with warm kindness and respect.[3] The Browns were part of his spiritual family, so much so that Wells Brown is later called his father. As we have seen, in a way he was. William took Wells Brown's name as a way of honoring the couple.[4]

> *There is no room in the family of God for racism, sexism, ageism—or any other "ism"—only "love-ism."*

Just as the New Slavemasters ravage all social, ethnic, and economic groups within the family of God, so deep, heartfelt caring crosses those boundaries, too. For all our differences, the Spirit is the same. And God is no respecter of persons (Acts 10:34 KJV). Through His Son Jesus Christ, He says: "Come to me, all you who are weary and burdened, and I will give you rest" (Matthew 11:28). In these words the Lord is saying: "All are welcome. Just confess Me with your lips, and believe in Me in your heart, and you are My child" (Romans 10:9–10). There is no room in the family of God for racism, sexism, ageism—or any other "ism"— only "love-ism," which we must express for all our brothers and sisters in Christ.

Our highest qualities can be nurtured.

God's spiritual family sees the world, and our behavior in it, in *spiritual terms*. Before we became children of God, if we got angry, we would explode at the person who had offended us. Once we are accepted into

God's family, we may still get angry, but there is no explosion. Instead we ask ourselves: *Is my anger justified? Is there a more godly way to handle this situation? How can I reveal Jesus in it?* It is no longer just

It is no longer just about our comfort; it's about Jesus.

about our comfort; it's about Jesus. It's about our Christian witness, about becoming a more effective member of God's family, and it's about helping others into it.

Although we love imperfectly, our goal is to love selflessly and unconditionally, which means that our commitment is to one another. And selfless love is certainly one of the highest qualities to nurture.

Babies are always welcome.

We grow our spiritual family with new members. Some will be teens and young adults, some will be older—all who proclaim Jesus as Lord and Savior.

And some, who may one day know Jesus, are babies. Babies are always welcome in the family of God. We never abandon, abort, or behave contemptuously toward them. They are precious gifts from God, and God has a life planned for each of them.

But there are other babes in the spiritual family, too. Paul addressed them in 1 Corinthians 3:1–2:

Brothers, I could not address you as spiritual but as worldly— mere infants in Christ. I gave you milk, not solid food, for you were not yet ready for it. Indeed, you are still not ready.

Babes in the kingdom of God are simply the new entrants through the gate (John 10:1–3). They have just grabbed Jesus' hand, just confessed their sins, just invested their faith in Him. Like human babies, they need help and nurture, and when they get it, like human babies, they grow and become stronger in their faith.

It falls to us, those who have reached a certain level of maturity in the faith, to help. We need to *disciple* these babes in Christ.

Discipling

Discipling is one of those wonderful activities that help both the discipler—or mentor—and the disciple. Discipling helps the new Christian reach maturity in the faith, while the older child in Christ, the discipler, grows in grace.

The Great Commission at the end of the book of Matthew (28:19) makes it clear that we are all called to be disciplers. But what goes into being a good discipler?

Good discipling starts with commitment. Promise yourself and God that you will be a good teacher, encourager, and guide. This commitment brings awareness and energy, and it starts the search for those in need. This is a humble search. We are all sinners; none of us is any better than any other. It is only through the grace of an all-powerful, all-loving God that we are able to help one another. We are not here to "lord it" over anyone. We simply want to pass the spiritual baton to the next generation of believers by helping to forge in their hearts what others who were strengthened and encouraged by God's grace helped forge in ours.

This baton has many facets—legacies of integrity, family loyalty, sexual purity, biblical faith, true spirituality—all under the heading of godly service. This is why mentors find their lives tested and improved, their separation from God narrowed. As they teach, so must they live— the sins they uncover in the disciple, they uncover in themselves. Then, as both discipler and disciple mature, they have an even greater impact on God's kingdom and a stronger part in His plan.

Alice, young John's spiritual "mother" and discipler, talked to me several times over the next few weeks. More relaxed about her relationship with John, she discovered quickly that John was very angry with his father. As she helped the boy to forgive, she began to see how she hadn't forgiven herself. She had aborted a baby almost twenty years earlier, and she still hated herself for it. But, just as John was angry with his father, she was angry with hers—her heavenly Father. Why had His punishment been so severe? She wanted children, and why had He made it so she couldn't bear them? She realized that her inability to forgive herself and God, and accept His plan for her life, had kept her from reaching out to those she could truly help—those thinking about aborting their children. John, with the blessing of his foster parents, began to go to one of our youth groups, and as time passed, he became a happier, more relaxed young man and an even more committed child of God.

If you are a babe in Christ, undoubtedly you are spiritually hungry. You want to devour all things Christian, yet you lack something very important—the insight and wisdom to know what is Christian and what may be a fraud, and there are a lot of frauds out there. Paul tells us about them in his second letter to the Corinthian church: "For such men are false apostles, deceitful workmen, masquerading as apostles of Christ. And no wonder, for Satan himself masquerades as an angel of light" (2 Corinthians 11:13–14). Even mature Christians can be fooled. So as a young Christian, you need to find a mature, trustworthy Christian to help you discern the truth. If you don't know such a person, go to your pastor and ask to be paired with one. Then, allow yourself to be discipled: work sin from your life as you grow in grace. Do all this patiently—go slowly, read deeply, learn judiciously—watering your spiritual seeds as a caring gardener.

SPIRITUAL CONNECTION: SATISFYING OUR SPIRITUAL HUNGER

I have mentioned that God created our physical family as an antidote to our physical loneliness. In my life, however, I am never less lonely than when I am surrounded by my *spiritual* family. That is no surprise to me. We humans were created for spiritual connection, first with God, then, since God's Spirit lives in the hearts of His people, with those in our spiritual family. We yearn for this connection. When it is absent, we feel incomplete and search for something outside ourselves to make us whole. We see this fact everywhere. Although there are relatively few born-again Christians, there are also very few who deny the existence of a spiritual world. Even when man's eyes aren't turned toward the one true God, they are turned toward ghosts, astrology, voodoo, or some other phenomenon outside of the senses.

And when true spirituality is present—when we do see God for who He truly is—our lives feel profoundly grounded, immeasurably safe, and we know that our lives possess great purpose. We are on a divine mission. Every day is a gift from God and part of His plan.

And when we share that sense of being grounded and having a divine purpose with people who also see God for who He truly is— those who are also part of His plan and who see themselves stepping along God's path at least partway with us—the connection is wonderfully rewarding. That doesn't mean the road is always smooth. Harsh words occur occasionally, and there are even betrayals, but over time God works within the lives of His people to smooth out the wrinkles and forge relationships that have real depth, strength, and meaning.

Alice found that to be true in her life. She found true peace in her relationship with John, because John blossomed around her. He turned into a writer; simple poems at first, but soon they expanded into short stories. Alice liked to read. Her closet was stacked with romances and mysteries, and having read and reread them all, over the years she had learned a lot about writing. With her input, John's writing came to life. By age twelve, he was actually being published in a local children's magazine.

When John finally trusted her totally, he began to write about the painful parts of his life, how his mother had just disappeared one day never to contact him again and how his father would frequently use his one phone call from jail to ask John to get one of his dad's pals to bail him out. When he stopped writing that story, John cried. That's when

Alice decided to be more than just a mentor and tutor. She started classes to become a foster parent. She then asked John's father to let her adopt him. She is now John's foster parent, and his father has not yet said no to the adoption request. She also works with a ministry that helps young ladies recover from abortion's spiritual scars.

One powerful element present in a Christian relationship but usually absent from all others is the fact that God is at work on both sides of it.

One powerful element present in a Christian relationship but usually absent from all others is the fact that God is at work on both sides of it. As their lives unfold, usually both parties move closer to each other and closer to God as their relationship matures.

When all is said and done, our spiritual family is our truest family— our family with our truest Father, our truest relationships, those connected by the strongest ties to our hearts, and the one with our truest purpose. As the strength of our spiritual family grows, so grows our ability to remain free and to keep the New Slavemasters outside the gate.

CREATING A CHURCH THAT BUILDS UP THE SPIRITUAL FAMILY

God, through Peter, described the spiritual family this way:

But you are a chosen people, a royal priesthood, a holy nation, a people belonging to God, that you may declare the praises of him who called you out of darkness into his wonderful light.
—1 Peter 2:9

That family is God's Church. And our churches leave legacies, too; they are critical in defeating the New Slavemasters and keeping those voracious wolves from their members' doors. We read of such legacies in chapters 2 and 3 of the book of Revelation. Of the seven churches mentioned in that context, five reel beneath the Lord's criticism; only the churches in Smyrna and Philadelphia are free of it. All of us in church ministry want nothing more than to hear the sweet music of God's praise. And that praise follows our diligence in but one effort, our support of those in our immediate spiritual family. We provide spiritual worship, advice, counsel, education, and encouragement to help God's family grow, mature, and become more effective soldiers in His spiritual army. When we stumble at this effort, we stumble at all of them. And when we stumble, our spiritual families stumble, and the work they are called upon to perform in God's kingdom suffers.

Let's commit ourselves to making our churches the spiritual buildings God created them to be—vital, effective, compassionate, and passionately committed to God's leading.

We will examine what I consider to be one of the more important elements in God's leading in the next chapter.

TRUE TO OUR CHRISTIAN SELVES

Jabez cried out to the God of Israel, "Oh, that you would bless me and enlarge my territory! Let your hand be with me, and keep me from harm so that I will be free from pain." And God granted his request.
—1 Chronicles 4:10

We have men-stealers for ministers, women-whippers for missionaries, and cradle-plunderers for church members. The man who wields the blood-clotted cowskin during the week fills the pulpit on Sunday, and claims to be a minister of the meek and lowly Jesus.
—Autobiography of Frederick Douglass, an escaped slave

I believe the most important reason God created His spiritual family is so that we may …

GROW IN OUR KNOWLEDGE OF HIM

In 1 Corinthians 2:16 the apostle Paul tells us:

> "For who has known the mind of the Lord that he may instruct him?" But we have the mind of Christ.

We possess the mind of Christ and can discern spiritual things. Chief among them is God Himself. Of course, our minds are too limited to comprehend completely an infinite God. But we are able to understand as much about Him as we need to—that He exists and that He rewards those who earnestly seek him (Hebrews 11:6). When the New Slavemasters take hold, God is there to help us gain and regain our freedom. That help often comes from the very words that describe Him—the Bible. To assure that we get the help we need from it, His Spirit is there to interpret it and apply its meaning to our heart.

When the New Slavemasters take hold, God is there to help us gain and regain our freedom.

This Word not only came *from* God; it *is* God (2 Peter 1:16; John 1:1). Every syllable paints a spiritual picture of Him on a vast canvas that stretches from the ends of the universe to the very center of the human heart.

That image includes His righteousness and justice, His love for His people that rests upon them, and His final judgment—eternal separation from Him for those who are *not* His people. We see His mercy and compassion; His wrath; and His infinite power, knowledge, and wisdom.

You may live in a few rooms in a crowded city and have to scrape for every penny you earn. You may think that God has forgotten you or, worse, that He is against you. You may be enslaved by drugs, debt, rage, or racism. You may feel defeated and alone. But you aren't. You are God's child—the child of the Creator of the universe. How sweetly will your cries to God sing out as you reach out to Him from the heart of trial? Just as sweetly as the witness of these heart-wrenching words written by Harriet Jacobs under the name Linda Brent:

Why does the slave ever love? Why allow the tendrils of the heart to twine around objects which may at any moment be wrenched away by the hand of violence? When separations come by hand of death, the pious soul can bow in resignation, and say, "Not my will, but thine be done, O Lord."[1]

How Powerful Is Our God?

How powerful is our heavenly Father? Let's think about it for a moment. A volcano erupts. In a single explosion millions of tons of earth are pulverized, liquefied, and scattered for miles—house-sized boulders are tossed about. Yet this kind of power is exhibited and confined within a relatively small planet that circles a relatively small sun within a relatively small galaxy in a universe that is made up of billions of galaxies—and God created it all. And in Colossians 1:17, we are told Jesus, His Son, holds all of it together. So how powerful is God?

Powerful enough.

Powerful enough to defeat His enemies, and ours, and powerful enough to work through us while we do our part in the struggle "against flesh and blood ... against the rulers, against the authorities, against the powers of this dark world and against the spiritual forces of evil in the heavenly realms" (Ephesians 6:12).

Powerful enough to change our hearts and minds so that we may, day by day, move closer and closer to Him.

What Will Be Our Legacy?

One goal we definitely have is to be a more effective witness for our Savior than the church our ancestors were forced to attend. Frederick Douglass observed:

The man who robs me of my earnings at the end of each week meets me as a class-leader on Sunday morning, to show me the way of life, and the path of salvation. He who sells my sister, for purposes of prostitution, stands forth as the pious advocate of purity. He who proclaims it a religious duty to read the Bible denies me the right of learning to read the name of the God who made me. … I love the pure, peaceable, and impartial Christianity of Christ: I therefore hate the corrupt, slaveholding, woman-whipping, cradle-plundering, partial and hypocritical Christianity of this land.[2]

How will the legacy we leave behind be described? More important, how will God describe it?

This strong condemnation of the church's hypocrisy in Frederick Douglass' time is deserved. Of course, our churches aren't in danger of such extremes. But 200 years from now, when all the politics and prejudices of our age are gone, what will people say of our churches, our Christianity? How will the legacy we leave behind be described? More important, how will God describe it?

Do we want to be seen as a loving people? Then we must love. Do we want to be seen as a forgiving people? Then we must forgive. Whatever legacy we want to leave, we must live it wholeheartedly, eager to embrace Jesus and all His people. The closer we come to living the legacy God wants us to leave, the greater our freedom in Christ and the less we have to worry about ever being enslaved again.

WHAT WILL BE YOUR LEGACY?

I want us to focus as our journey together ends for now. This book's purpose is to help you break free from and remain free of the New Slavemasters. To do that, I would like for you to settle on how you want to be remembered. What is that legacy? Write it down. Then study it.

Now throw off whatever enslaves you and expand your legacy. Become aware that whatever you hope your legacy will be, God is powerful enough to make it greater. Whatever impact on God's kingdom you hope to have, it can be greater. Whatever glory you want your talents to bring God, He can bring Himself even greater glory.

I am a prime example of God's using one of His children in ways that child never, ever thought possible. How could the son of a poor sharecropper, one of fourteen children, the great-grandson of a slave ever imagine that God would make him a bishop in such a large and prestigious denomination? How could he have ever dreamed of being even a small part of the work within God's kingdom?

Had I wrote out the legacy I hoped to leave, I may have visualized being a husband and father, perhaps the pastor of a small congregation in Arkansas.

This is not to minimize the work done by such people in such places. These pastors, parents, and teachers are on the front lines. However, even to hope to be used as God has used this humble servant would have been beyond anything I possibly could have imagined. Yet God, as Jabez prayed, has enlarged my territory and may enlarge it even further. Every day I stand in awe of Him and how He exhibits His mighty power in my weakness (2 Corinthians 12:9).

May God help you to remain free, and may He bless your legacy. May the legacy you envision for yourself now be a mere shadow of the legacy He has in mind for you. As you fulfill that legacy, may your life be an abundant reflection of your growing faith in Jesus Christ, our Lord.

NOTES

WORKS CITED

BOOKS

Bennett, Lerone Jr. *Before the Mayflower: A History of the Negro in America—1619–1966*, Third Edition. Chicago: Johnson Publishing Company, Inc., 1961, 1962, 1964, 1966.

Bibb, Henry. *The Life and Adventures of Henry Bibb: An American Slave*. Boston: Anti-Slavery Society, 1849.

Brent, Linda. *Incidents in the Life of a Slave Girl, Written by Herself*. Boston: self-published, 1861.

Brown, William Wells. *Narrative of William W. Brown, an American Slave*. London: C. Gilpin, 1849.

Clinton, Timothy. *Before a Bad Goodbye: How to Turn Your Marriage Around*. Nashville: Word Publishing, 1999.

Douglass, Frederick. *A Narrative of the Life of Frederick Douglass, Written by Himself*. Boston: Anti-Slavery Office, 1845.

Dow, George Francis. *Slave Ships and Slaving*. From the Introduction by Captain Ernest H. Pentecost, R.N.R. This Dover edition, first published in 2002, is an unabridged republication of the work originally published by The Marine Research Society, Salem, Massachusetts. In 1927, it was published in Canada by General Publishing Company, Ltd., 894 Don Mills Road, 400-2 Park Centre, Toronto, Ontario M3C 1W3; it was published in the United Kingdom by David & Charles, Brunel House, Forde Close, Newton Abbot, Devon TQ12 4PU.

Hart, Archibald D. *Children and Divorce*. Nashville: Word Publishing, 1982.

Heschel, Abraham J. "The Religion of Equality of Opportunity, The Segregation of God" in Mathew Ahmann, ed. *Race, Challenge to Religion*. Chicago: Henry Regnery Co., 1963.

Simpson, G. E., and J. M. Winger. *Racial and Cultural Minorities: Analysis of Prejudice and Discrimination*. New York: Harper & Brothers, 1953.

Whiteman, Thomas A., and Randy Peterson. *Starting Over: A Step-by-Step*

Guide to Help You Rebuild Your Life after a Breakup. Colorado Springs, Colo.: Pinon Press, 2001.

PERIODICALS

Almeida, Christina, Associated Press Writer. "Middle-class Vegas teens in gangs, say police." *Salt Lake Tribune,* September 29, 2003. Copyright 2003 by the Associated Press.

Graham, Billy. "Racism and the Evangelical Church." *Christianity Today,* October 4, 1993.

Koranteng-Pipim, Samuel. "Saved by Grace and Living by Race: The Religion Called Racism," *Journal of Adventist Theological Society,* 1994.

McBride, Wesley, President, California Gang Investigators Association. Statement to Committee on Senate Judiciary, September 17, 2003.

U.S. Department of Health and Human Services, National Center for Health Statistics. "Non-marital Childbearing in the U.S. 1970–99."

Wallerstein, Judith, and Sandra Blakeslee. *Second Chances: Men, Women, and Children a Decade after Divorce.* New York: Tickner and Fields, 1989.

Yang, Debra, Honorable United States Attorney, Central District of California. Statement to Committee on Senate Judiciary, September 17, 2003.

NOTES

Chapter One
1. Douglass, 296.

Chapter Two
1. Bennett, 4.
2. Ibid.
3. Ibid.
4. Ibid.
5. Dow, xviii.
6. Ibid.
7. Ibid.

Chapter Three
1. Brown, 400.
2. Ibid.

Chapter Four
1. Douglass, 281.
2. Ibid.
3. Ibid.
4. Brown, 417.

Chapter Five
1. Brown, 411.
2. Ibid., 394.

Chapter Six
1. Graham.
2. Heschel, 56.
3. Simpson and Winger, 546.
4. Koranteng-Pipim, 41–45.
5. Brown, 379.
6. Ibid.

Chapter Seven
1. Douglass, 303.

Chapter Eight
1. Douglass, 297.
2. Ibid., 303.

Chapter Nine
1. McBride.
2. Yang.
3. Almeida.
4. McBride.
5. Douglass, 319.
6. Ibid.

Chapter Ten
1. Brent, 773.
2. Ibid.

3. U.S. Department of Health
   and Human Services.

Chapter Eleven
1. Bibb, 445.

Chapter Twelve
1. Douglass, 281.

Chapter Thirteen
1. Brown, 416.
2. Ibid., 412.
3. Ibid., 416.
4. Ibid.

Chapter Fourteen
1. Brown, 402.
2. Ibid.

Chapter Fifteen
1. Bibb.
2. Ibid., 494.
3. Ibid.
4. Ibid.

Chapter Sixteen
1. Bibb.
2. Ibid.
3. Ibid., 458.
4. Ibid.

Chapter Seventeen
1. Douglass, 282.

Chapter Eighteen
1. Douglass, 337.
2. Ibid.
3. Ibid.
4. Ibid.
5. Brown, 410.
6. Ibid., 389.
7. Bibb.
8. Brown.
9. Bibb.
10. Ibid.

Chapter Nineteen
1. Douglass, 281.
2. Brent, 773.
3. Brown, 393.
4. Ibid., 382.

Chapter Twenty
1. Brent, 774.

Chapter Twenty-one
1. Bibb, 459.
2. Ibid.

Chapter Twenty-two
1. Brent, 823.
2. Ibid.
3. Ibid., 804.
4. Ibid., 822.
5. Ibid., 828.
6. Ibid.
7. Ibid., 832.
8. Ibid., 841.
9. Ibid., 844.
10. Ibid., 850.

Chapter Twenty-three
1. Brown, 397.
2. Ibid.
3. Ibid.
4. Ibid., 398.
5. Ibid., 397.
6. Wallerstein and Blakeslee, 3–4.
7. Clinton, 4.
8. Ibid., 34.
9. Wallerstein and Blakeslee,
   29–30.
10. Hart, 19.
11. Wallerstein and Blakeslee.
12. Whiteman.

Chapter Twenty-four
1. Brown, 404.

Chapter Twenty-five
1. Douglass, 318.
2. Brown, 420.
3. Ibid., 420.
4. Ibid., 419.

Chapter Twenty-six
1. Brent, 782.
2. Douglass, 363.

READERS' GUIDE

For Personal Reflection
or Group Discussion

THE NEW SLAVEMASTERS

To break the chains that keep you from freedom in Christ, you must identify and conquer your New Slavemasters. Author Bishop George McKinney describes how the New Slavemasters—drugs, materialism, racism, instant gratification, and more—are akin to slavery of old. They are tools in Satan's arsenal to prevent us from living a full life and leaving a strong legacy.

However, just as the old slave masters lost their hold on people's lives and hearts, we, too, can experience the victory through Jesus Christ. As Ephesians 6:12 says, "Our struggle is not against flesh and blood, but against the rulers, against the authorities, against the powers of this dark world and against the spiritual forces of evil in the heavenly realms." Isn't that the battle we so desperately need the wisdom and power of our heavenly Father for? Don't we want to be able to stand firmly on the freedom we have through Christ?

This study guide, and indeed this entire book, is written to support and encourage you to "fight the good fight" against the New Slavemasters that assault you and your family. The following questions can be used for individual or group use. Read them during your personal devotions, with a prayer partner or Bible-study group, or in Sunday school. However you use this study, may you gain a deeper understanding of the love and dreams your heavenly Father has for you.

Chapter One—*Crack!*

1. The book begins with the story of a family tragedy and how each person was impacted by it. What lies became truth to Edward's family in the wake of his death? How did those lies lead to action on the part of family members?

2. New Slavemasters, like slave masters of old, try to control and inflict pain in our lives. What are some of the most influential New Slavemasters in today's culture?

3. Bishop McKinney says Satan not only has a plan for our lives, but also has laid out how he will get to us. What are his goals for us, and what does he use to accomplish them?

Chapter Two—A Proud, Dynamic, Sensitive—Dangerous People

1. According to Lerone Bennett Jr., people in early Africa contributed to the beginning of civilization. What were their characteristics, and why was this race dangerous to God's enemies?

2. How did men become accustomed to using "beasts of burden"? How did this lead to using slaves for labor?

3. According to Bishop McKinney, nature's law made it easy for Satan to plant the idea in the minds of African people that slavery was moral and legal. Describe this "law."

4. What was the beginning of slavery in the United States? What do you see as its long-term effects?

Chapter Three—Alone and Weak

1. Making us feel utterly alone is one way Satan tries to turn us away from

God. When did you last feel all alone? How did you feel about God during that time?

2. According to Bishop McKinney, what does Satan hope to do in our relationship with God? What does he use to accomplish this? When has he tried to intervene in your life?

3. In this chapter, the author describes seven lies Satan uses to change our perspective about God, others, and ourselves. How does Satan use the first two lies to influence how we view other people?

4. If we think other people's motives are callous and self-centered, we begin to see ourselves as their victim. What can be the results of seeing yourself as a victim?

5. Satan rejoices when we think we are unlovable to God and to others. How do we know God loves us and wants the best for us? How can we continually remind ourselves of his love?

Chapter Four—New Slavemaster: Drugs

1. Drugs and/or alcohol can destroy relationships in many ways. Why do you think people get involved with these destructive influences?

2. Why would Satan want to target the family as a means of furthering his goals?

3. Bishop McKinney compares how slavery broke up families in the past with how alcohol and drugs destroy families today. What are the similarities between the two methods?

4. In this chapter, we learn that Satan wants us to lose "who we are" so that those closest to us no longer know us or want to be around us. How do drugs and alcohol contribute to this identity loss? Why is it hard to stay connected to someone who is deeply involved in drugs and alcohol?

Chapter Five—New Slavemaster: Materialism

1. What evidence do you see that our society is materialistic? In your own life, where do you find materialism?

2. In this chapter, Barbara was driven by circumstances in her life to want "things" for fulfillment. What were these circumstances? How did they contribute to her opinion of what she needed in her life?

3. Bishop McKinney makes a distinction between the fulfillment one gets from material things and the fulfillment one gets from relationship with God. How can possessions make us feel fulfilled? How does that compare to fulfillment in the Lord?

4. The New Slavemasters' ultimate goal is to "keep us from seeing God." What do you choose to fix your eyes on?

Chapter Six—New Slavemaster: Racism

1. Billy Graham said, "Racism in the world and in the church is one of the greatest barriers to world evangelism." What evidence do you see in the Church, both globally and locally, that supports this statement?

2. What is racism? How does Satan use it to keep people from God? What are some examples of racism and their results throughout history?

3. According to Bishop McKinney, what makes racism a sin? What is racism's impact on the one who is racist and the one who experiences racism?

4. If the Church is charged with stewardship of what God provides for His people, how can the Church make sure that all people have equal access?

Chapter Seven—Two New Slavemasters: Instant Gratification and the Mindless Pursuit of Pleasure

1. "Slavemasters can ... start out feeling like friends, boon companions, then suddenly turn on you." List some ways people seek instant gratification.

2. What benefits did Gerald draw from pornography? How did he feel once his wife discovered his addiction? What was the effect on his wife?

3. From what do instant gratification and the pursuit of pleasure keep you? What are the effects on your spiritual life?

4. The author says to turn to Jesus and "through Him to the Father, you will be seeking what truly satisfies and sets you free." How is this process not instant? How do you turn to Jesus and find what truly satisfies?

Chapter Eight—New Slavemaster: Rage

1. On the evening news, we see people strike out at others around them. What are some examples of how rage influences violence and war in the world?

2. People who have suppressed rage may never show it until they explode. How does rage begin and grow? What does it steal from people's lives?

3. What are the surface indicators of buried anger?

4. If the New Slavemaster of rage enslaves someone, what lies is Satan telling that person?

5. What goal does Satan reach by keeping anger in our lives? How does that anger interfere with our relationship with God?

Chapter Nine—New Slavemaster: Gangs

1. Gangs have had a presence in every U.S. state since the 1980s. What are some activities that can be attributed to gangs in your community?

2. Though gang members seem tough and determined, the author says they all share basic needs. What are those needs?

3. Satan uses four lies to bring and keep young people involved in gangs. What are those lies? Why do gang members easily believe them?

4. For Taylor, literal gunshots woke him from his blindness to the workings of the gang. What else can God use to pull us from our particular bondage?

Chapter Ten—The New Slavemaster's War Against the Children

1. "Satan … knows the easiest way to keep a people enslaved, isolated, and weak is to defeat their children." How does Satan accomplish this?

2. With 1.5 million abortions a year, our society suffers. What pain do the aborted children's mothers and fathers feel? How has Satan packaged abortion to be an attractive alternative to so many?

3. If Satan gets involved in the shaping of children, he has a stronghold—in many cases for the rest of their lives. What can be the long-term consequences of this for our children and our communities?

4. "God *is* love, and our good works express it. Our grandest work, of

course, is to point to Jesus those whom God brings us, especially our children, and to help those who already know Him to grow in His grace and love." If love is the answer, how will you share the love of God to those who have not experienced it?

Chapter Eleven—The Truth

1. Teri was a woman ready to give up until she heard Celia's testimony. Discuss a time God supernaturally gave you hope or encouragement through a person or situation you did not expect.

2. When is it hardest to feel God's protection in our lives?

3. It is hard to be angry and still believe that God is going to work in your life. Why can't you have both rage and faith at the same time? How are the two incompatible?

4. "The truth sets us free" (see John 8:31–32). How do we go about making truth a part of our lives?

Chapter Twelve— God's Truth Teller: The Family

1. How does the story of God's creation of the Garden of Eden and Adam and Eve show the importance God placed on the family?

2. What attacks did that first family have to face? How has God continued to use the family as His building block for human culture?

3. How did God use Bishop McKinney's family? Rayna, Toby, and Tanya? How have you seen God work in your family?

4. Have you identified a New Slavemaster(s) that is working overtime in

your life? Are you ready to accept the freedom God has for you? What do you need to do to take the first step toward freedom?

Chapter Thirteen—Your Legacy

1. Bishop McKinney gave Gerald another reason to fight his addiction to pornography. What was the reason? Why do you think Gerald was then willing to change?

2. Many addictions, including pornography, give their victims a sense of control or power. Yet when a person commits to change this area of his life, he finds something even more powerful. How does focusing on how you want to be remembered help a person overcome his addiction?

3. How does doing the right thing help us overcome the New Slavemasters? Give an example. What does God do when we choose the right path?

4. Consider your life critically. How do you want people to see you? What is the legacy you want to pass on to your children?

Chapter Fourteen—The Freedom Family

1. Bishop McKinney's church was destroyed by arson, but not his dream. Did you ever have a dream that almost came true as you visualized, only to see it finally come together in a way you never anticipated?

2. After the fire, God made St. Stephen's a greater influence for Christ than ever before. Share a time when God gave your family greater influence after a struggle or challenge.

3. Bishop McKinney acknowledges there will be "trials, temptations, monumental difficulties, and many disappointments." How has a hard time better prepared you to raise your family?

Chapter Fifteen—Husbands and Wives: Keeping the New Slavemasters at Bay

1. Husbands and wives must navigate many temptations and challenges in marriage. What are some of the most difficult? How has God planned for support and help in marriage?

2. Ephesians 5:25–33 sets the bar high for the marriage relationship. List the commands for husbands and wives in this passage. Who does Paul say the model is for marriage? What would you say the "profound mystery" is?

3. The urgency in the Lord's voice from Deuteronomy 6:6–9 challenges the husband to be the spiritual head of the family. What are some ways a father can teach his family to love God and His Word?

4. "Respect acknowledges that a person has characteristics and abilities that we, and the One we serve, value. We, as God's children, should respect all His children." How do you show respect to another person? What most often gets in the way of showing respect to your spouse?

5. Bishop McKinney contrasts respect with contempt in a marriage. What is contempt? How can you keep contempt out of a relationship?

Chapter Sixteen—The Two-Parent Fortress

1. In this chapter, Bishop McKinney discusses how "two perspectives wrapped around a common course of action make the worst moments manageable." How can different approaches to parenting work together?

2. With two parents in the home, there is more time and there are more resources to address unexpected emergencies or financial situations. Why is this important for children?

3. Bishop McKinney recommends adoption to single moms so that children will have the opportunity for a two-parent family. What are the benefits for the child and the mother? Do you agree or disagree with this position?

4. Many couples choose to live together instead of getting married. What does marriage offer that living together does not?

5. What qualities make a family a "safe harbor in times of distress, the perfect classroom in times of confusion and doubt, the reservoir of understanding in times of need"?

Chapter Seventeen—The Single Parent

1. Bishop McKinney says, "Successful parents have a narrow focus; a firm commitment; courage; and, above all else, reliance on a powerful, yet tender, loving God." What is the narrow focus? How does society distract parents from this focus?

2. Children need stability. How can you ensure physical stability in your home?

3. Often the other parent can spark strong emotions in the custodial parent. What are some practical ways you can deal with the other parent in regards to coparenting?

4. If the noncustodial parent is not involved with your children, you must address their feelings of abandonment. How can you support your children through this difficult time?

Chapter Eighteen—The Single Parent: Spiritual Stability

1. "It is a parent's responsibility to make sure the children place Jesus as their firm foundation." How can a parent establish a firm foundation in his or her own life first?

2. Bishop McKinney gives examples of how Scripture can be taken out of context to support and justify a person's agenda. How can we keep ourselves from being caught up in this kind of Bible use?

3. The local church can help lay the foundation for spiritual stability. What activities and support can the local church offer families?

4. What suggestions does Bishop McKinney offer for establishing prayer as a way for your children to see God working in their lives and yours?

Chapter Nineteen—The Single Parent: The Sexual Predator Seeking Whom He May Devour

1. Why did God create sex? What is its role in the marriage relationship?

2. Sex has heavy emotional, psychological, and spiritual consequences. What happens when sex is experienced outside the marriage bond?

3. How can you tell if you are being courted according to God's way? What are the characteristics of a relationship with someone who truly loves you?

4. What goals does a young person need to make early to assure his or her relationships are glorifying to God?

Chapter Twenty—Families Within Families: Parents of Young Parents

1. The author says that when there is a family within a family, "it's like the New Slavemasters violently rubbing two very dry sticks together: the forces spark, ignite, and ultimately consume and destroy." What are these forces?

2. The goal of a Christian family is to keep the New Slavemasters at bay. How can you do this?

3. You are the parent of a young woman who still lives in your home—and who has her own child. How can you help develop and encourage her roles as spiritual leader and caregiver to her child? What boundaries do you need to set?

4. What are some ways to care for your other children in the midst of your "family within a family"?

Chapter Twenty-one—The Unmarried Father: The Male Fortress
1. "The New Slavemasters are delighted when men see themselves as little more than sperm donors, willing to casually separate themselves from the children they spawn." What do these separated children miss by not having a relationship with their father? How are these children more at risk for the New Slavemasters?

2. It is a father's moral responsibility to address his children's needs. What physical needs should a father take care of?

3. A father also needs to care for his children emotionally. How can a father show emotional support to his children when he is not living with them?

4. For children, their earthly father introduces them to their heavenly Father. In what ways can a noncustodial father teach his kids about their place with God?

Chapter Twenty-two—The Jumbled Family: The Fortress of Decision
1. A "jumbled family" is created when family members other than the parents

raise children. How can God use a jumbled family for His glory?

2. Bishop McKinney offers eight things that a jumbled family should do as it takes on the responsibility of raising children. What are they? How can each of them bring a peace to the challenge ahead for the surrogate parents?

3. Do you know a jumbled family? What support can you offer in the midst of the changes and challenges it faces?

Chapter Twenty-three—Footholds

1. One place the New Slavemasters attack is marriage. What are some areas that are vulnerable to attack?

2. If facing a divorce, why should a couple explore staying married? What support and help do they need to rebuild their marriage?

3. The author discusses some of the effects divorce can have on the couple and their children. What are they?

4. The divorce rate among Christians equals that of non-Christians. How can the Church better address the issue of divorce? What could the Church offer Christian couples to help build stronger marriages?

Chapter Twenty-four—Iron in the Fortress Walls

1. All around our world, evil tries to permeate into our families. How do we identify evil? How can we establish a perspective that helps us identify evil when it comes?

2. "As your family members mature and change, do whatever is necessary to

keep them vital, spiritually productive members of God's kingdom," the author challenges. List the suggestions he gives for doing this. Can you think of others?

3. Consider your family and its needs; then pray this prayer:

> We confess, O God, that the battle is not ours; the battle is Yours.
> But You have chosen to use these frail human vessels. We bring to
> You, O God, all our brokenness. We bring to You all that we are and
> ask You to cleanse us, to forgive us, and then to fill us with Your
> Spirit. Use us in the fight for the recovery of a godly family life.
> This is our prayer, in Jesus' name. Amen.

Chapter Twenty-five—The Spiritual Family: The Family of God

1. How does Bishop McKinney define "spiritual family"? Who are the members of your spiritual family?

2. "Discipling is one of those wonderful activities that help both the discipler—or mentor—and the disciple." How does discipling work to build a person's relationship with Christ? Do you need to find someone to disciple you, or is there someone God has brought into your life to disciple?

3. If spirituality is a void we all have, how does society try to fill that void? How can we make sure that we are satisfying our spiritual needs through Christ?

4. God's Church is the home for the spiritual family. How can you contribute to God's work within the Church?

Chapter Twenty-six—True to Our Christian Selves

1. Remember Ephesians 6:12? God is powerful enough to fight any enemy

that would come against us. What is the enemy in your heart today? Do you believe God is powerful enough to defeat it? Commit to moving closer to Him today.

2. What would God say about the legacy your church is leaving right now? What changes need to happen for the legacy to be one where people live "wholeheartedly, eager to embrace Jesus and all His people"?

3. As you personally consider the impact God wants you to have on His kingdom, what is enslaving you? Will you throw off those footholds the New Slavemasters have planted?

4. What do you want your legacy to be? Write it down, and invite God to help you remain free and to bless your legacy.

The Word at Work Around the World

A vital part of Cook Communications Ministries is our international outreach, Cook Communications Ministries International (CCMI). Your purchase of this book, and of other books and Christian-growth products from Cook, enables CCMI to provide Bibles and Christian literature to people in more than 150 languages in 65 countries.

Cook Communications Ministries is a not-for-profit, self-supporting organization. Revenues from sales of our books, Bible curricula, and other church and home products not only fund our U.S. ministry, but also fund our CCMI ministry around the world. One hundred percent of donations to CCMI go to our international literature programs.

CCMI reaches out internationally in three ways:

- Our premier International Christian Publishing Institute (ICPI) trains leaders from nationally led publishing houses around the world.

- We provide literature for pastors, evangelists, and Christian workers in their national language.

- We reach people at risk—refugees, AIDS victims, street children, and famine victims—with God's Word.

Word Power, God's Power

Faith Kidz, RiverOak, Honor, Life Journey, Victor, NexGen — every time you purchase a book produced by Cook Communications Ministries, you not only meet a vital personal need in your life or in the life of someone you love, but you're also a part of ministering to José in Colombia, Humberto in Chile, Gousa in India, or Lidiane in Brazil. You help make it possible for a pastor in China, a child in Peru, or a mother in West Africa to enjoy a life-changing book. And because you helped, children and adults around the world are learning God's Word and walking in his ways.

Thank you for your partnership in helping to disciple the world. May God bless you with the power of his Word in your life.

For more information about our international ministries, visit www.ccmi.org.

Additional copies of
THE NEW SLAVEMASTERS
and other Life Jouney titles are
available wherever good books are sold.

If you have enjoyed this book,
or if it has had an impact on your life,
we would like to hear from you.

Please contact us at:

LIFE JOURNEY
Cook Communications Ministries, Dept. 201
4050 Lee Vance View
Colorado Springs, CO 80918
Or at our Web site: www.cookministries.com

LIFE JOURNEY®
Bringing Home the Message for Life